Morgan will have you laughin̴ to think beyond your self-imposed limits. Her bold, fresh thinking and personal experiences give women who have the "Superwoman personality" the tools to truly have it all.

Denise Stillman, MBA, Owner, "Field of Dreams" Movie Site, and Author, *Courageous Clarity: Four Keys to Unlock the Leader Inside*

Morgan Field is poised to become one of the self-development leaders of our time. She has the ability to cut to the core of an issue and express love and compassion when delivering harsh truths. Her understanding of the world beyond the physical and her insistence on walking her talk make her a strong leader especially equipped to help women find their way back to their true path.

Avril Marchegiano, Holistic Therapy Practitioner for Animals, www.AvrilTheIndigo.com

Epic Sexy You is for every woman who has struggled with identifying healthy relationships and for every young girl who desires to become a strong independent woman. This book will shift a woman's positioning in her own life, moving her from passenger-seat rider to Indy car driver.

Courtney Lynne Butler, Women's Empowerment Coach, Owner of Transform Her LLC, www.courtneybutler.com

Hell YES! This book is NOT your typical self-help cheerleader crap. Morgan is massively positive but she's also the real deal. She shares her journey in ways that stopped me in my tracks. I will never look at my own indecisiveness and tolerance of bad behavior in the same way. Officially a "must-read" for all my clients!

Shawna Burkhart, Executive Life Coach and Psychotherapist, The Honest Edge, www.thehonestedge.com

I have always told my clients that "selfish" is not a bad word. Morgan takes that concept and explodes it with wit, inspiration and an authentic, can-do spirit that will cause you to stand up and shout, "Why me? Why the hell *not* me?"

Julie Bauke, Chief Career Happiness Officer, The Bauke Group, www.thebaukegroup.com

When I went on a retreat with Morgan to Costa Rica, she introduced me to some of the life-changing tools she reveals in this book. I began to implement them into my life, and I am blown away by how much my life has already changed. I am healthier and happier. A simple shift of unapologetically taking charge in all aspects of my life has led me down the path of achieving things that I didn't even think were possible.

Ana Dominguez, Creator and Editor, "The City Sidewalks," www.thecitysidewalks.com

Morgan writes as she speaks, with honesty, integrity, and from her soul. She shows you how to break the negative patterns for good by providing examples from her own journey and using simple, easy-to-understand, yet direct language. If you do the work the results truly are epic and instant.

Elaine Batho, Health, Fitness and Healing for Your Body, Mind, and Soul, www.healingfitandwellness.com

You there, yes you, on the couch: Whether you are in a rut, a living zombie, or simply ready to challenge yourself, read this book. I know I always wanted better for myself. It wasn't until the universe decided to bless me with Morgan that I felt certain I would live it.

Leecis Perry, Founder of leecisllc, Exceptional Facial and Waxing Services and Original Epic Sexy Goddess tribe member.

EPIC
SEXY YOU

No Limits. No Rules.

MORGAN FIELD

EPIC SEXY YOU
No Limits. No Rules.

Published by
Epic Sexy You Publishing
Chicago, IL

ISBN 978-0-9972224-2-5 Print
ISBN 978-0-9972224-7-0 E-Book

Printed in the United States of America

AUTHOR WEBSITE
www.EpicSexyYou.com

EPIC SEXY CONTENTS

Use this table of contents to quickly locate and revisit anything you are jonesin' for a fix of!

I Used to Be a Sucker

I used to not give a shit about myself quite frankly and didn't even consciously realize it. This picture was taken about 15 to 20 pounds in on my way to a full 35+ pound weight gain. Yes, I was wearing braided pigtails. And yes that is the world's strongest drink in my hand, which, as you can clearly see, I can't get to my mouth fast enough.

INTRO

Meet the Not So Epic Sexy Me

Let me start by saying this…

No, I have not always had this "pinch me, am I dreaming" kind of life where I live on my own terms, with no rules and no limits, unapologetically me, madly in love with the world's most awesome man of all time, and equally madly in love with myself. I have not always looked or felt sexy as hell or been completely in my power with the utmost, unshakable confidence. Actually, I now live a life that was once so far beyond my wildest dreams that my mind is still blown on a daily basis.

You see, I used to be a sucker, settling for the constant and predictable experience of mediocrity. Well, actually, if I am being honest, I was settling for far below mediocrity. I was too "busy" to actually LIVE life and fully experience it. Truth be told, I was a hot mess. I was a highly functioning, massively codependent, wild and fiery, drunken hot mess. I was addicted to cigarettes, junk food, alcohol, pleasing others, toxic men, and work.

If I was happy, I would drink. If I was sad, I would drink. If there was reason to celebrate, such as my birthday, a friend's birthday, St. Patrick's Day, Black(out) Friday, Monday, Tuesday, Wednesday, or any other day ending in "y," I was sure the occasion called for drinks! Or more like "shots!" and a lot of shots at that.

I was a professional number, with zero coping mechanisms outside of my numbing, distraction, and escapism addictions. My predominant emotions were anger, frustration, sadness, depression, insecurity, unhappiness, bitterness, and an epic fear of intimacy. Intimacy was the one thing I craved more than anything else. Yet the fear of rejection terrified me. That fear kept me paralyzed in an endless cycle of toxicity and dating unavailable men.

If a man was emotionally or geographically unavailable, an addict, a liar, a cheater, a narcissist, or any variation of toxicity, it seemed I was magnetized to him. Like a moth to a flame. I was the moth that got burned over and over and over again; nevertheless, I was drawn back to that damn flame! I had the disease to please. I put everyone and everything above my own needs. For the life of me, I couldn't make a decision. I sacrificed myself to give to others and thought it was selfish to be any other way.

I threw myself into work, because it was the very thing that I was completely awesome at (which of course made me feel really good about myself). I was always too "busy" to focus on getting good at the one thing I wanted more than anything else. What I really wanted was to have a loving and healthy relationship. I wanted to live and experience the *Epic Love Story*.

I always promised myself I would get to it "tomorrow," "next month," or some form or fashion of "later." I put off the dream so I could focus on my career. Or so I told myself. It was a convenient story that supported me in staying in my comfort zone, where rejection was not even a possibility. I avoided growth and stayed stuck, firmly rooted in the comfort of everything I was already really good at. I focused all my energy on getting even better at those things to the detriment of what I wanted most.

I was wildly successful financially, and was at the highest level in my company, yet I felt empty inside. I was single, overweight, exhausted, fatigued, and depleted. I was emotionally, mentally, and physically drained and unhappy, to say the least. I knew there was more to life, and I was ready to go find these elusive things I had heard about: *Fulfillment. Happiness. Bliss. Joy. Thriving.*

So, I set off on a journey.

This book will take you on your own unique journey of discovery and exploration as you learn what works best for YOU. Our journey together will help you stop looking for love and happiness outside yourself. It will help you take your power back. Most importantly, it will lead you to the ultimate love affair – a love affair with *yourself.*

Here's the thing: when you fall madly, deeply in love with yourself, you will finally claim fulfillment, love, and true success on your own terms. All of this is yours for the taking. It's all waiting for you right now on the other side! This is a journey to *living* an ignited life, leaving mediocrity in the dust, and truly *thriving*! I invite you now to start fresh, with a beginner's mind.

Give yourself permission to ditch any limiting, preprogrammed, generationally-recycled conditioning regarding the rules of survival. Come join me on this journey to thriving. This is your journey to an Epic and Limitless Life. You will connect with Epic Sexy You and bring her with you everywhere you go for the rest of your life. To support you with this journey of metamorphosis and sustainable transformation, look for Thrival Perspectives throughout this book.

Settling is for Suckers… Don't be a Sucker!

Catch ya on the flip side, sister, where Epic Thrival awaits you!

XOXO
Morgan

Me Too and Me First

As a woman, you tend to nurture, love, and give a *lot* of yourself to those around you. Sometimes, maybe a lot of times, you might be left feeling depleted, exhausted, spread too thin, and like you are nowhere to be found on your own priority list! Who has the time for that anyways?! Right? Especially considering all of the roles that you play.

Those roles seem to require giving to everyone and everything else but ourselves. Mother, Daughter, Sister, Wife, Girlfriend, Friend, Grandmother, Career Powerhouse, Suzy Homemaker, Maid, Chef, Mommy, Chauffeur.

The list goes on. And on. Does it ever end?

There is no doubt about it: giving to others absolutely feeds your soul. Still, there comes a point when you've given all you've got, and then you give some more because that's what you feel like you are *supposed* to do. How else can you be a good mom, daughter, sister, wife, (insert any other role you play here) if you don't give? Even when there is nothing left to give, you know you had better find a way to be there for everybody else.

It doesn't end there, because you also know you'd better make sure to smile through it all. Whatever you do, you do *not* let others know you are suffering. You might impact their happiness. If you dared to express what you really felt, you might become a burden, and that would be completely inconsiderate, rude, and selfish.

Here, let me help you. I'll lift up the proverbial rug for you, while you sweep yourself under it so we can hide that mess! Everything is "fine," right? Super! Great!! Keep on going, sister!!! You can make time for yourself tomorrow. Or next week. Or

4

maybe a month from now. Actually, maybe next year is a better time for you to start living your life. Right now, things are pretty "busy." Yep, I know the story. We all know it.

As women, there is an unconscious pattern we are repeating. It has been passed down from generation to generation. This energetic pattern of giving from a place of obligation robs us of the lives we are meant to live. We repeat it in supposed service to others and sacrifice our own needs and desires in the process.

Self-sacrifice is a low-vibration energetic pattern that limits us from being able to experience ourselves and this journey of life in a fully expansive way. You see it, don't you? You keep on keeping on to the detriment of living your own life. To the detriment of your happiness. To the detriment of your soul's expression. To the detriment of your dreams. You give up living, expressing, and being your Epic Limitless Self.

There is another way to give. There is another, much higher vibration option available to you. This option allows you to unleash Epic Limitless You *and* give to others. This is an option where you give, love, and nurture everyone around you, *and* you get to be equally generous with yourself.

I call this energetic vibration "Me Too!" "Me Too" is a state of being as generous with *yourself* as you are with others. It occurs when you are handing out the love, care, and nurture to yourself as well as to others in your life. "Me Too" means we ALL WIN! Which means *you* win too. You may be thinking, "Wait. You mean I get to win too? Me too?! Tell me more about that!"

Let me tell you a little story, and we'll get this PAR-TAY started. The story I am about to tell you

5

is about shedding the age-old skin and energetic signature of self-sacrifice, where the rules teed us all up for a game where somebody had to lose.

In this familiar game, the rules state that you must energetically settle for less than what you want so that someone else can be happy instead. When someone gets what she wants, someone else has to settle for less. Settling is for suckers! I know. I used to be a sucker, remember?

• • • • •
THRIVAL PERSPECTIVE
• • • • •

Self Love is hands down the most crucial brick in the foundation of creating a life that you LOVE living.

I'm going to share a story from my own life that illustrates this point. This story will paint that picture for you. You will find bits and pieces of yourself in this story. You will laugh with me in the face of what self-sacrifice looks and feels like for yourself and for others. It's kind of a silly pattern. The more conscious we become of this pattern, the more opportunities we have to free ourselves of it and choose a higher vibration.

It is important to note that, in this higher vibration, there is also nothing wrong with sprinkling in a little bit of the beautiful, magical, "Me First" existence every now and again. With this higher vibration, you can choose "Me First" in a way that is free of narcissism, arrogance, or destructive self-centeredness. "Me First" can be completely void of any ill intent toward others. It is *not* a "screw you" kind of vibe. Instead, it is more of a "YAAAY ME" feeling.

"Me First" is about taking time for yourself when you need it. This decision to choose you allows you to replenish, restore, and rejuvenate in a way that is incredibly beneficial to you *and* to everyone else around you. When the foundation of who you are is grounded and firmly rooted in Self Love, you can truly give to others in a way that is beyond what you can even imagine.

What the Hell Are These Things Called Boundaries? How Does That Work?

Sister friend, on this journey you will discover and explore all the limitless ways that you can have it *all*! Every single thing you want is yours to enjoy. All of it is available to you.

As you read the following story, please resist the urge to listen from a low vibration of self-sacrifice. That old, familiar vibe will want you to believe the lie that you can't fill other's love buckets while you are on a journey of Self Love. What this story and our entire journey together are really about is making sure that you intentionally, purposefully, and consciously fill your own love bucket on a consistent basis. When you fill your own love bucket first, you can then give to others from a truly loving desire, as opposed to giving from guilt and obligation, which can lead to resentment.

You will see in the following story, and the majority of stories in this book, that I had to stumble my way through my own journey to Self Love haphazardly, unconsciously and clumsily unleashing my Epic Limitless Self. I'd like to offer you another option, a faster path. I want to share direction, insight, and clarity on how you can get what you want a shit ton faster than what it took me! Less tears, less years, less heartache, less pain, and less temper tantrums.

OK, maybe the last thing is just me! As we begin our journey, let me share a story...

Let's call this story, "What the Hell is Self Love?!" That's the question I was asking when I began my journey. Here's the story I lived.

About five years ago I was a manager in a sales organization, leading a team of traveling sales reps. One day my boss pulled me aside and said, "Morgan, can I ask you something?"

"Sure, of course. What's up?" I asked.

"Do you ever say 'No' in your personal life?"

I was a little stunned by her question, and, frankly, I was not quite sure how it was relevant to our convo or my performance at work. But I listened to what she had to say.

"See, I've observed that you never say 'No' at work, and I can see that it takes its toll on you. You put all of your time and energy into this job and into your team. You work crazy hours," she said. "And you do not have any boundaries with your team, so it's a free-for-all. Your life, your energy, and your time are completely theirs for the taking. I care about you, so I am just wondering if this pattern of behavior is happening in your personal life too?"

It was like this woman had a magical crystal ball. *YES* it was happening in my personal life too. My mind was churning. What the hell were these foreign things she had mentioned called boundaries? I knew there was some truth in what she was saying, and I kept listening.

"I have a challenge for you if you are up for it," she said. "It won't be easy but it *will* change your life."

Life-changing? Challenge? Hell Yes! I'm in, I thought.

"It's Friday," she said. "Go home on time tonight. Leave the office no matter who needs what. Just tell them no. Let them know that you will get to it on Monday morning. Then, for every single person who asks you for something this weekend, say no. Do not tell them why. You do not owe them an explanation. It's a no because you don't want to do it, and *that* is a perfectly good enough reason to say no."

There was more. "This is a weekend of no..." she said, "This is a weekend for *you*. Then, after the weekend is over, every day for the next week, do at least one thing for yourself *every single day*. Make you a priority."

"While you're at it, make signs for yourself that say, *I am a priority*. Put them all over your house, everywhere you look. Everywhere you go, make sure there is a sign there – in your bathroom, on your desk, by the TV, on the fridge, on the kitchen cabinets, and on your phone. Put a note somewhere you will see it first thing when you wake up. Put notes everywhere."

Wait a second. I can say, "No" to people? My mind was reeling. This was a foreign concept to me. Someone is not only giving me *permission* to say, "No," but also *challenging* me to make it into a *game*?

Game on! It was at this point I set off for what ended up feeling like the longest two days of my life.

When you accept a challenge, the universe, in an effort to help you get *exactly* the growth you need and crave, delivers in the most epic ways possible at the *exact* time that you need it! This book has made its way into your hands at this exact moment in your life. How cool is that that the universe has your back and always provides you with the support you want and need?

The Longest Weekend

The first challenge came the second I got home. My phone dinged to signal I had a message. It was a text from my girlfriend inviting herself over to stay the night at my place. You see, when you never say no, people stop even asking. They just rightfully assume they can have whatever they want from you because you are the "YES" friend, the bottomless pit of endless giving friend.

I didn't actually feel like having company over. If I was giving myself permission to do what *I* wanted to do, I just wanted some solo me time on the couch. Maybe I'd order pizza, watch a movie, and just be with me, myself, and I. So I said, "Not tonight."

As you can imagine, when it is your first time *ever* saying no to someone, consciously, intentionally, and purposefully putting yourself first and making yourself a priority, *all* parties involved are quite confused by your new vocabulary. Even you! My friend dismissed my "No" immediately.

"I can come over and we can go out for some drinks. Then we can head home and watch a movie. It will be so much fun, just like the old days!" This was her reply.

Before I tell you about what happened next on that fateful Friday, let me take a second to paint a crystal clear picture for you of what went down two days prior. This will give you a solid idea of what our friendship looked like.

This same friend and I had gone to dinner two nights earlier. When she showed up for what I thought (and we had agreed to) was just going to be a dinner date, it became clear she had a different idea about the evening. My friend had actually packed her bags for a sleepover that she hadn't even filled me in on until she arrived. She looked at me and said, with the biggest smile on her face as she was holding up her packed bag, "Slumber party! I knew you wouldn't say no."

I kid you not, those were her exact words to me. I did not have the word "No" in my vocabulary, so I reluctantly agreed to her plan, even though I did *not* want to have a slumber party on a night when I had work the next day. This is just one example to illustrate what was running rampant in every single area of my life! *I* was literally nowhere to be found on my own priority list, and I literally *never* said, "No."

This friend was contemplating a divorce. She wanted to get out of her house and have some fun. She wanted to go out drinking since she had the following day off work. She kept pushing *her* agenda on me. *I* did not have the same agenda as *I* had work early the following morning, and I wasn't even aware of a sleepover until the second that she notified me of it, which was *after* she had already showed up for our dinner date.

By then, I felt as if it was already too late for me to say no. I hadn't been given the "No" Challenge yet, so the truth is I didn't feel like I even had permission to say no to anyone. Like ever. As in never ever. Just want to make sure we are on the same page here. I was hopelessly lost in the Neverland of neverness, and I never ever said no.

That night we went to dinner, skipped drinks (by some miracle, I had somehow managed to say no to that part of the game plan), and we went home to watch movies. She fell asleep on the couch, which was actually awesome because I don't sleep well with someone in my bed (unless that someone is my man or my dog.)

What I didn't consciously know then but know now is that I am an energy reader, and I easily absorb other people's energy. It's a lot on me energetically to be in the presence of another person's energy 24/7. Sleeping is my own private time. It's a time to decompress and rejuvenate my own energy field, solo! So I am *not* a fan of sharing my bed in general, and this night I needed a good night's rest so I could get up early in the a.m. for work. I left her on the couch as she was sleeping peacefully and went to bed, solo.

At about 4 a.m. that morning, I woke up with someone making noise in my bedroom and walking towards the bed. I let out a horrified, blood-curdling scream, which was met with my friend's uncontrollable laughter. I had forgotten that she was there. It was four in the morning, I was disoriented, and I was terrified that someone was in my room, walking towards my bed to come join me. I had no idea who it was until she laughed and I suddenly remembered that my friend had been sleeping on my couch.

To *her* it was funny. Now that I was awake, it was an opportunity for her to turn the lights on and chat, because she was wide awake and wanted some company. *I* had work the next morning. I was livid and pissed. I couldn't understand how a friend could be so oblivious to *my* needs. But these were needs I never even spoke of, so how the hell could she know?! Right?

Still, at the time, all I was thinking was that she had invited herself over without even asking. She had showed up for dinner with her bags already packed. She had come into my room at four in the morning on a night before I had to go to work early, because she wanted to sleep in the bed instead of the couch.

And, oh, by the way, now that I am up, she seemed to be thinking, let's chat! All I could think was, *AHH! Why is this happening to me?*

It's pretty obvious that I clearly had ZERO boundaries, never spoke my mind, never said, "No," and never stood my ground! So, let's go back to the Friday that followed, two nights after that evening...

Until this, the longest weekend, I had been completely unaware that my own lack of boundaries and my failure to express my needs, wishes, and desires were contributing to the situation. Since my boss had given me the permission to say, "No," I felt liberated and free. So I said "No" to her inviting herself over again.

It was the very first time in our entire 10+ years as friends that I had ever said no to her. Actually, I think it was the very first time I had ever really truly wholeheartedly given myself an opportunity to ask myself what I wanted and then spoken up for myself and said "No!" to anyone. Ever.

She didn't even hear it. She completely ignored it and kept on planning our "slumber party." Honestly, I would not have been surprised if she was already on her way. I *never* said no, and I had conditioned those around me to expect that I would give to them, even when I had no more to give. But this time I stood my ground. I said, "No." Again.

She tried to guilt me into a "super fun sleepover," reminding me that she was going through a divorce and needed me. Ouch. Low blow. These were hard to take. Still, I kept saying, "No." I started to realize that if I didn't stop this pattern now that I would have a permanent roomie in no time! I had to say, "No!" if I didn't want more 4 a.m. moments of shitting my pants in bed.

She wanted to know why I was saying no. Me wanting a night in *for* myself and *by* myself didn't seem to be a good enough reason for her. Now, looking back at it all, her confusion makes perfect sense because this was a brand new version of me that was showing up in our relationship. I may not have taken this new me very seriously either. Or maybe I would have just thought I was having an "off" day.

I never would have expected such an epic energetic shift in less than two days. Neither would my friend. We had spent more than ten years in a consistent pattern of relating that I was now disrupting. Understandably, she wanted to know if I had a man over. Was that why she couldn't come? My friend was soooo confused by this new concept of me taking "Me Time." It was new to me too.

By the time we ended our conversation, I had said "No" more times than I could count. I was in so much pain from the shock to my system, for this was the first time that I had ever said "No" to someone I loved. I had told my friend no even though she was telling me she needed something from me. It was the first time that I consciously, intentionally, and purposefully put myself and my needs above the needs of another person. It was the first time I intentionally said "No" to someone else because I was choosing to say "Yes" to ME.

I crumpled onto the floor and had the most epic temper tantrum of all time. I remember it like it was yesterday. Literally I was like a small child, uncontrollably shaking my body in protest and bawling my eyes out.

Why did this hurt so much? Why didn't my friend honor my boundaries? Am I doing this "boundary" thing wrong? WTH???!!! Ladies, trust me when I say it wasn't pretty.

It was one hell of a weekend as you can imagine and, predictably, yet another test presented itself that same weekend. Another friend called and asked me for help with moving a couch I had in my place, one he wanted to take over to his place.

"This weekend isn't good for me. How about next weekend?" I said. Again, this was the first time he had heard a version of anything other than, "Yes!" come out of my mouth, so he too pushed the boundaries. He told me I was selfish and inconsiderate and rude.

Let me just paint a clear picture for you on this one too. This was a couch I had had in my place for approximately six months. It was a temporary couch I had put in my place as a space holder until I got my furniture. About five months prior to his request on this fine day, I had asked him if he wanted it. He said, "No."

Around the same time, five months prior, I asked him if *he* could help *me* load it into a truck and donate it to Salvation Army. He always had an excuse why it wasn't a good time. Five months of my asking for help, with no response or action on his end. *Five full months!* Then, on this very weekend, he decided that he wanted the couch after all and he wanted it immediately.

At the time, it seemed to me he was implying that, if I was a good friend, I would help him carry the couch out and load it into a truck to take it over to his place. And the fact that I wouldn't do it *immediately,* right that very moment, on his terms, meant I was an awful person and the world's most selfish and shitty friend of all time. OK, at least that was how I felt at the time because this was my first time at the "No" rodeo and everything feels pretty damn heavy and dramatic on your first bull ride!

In the past, I would have heard his words and believed them. But a funny thing happens when you give yourself permission to love yourself and do only things that are an absolute "Hell Yes!"

In the past I would have accepted what he was saying without questioning it, because it was impossible for me to trust my own judgment. It had become impossible because my Heartspace GPS, my Goddess Power Source, was turned off due to the lack of Self Love, and Self Love is the actual power pack for that damn thing!

When you give yourself permission to say "No" to anything that isn't an absolute "Hell Yes!" for you, other people will say things that make *no* sense. When you give yourself permission to put yourself first, for the first time ever you will see the holes in their stories. Let me repeat this. If you have your pen and paper handy, write this golden nugget down right now:

A healthy relationship will honor your "No."

Once you start saying, "Yes" to you and "No" to others, you hear the same exact words that people have always said, including words that previously manipulated and guilt-tripped you into doing what they wanted you to do even when you *really* didn't want to. The difference is this: now you stop and ask yourself if what they are saying is even true. You learn that a healthy relationship can honor a "No."

• • • • •
THRIVAL PERSPECTIVE
• • • • •

It is impossible to truly LOVE yourself if everyone else comes BEFORE you.

However, when you are someone who has never said "No," the first few times that you do say it, people tend not to believe you. They will continue to not believe you until you *show* them with your actions and follow through, standing your ground no matter what they say or do. I said "No" all weekend. I only did what *I* wanted to do. Although it was painfully uncomfortable and I had the most violent temper tantrum as a result of the energetic shock to my system that came from saying "No" for the first time, that weekend changed my life.

The longest weekend of my life introduced me to what Self Love is by helping me to form my own definition of it. I discovered how it makes me feel when I love myself. I saw firsthand why *not* choosing to love yourself can destroy your life. I saw clearly how saying yes to everybody but yourself can keep you from *every single thing* that your soul craves most.

Let's talk about why mastering Self Love is your key to having everything you desire and deserve. It's time to take your power back.

It's time to become the master creator of your own happiness through the beautiful vehicle of Self Love. We will be playing with, discovering, exploring, and customizing this foundational concept of Self Love throughout this entire journey. Let's take a second right now to allow you to begin to connect with what Self Love means for you, what it could mean for you, and what you want it to mean for you. We will give our attention to this so you can intentionally, purposefully, and consciously include it in your daily rituals, shed perceived limitations, and step into a limitless existence.

Define Self Love, On Your Own Terms

Here is what Self Love means to me. As you read this list, consider the ways in which *you* are defining Self Love.

✓ Self Love means **creating a truly epic relationship with myself**, first and foremost so I can create the unshakable foundation of an unapologetic self on which I can build my desired relationships and my Epic Sexy Existence.

✓ Self Love means **honoring my desires**, my wants, my needs, and my soul's cravings.

✓ Self Love means **listening to the quiet whispers** and requests from self and then following through by taking action to make it *all* come to life.

✓ Self Love means **speaking up for myself**. Self Love means that I am a priority too.

✓ Self Love means **doing things because I *want* to do them**, not because I feel like I should do them or just because it's what others want from me.

✓ Self Love means I always **take my own feelings into consideration**. Self Love means I say "No" when I mean no, and I only do things if they are a big fat huge, "Hell Yes!"

✓ Self Love means consistently choosing me as **my own Numero Uno priority** so that I can ensure to get my *Thrive* on and have the most epic existence of all time.

✓ Self Love means **living life feeling ignited**, which empowers me to love others from a place of fullness inside myself.

✓ Self Love means continually **checking in with myself** to ask, "Am I happy? What can I do to make myself even happier? What do I want? What do I need? How can I take my thrive factor up a notch? What am I craving?" Once I discover the answers to these questions, Self Love means taking action to make those things happen.

✓ Self Love means continuously **learning new and improved ways** of loving and caring for my body, mind, heart, and soul! It's about pampering myself. It's about treating myself, deepening my trust with myself, keeping promises to myself, going deeper into understanding myself, and improving myself in every way.

✓ Self Love means I choose **a journey of growth**, a journey of love, expansion, exploration, curiosity, experimentation, liberation, freedom, fun, adventure, play, connection, transformation, and endless inspiration. Self Love is an epic journey to complete and utter happiness, fulfillment, and the ignition of my soul!

As you are creating your own definition I challenge you to really screw what anyone else says. In fact, screw what I say too! The *only* person that needs to "get" your definition of Self Love is you. Feel free, however, to get curious and extrapolate ideas from others.

✓ **Who comes to mind** when you think of someone who is epically awesome at Self Love in the way you would like to be?

✓ **What is it this person does** that signals that he or she is awesome at Self Love?

✓ **What ideas can you use** to start building on your own definition of what Self Love is: what it means, what it looks like, and how it feels?

Epic Sexy Q&A

On that note, get out a pen and paper and take a minute to explore the following questions.

✦ What do you want Self Love to **mean** to you?

✦ How do you want to **define** Self Love?

✦ How do you want Self Love to make you **feel?**

✦ What do you want the **purpose** of Self Love to be?

✦ How do you want Self Love to **impact** you mentally, physically, emotionally, and spiritually?

What do you want Self Love to look like when you put it into action?

Epic Sexy Self Love Activities

Let's create a Self Love Activities List so you will know what Self Love looks like for you. Here are some things that came up for me when I was doing my own exploration of this:

✓ Giving myself permission to **put aside the "To Do" list** items; put work aside; say "No" to friends, family, and even my man; put aside errands; and just do what ever *I* want to do in that very moment.

✓ Giving myself permission to **watch a movie**, guilt-free.

✓ **Relaxing** and rejuvenating with the intention of pampering my inner goddess.

✓ Connecting with self through **self-exploration**.

✓ **Working out** is Self Love for me. It is the act of honoring and loving myself by taking care of my body and the Epic Goddess of a vessel that I am.

✓ Juicing, cleansing, and **drinking loads of water** with ample awareness. Listening to my body.

✓ Giving myself permission to put down work and **just *play*!** Reading. Watching movies. Taking a mental break or engaging in an activity that is mentally stimulating, whichever I might be craving on that particular day ;)

✓ Giving myself permission to **spend money** on Self Love and pampering.

✓ Believing that I will always have an **overflowing abundance** of money.

✓ Giving myself full permission to **spoil myself** with energetic cleansings and explore the spiritual realms by investing in healers, life coaching, and spiritual readings.

✓ Spending money on **organic makeup** and skincare so I will experience health and vitality as I glow from the inside out.

✓ Investing in organic, holistic, and **natural body scrubs**, spas, steam rooms, and facials.

✓ **Treating myself** to floating in the Water Weightless Machine Thingy (totally the technical term).

✓ Practicing self-care by investing in **dental cleaning appointments** twice a year and haircut trims every six weeks. Having my nails painted. Going tanning. Just like the maintenance I get for my car, I make sure that I am taking care of all of the things that make me feel beautiful and as if I am a priority. This gives me limitless energy to experience a fully expansive life.

✓ Honoring my spirit-led soul space of **being on a beach** at minimum once every quarter.

✓ Treating myself to a **mani/pedi**, a massage, or shopping!

✓ **Enjoying baths**, candles, music, and reading.

✓ **Yoga!**

✓ Meditation, **visioning**, and journaling.

✓ **Technology cleansing** days.

✓ "Me" Days, and **"No" Days**, meaning "No" to others and a big "Hell Yes!" to *me*.

✓ **Writing** as therapeutic release.

✓ Giving myself full permission to **make up my own rules** and to change them however I feel like it.

✓ **Organizing and cleaning.** These activities fall into this realm of Self Love, as I recognize how much I love the feeling once it's done. It's such a treat, like a good ol' car wash! Maybe the extra treat to spoil myself rotten is to hire someone to clean my place for me. Woo!! Winning!

✓ Buying myself some **flowers**. Even if I have a man, I can still pamper myself.

✓ **Cooking!** I enjoy playing with a new recipe or making myself something delicious and nutritious that is going to make me feel light, energized, and loved.

✓ Jamming out to music and doing **happy dances of joy** around the house, taking dance breaks in between work, blasting music in my car and singing along, even when others look at me like I am crazy. I am having an epic time, and quite frankly they are having a great time laughing at me. Win-win!

✓ **High-fives** with myself, patting myself on the back, and hugging myself.

✓ Taking myself on **a date** (even when I have a man).

✓ **Getting dressed up** *for me.*

✓ Wearing **sexy underwear** just *for me.*

✓ Strutting around the house in my **best lingerie**, just for *my* enjoyment (even when I am *in* a relationship, and he is not around!)

✓ Using the very **best linens**.

✓ Pulling out the **best dishes**, setting an ambiance even when I'm eating solo.

✓ **Keeping promises** to myself.

✓ Positive self-talk: **"Guuurrl, you rock!** You are so pretty!! You are such an epic badass. You are so sexxxyyy! WOO!"

✓ Giving myself permission to **openly receive help**, gifts, treats, and compliments from others. And only giving to others when I *truly* want to, free of guilt or obligation.

✓ Celebrating my awesomeness. Making sure that I take the time to acknowledge and validate my **epic awesomeness** and celebrate all of the things that I am learning, doing, and becoming. Celebrating by doing any of the above thaaangs.

Take your first step in this journey of Self Love, and start your journey today. Take a minute to write down your own list of Self Love activities. Pick ONE thing from your list that makes you feel really great, and do that thing. One by one, we are laying the bricks of the foundation to your Epic Sexy Self, starting now.

Are you ready to build a never-ending habit of Self Love? For one full week, I want to invite you to do one Self Love Thaang per day. It could be something as simple and small as giving yourself one compliment a day! Or play with picking different thaangs for different days – a bath one day, painting your nails another day, and creating a vision board another day. Or a facial one day and a body scrub another day. Meet yourself where you are.

If you are at zero things currently, than maybe pick something that takes less than five minutes a day to do, like read three pages in a book you love, say "thank you" when someone gives you a compliment, or let someone open the door for you. Whatever you choose to do, make sure it is totally achievable so that you are setting yourself up for success as you lay this foundation of Self Love and resist the urge to go from zero to 100 in 2.5 seconds, which could lead to another unkept promise and further damage to your relationship with yourself.

Play with constantly increasing the frequency of your habits of Self Love and watch how your life evolves into a more loving, fulfilling, happier, blissful, and ignited existence as a result.

One client I was working with came up with a super Epic Sexy Idea. She created a list, writing each thaang down onto small pieces of paper, folding the pieces up, putting them in a box, and then picking one Self Love action each day. It became a game! A surprise!! This was something to look forward to each day. Just play with this. Make it *fun*. Do what *feels* good to *you*! ;) xoxo

Bring Sexy Back

As we have just learned in our exploration of Self Love, how you *define* something will have the most profound impact on your ability to *create* that very thing in your own life. We started with Self Love as it is the key foundation to unleashing a limitless life and Epic Sexy You. As a woman, another foundational principle is to get your sexy back. Or discovering your sexy for the first time!

The reason Epic Sexy You is named what it is is because, for the first year that I was working with women, I kept seeing a pattern. Women went from "surviving" their days, to incorporating epic adventures that led to a new way of being and a new ignition in the depths of their soul. These women who came to me wanting more in life but not always knowing what was missing or how to make the shifts were now fully alive, not just living but *thriving*!

My clients kept saying, "For the first time in my life, I feel *sexy*." I was feeling it right there alongside them, and I was experiencing similar results myself! We were all falling in love with ourselves. We were getting comfortable in our skin. For most of us, this was the first time ever in our lives we had felt this way. We were having so much *fun* on our endless and epic adventures. This was the new standard for our lives, and there was no going back.

People were moving to new places, places they had wanted to move for years. One woman had wanted to move for sixteen years! *Sixteen. Years.* In less than three months of coaching, she made that happen. She finally took action and up and moved.

Epic Sexy You named itself. It found me. It found all of us. It came from the amazing women coaching with me. The name is a direct result of what I and other women were experiencing through the work we were doing together. When I started telling people the name of the business, things were at times wildly misunderstood, particularly with the word "sexy" being included in the business. Let's face it, "sexy" is a taboo word in our society. The word itself conjures thoughts of scantily-clad or naked women.

Google the word "sexy" and just see what type of results you yield. It's as if the very word "sexy" means that you have to objectify the female body, which can leave you feeling downright dirty if you accept the *sexual* connotation of the definition that society is imposing upon you. Here is the keyword in that sentence: *sexual*. Not, *sexy*.

The business is not named Epic *Sexual* You. It is named Epic *Sexy* You, which is about leaving mediocrity in the dust once and for all and living an *epic,* legendary life, one where you pinch yourself because you almost can't even believe it's real, you love the skin you are in, and you give yourself permission to get your sexy on.

All the epic thaaangs you're creating, experiencing, and doing as you chase your dreams and get all of the puzzle pieces of your life in order, set you up for a life well lived. Then, when all comes to a natural close, you can slide into your grave knowing that you gave this go-round everything you had. There will be no regrets, no wondering what if. Along that journey, you better bet your ass that you looked and felt *sexy* the whole way through.

So, let's get your sexy back, girl. Don't get me wrong. When you are sexy, you unleash your inner sex kitten and you are able to take your sexuality to a whole new level. But Epic Sexy You happens from the inside out. No self-sacrifice. No deprivation. No diets. No counting calories. Inside out means we clean up all the internal blocks. Then the outside begins to match the inside rather effortlessly. As a result, you are left looking and feeling *sexy.*

THRIVAL PERSPECTIVE

An EPIC SEXY LIFE is your birthright. When you own your power, you are comfortable in your own skin. Nothing and no one can take that away.

✦ *Let's Define Sexy* ✦

Society's definition of "sexy" is one that often brings shame if we talk about being sexy or even feel sexy. Often times we are left dealing with sleazy, creepy guys who think that if a woman talks about looking and feeling sexy that this gives them full permission to sexualize or objectify her. Let me tell you, sister friend, accepting this crap is *not* doing us or our young soul sisters any favors.

We *are* sexy! We are meant to embrace sexy, to feel sexy, and to be sexy in our own skin. In order to do this, you need to create your own definition of the word, one that empowers you to feel comfortable and confident, fierce and free. Find a new definition of sexy that leaves you feeling liberated, accepted, and loved. Choose a definition that unleashes your inner sex kitten *on your own terms*, not somebody else's idea of sexy.

Think about it. When you have said to yourself, "Wow, that person is sexy," was it because they were half-naked and you were merely admiring their physical appearance? Perhaps there have been occasions when that was true, but what about the majority of the time you notice sexy? What was the specific set of conditions that caused you to be moved to use the word "sexy" to describe someone? What was the formula?

Obviously a piece of it was attraction, even if that person wasn't typically your type. Even when that person happened to be fully clothed. Yet, what else was going on that *moved* you in that encounter? What was it that captivated you about them? Often times, we even acknowledge and admire another soul sister for getting her sexy on, don't we?

For me, I think it is super sexy when someone is confident. They do *not* care a single iota about what people think, and they are just following the beat of their own drum. They are smart, intellectually stimulating, and passionate about life!

It is sexy when someone takes care of his or her body, treating it like the temple it is, putting clean fuel into the body, and sculpting it as if it was a priceless piece of art. When someone is strong body, mind, *and* soul, that's sexy! When a man or woman unapologetically owns every perceived flaw and embraces every single ounce of who he or she is, that is Epic Sexy.

Those who give you permission to just fall madly deeply in love with them are sexy too. I don't mean fall in love romantically, but just soul spirit crushing hard on them. They are fun to be around. They light up the room. They have a little sparkle in their eye, like they have a secret to life. Maybe, if you are lucky enough, they just might let you in on that little secret.

Sexy people have their own swag. They stand tall, they walk like a *boss*, they strut their stuff, and they own the room. They've got their own style and they can pull *anything* off because they own it. To me, that is *sexy*.

Sexy people are kind to others. They are thoughtful, generous, attentive, loving, and loyal. Oh, and they are *funny*! Laughter is so sexy to me. Sexy people don't take themselves or life too seriously.

At the same time, sexy people know what they want and they go after it. They *make* things happen. For me, sexy is about loving yourself and bringing the best you with you everywhere you go. Sexy is about owning your power, being unapologetically you, and fully knowing, embracing, and owning your beauty, both inside and out!

I can tell you what is *not* sexy to me: feeling bloated or irritable, being unhappy and angry, losing your temper, feeling exhausted or sick, being gassy, complaining constantly, judging others, gossiping, being negative, and constantly finding a problem for every single solution. It's not sexy when you are poisoning your temple with cigarettes and junk food and escaping the present moment by numbing yourself with food, drugs or alcohol, and TV. It's not sexy to be arrogant, narcissistic, and condescending, and lying and cheating are a world away from sexy.

I could go on, but I think you get the point. And these are just *my* definitions. This is what sexy is and is not too sexy *according to Morgan*. Now it's your turn.

Are you ready to bring your sexy back? We'll start with a little Epic Sexy Q&A. Get your journal out and let's do this thaang.

Epic Sexy Q&A

Write down your answers to these questions.

✦ What do you think is sexy in a **potential lover**?

✦ What do you view as sexy in **people you admire** and would like to have more of? Physically? Mentally? Emotionally? Spiritually? In your own personality or character? In your actions?

✦ If you were to create a new, **empowering definition** of the word "sexy," one that would inspire you to *be* sexy, to embrace it, live it, and own your full power, what might that definition look like? Do a brain dump onto the paper in front of you. See what comes out. Look for anything in your definition that feels like a "should" do or a "have" to. Scour for anything that makes you feel "less than" or "not enough" and put a big fat X through it! This is about chasing the feeling of sexy in whatever way feels best for you, on your own terms. No Limits. No Rules.

✦ What would it take for you to **want to look and feel sexy** just for *you*, not for anyone else but you? What would have to happen in order for you to truly want to be sexy for you?

✦ *Own Your Power to Choose* ✦

If you are exploring this journey of growth and laying the foundation of Self Love with a younger soul sister, perhaps a daughter, niece, little sister, or a cousin, decide for yourself what word fits that you would like her to explore. Empower her with options and let her pick the word(s) that *she* likes best, the one that she finds most empowering.

Here are a few focus words to consider: *Beautiful. Confident. Radiant. Stunning. Gorgeous.* It doesn't matter so much what word you use. It is all about the messaging and letting your soul sister know that there is nothing wrong with being absolutely, positively *Sexy, Beautiful, Confident, Radiant, Stunning*, and *Gorgeous*.

• • • • •
THRIVAL PERSPECTIVE
• • • • •

Love the hell out of yourself, unleash EPIC SEXY YOU, and create a limitless life.

Sexy is owning all of who you are, inside and out, and being unapologetic about that. It is refusing absolutely to allow another being, a book, or societal definitions to define who you are. The only person who can define who you are is *you!* The only one who can take that power away is you. Let others have their power and own who they are. Let them *own* their beauty and not bring shame to it. The absolute *best* way to help someone find her way is for you first to find *your* way. I am *super* excited, honored, and feeling beyond blessed to be on this journey with you. Let's do this!

How to Use This Book

First of all, if you are reading this, it is because this book found you. It is the *exact* right time, and the *exact* resource that you need to take your life to a new unimaginable height that your soul has been craving to go to for *years*. The time is *now*.

This is the right time, the right place, and the right version of you to finally make your dream life come to fruition and live full out. You manifested this book through your desire for *more*. You are ready to leave mediocrity in the dust and claim the epic existence that you deserve. Forget surviving. We are here to get our *thrive* on! Let's get this party started, shall we?

✦ *Epic Sexy Thrival Tips* ✦

Epic Sexy Thrival Tips are found in each of the four sections of this book. These tips provide ways to help you take your Thrive Factor up a notch. These tips are rooted in action. They are meant to be *done*, not simply considered. If you put in the time and energy, do the exploration, take action, and implement these *Epic Sexy Thrival Tips* and recommendations, your life will change.

When you translate these ideas into action, try them, and put them into practice... When you experiment with them, play with them, *experience* and *feel* what works best for *you*... Well then, sister friend, you are going to experience nothing short of an *epic uplevel* in your life. I *guarantee* it. Over time, and through your consistent habit of action with these *Epic Sexy Thrival Tips* you will develop a "pinch me, I must be dreaming" kind of life!

To be crystal clear, if you simply read this book, you will get a mini-bump uplevel in your life. However, if you actually *do* the things outlined in this book, then consider yourself mind-blown and life-changed. Watch yourself walk into a "watch out world, here I come" existence. It's your choice. Which do you prefer?

✦ *One Thing at a Time* ✦

Remember, pick *one* thing at a time and play with it for a week. Pay attention to how this thing makes *you* feel. If you experience an uplevel or insights, keep doing it. Once you've got the hang of it, add a second Thrival Tip simultaneously to further increase your Thrive Factor. Then repeat.

If you come across something that doesn't feel good to you, then move on to something else that is a better fit! There is no one-size-fits-all solution here. This is about finding your own unique and *customized* recipe for your Epic Sexy Life.

✦ *Write it All Down* ✦

I would recommend you get a journal you can use for this journey. Choose a journal that makes you feel like the badass ninja warrior goddess that you are.

If waiting to find the perfect journal will slow you down or perhaps be a potential reason as to why *not* to kick-start this journey, then just grab anything you can find and get started *now*! You can always add your pages of exploration and fold them up into your journal when you get it. There is no "right" way to do it, and the only "wrong" way is if you do *nothing* at all.

✦ *Start Right Now* ✦

Start *today*! Do not allow yourself to get stuck in the habit of "I'll do it tomorrow." Tomorrow, of course, never comes. Start now. When you create the habit of putting these Thrival Tips into *action*, you can expect to have your whole life trajectory changed. Today is the only day. Begin now.

✦ *Progress Not Perfection* ✦

Focus on the progress, not perfection, Remember, Epic Sexy You is a journey not a destination! Do *not* let waiting for "perfection" get in the way of your Epic Sexy launch. Perfection is not a realistic, achievable, or attainable thaang, so just remember to focus on progress, movement, momentum, baby steps, and growth. That is what your journey is all about.

✦ *Opening Quotes* ✦

At the beginning of each of the four sections of this book you will see an opening quote. These quotes are intended to inspire and ignite you as you kick-start your own Epic Sexy Journey and awaken, embody, and amplify the fire within you. Use these quotes to amp up your experience. Create sticky notes, with these quotes on them, as reminders to keep you laser-focused, ignited, and inspired along your journey.

Get creative, and come up with your own way to use these reminders. Put them all over your house. Put them in your office, and immerse the living areas of your home with them. Have them in your phone for quick and easy reference. Take action to keep you laser-focused on your journey to Epic Sexy You.

✦ *Navigation Made Easy* ✦

This book is not the kind of book you read once and then put back on the shelf to collect dust. Nope. It is filled with infinite expansion exercises for you to come back to over and over and over again, so you don't have to stumble your way through the dark or haphazardly create your dream life, like I did.

The table of contents navigation tool, which can be found in the front of the book, will be helpful in the event that you'd like to revisit a section and quickly find a little somethin' somethin' that you are jonesing for a fix of ;) Know that this tool is waiting for you, so you can relax and enjoy the journey you are about to embark upon. Trust that you have a simple, easy way to quickly find what you are looking for whenever you need it. Come back to this book frequently. Schedule regular dates with yourself to check back in, see how you are doing, explore what has changed in your soul cravings and Heartspace desires and play with this soul work some more!

✦ *Share Share Share* ✦

My mission in life is to help empower you to create an epic sexy community, a tribe of souls who will inspire you to be the absolute best version of yourself. I want you to find soul brothers and sisters who will help you break patterns that are holding you back from an epic existence. I want you to claim your power, own your unshakable confidence, and have partners who want you to shine as you reach the epic heights of greatness that you deserve to experience.

Today is the first day of the rest of your life, and I am beyond honored and blessed to be on this journey with you. I encourage you to create your own beautiful accountability and support system that will allow you to learn and expand at an expedited rate.

You can share this journey with your mother, your aunt, and your sisters. Walk alongside your daughters and your very best friend. Invite your grandmothers, your cousins, your sister-in-law, and your mother-in-law to join you. Share it with your nieces, your goddaughters, your female coworkers, employees, or clients. Share the journey with your husband, your boyfriend, your father, your brothers, your best friends and with any and all of your epic sexy soul sisters and soul brothers who are up for the challenge! Invite them to join you on this journey of expansion as together you experience an epic uplevel to heights beyond your wildest comprehension.

E-mail me at morgan@epicsexyyou.com Share your stories, your Aha moments, insights, epiphanies, lessons learned, and what's working so that we can all grow, learn, and celebrate together!! Let me know what you are struggling with, what you are craving more of, and what you could benefit from as your next steps. These insights help me create custom content, events, retreats, and programs to support you in your journey to a sustainable Epic Sexy Limitless You.

Get Social. Join the Epic Sexy You movement, and get social with your sharing!! Use #epicsexyyou to connect, explore, and celebrate with fellow Epic Sexy Souls along your journey. Sharing ingrains every lesson you learn deeper into the fiber of your being, which yields optimal sustainability. This is about finding Epic Sexy You and *never* going back.

Create Your Own Epic Sexy You Movement! Share your journey with others. Start your own book club. Learn, grow, expand, evolve, and celebrate together. Hit me up, and if divine timing serendipitously aligns our calendars, I'll pop in for a Skype Q&A book club quickie in my glamorous gold sparkly gown.

Share Your Pics on Social Media. Use #epicsexyyou or e-mail them to me at morgan@epicsexyyou.com.

Share Your Journey with the Epic Sexy You Tribe!

Instagram: **@epicsexyyou**
Facebook: **facebook.com/epicsexyyou**
Twitter: **@EpicSexyYou**
YouTube: **EpicSexyYou**
Pinterest: **pinterest.com/epicsexyyou**

Throughout the book, look for helpful tags to remind you to share the love. They will look like this:

GET YOUR SHARE ON *#epicsexyyou*

Whenever you see this invitation, pause for a moment. Reflect on who else in your life needs to know this truth. Then get your share on, girl!

✦ *One Thing, Again* ✦

Yes, I know I already said this one, but I cannot stress enough the importance of just picking *one* thing at a time to have as your laser focus for your attention, efforts, energy, and awareness. Do not overwhelm yourself or collapse into a state of inaction. Just pick *one* single Thrival Tip to play with at a time.

Try that tip, and experiment with it. Have fun with it! Learn, stretch yourself, expand, and grow. When you get the hang of the first Thrival Tip, add another one to the mix while still maintaining the original tip. I can assure you that when you *do* these things that your life will change *forever*.

As you progress on your journey and build momentum by creating a you that you *love* being and a life that you *love* living, it will be normal to have fears that you will backslide at some point. Trust me when I say that you will *not*. If you continue to focus on your progress, layering on one Thrival Tip after another, all the while sustaining the ones you have previously added, you will expand beyond the point of regression. You will never go back to where you started. Never ever. That's a *promise*.

Sure, you will have bad days and bad moments, but your average resonating existence of loving your life and loving yourself will increase the more you do these things. Soon, you will forever and sustainably experience a higher quality of life. You will find yourself living an extraordinary life beyond what you can now imagine. So what are you waiting for? Get it, girl! Let's Do this!

The Greatest Love Affair

First and foremost, above all else, *you* need to believe that you are worth it – "it" being whatever it is that you want. Maybe you want an epic love story, a thriving career, your own epic empire, or an amazing relationship with everyone around you. Insert any and all of your wildest dreams.

If you do not believe a.) you are worthy of an Epic Sexy Life, and b.) that your "it" is even possible, then you cannot even begin to create your epic sexy existence. It is impossible to find your way to Epic Sexy You without this foundation. Your relationship with yourself is hands down *the* most important love affair that you will ever have in this lifetime. It can actually even be the most fun one too, if you allow it to be.

Let me give you an example. I remember when I decided I wanted to quit smoking. I had tried quitting about one hundred and seventy-five gazillion times prior to this time. I remember reading an article that changed it all for me. In the article, there was a question that read something to the effect of the following:

Think of someone that you love more than anyone else on this planet. My nephew popped into my head.

The article went on to say, "Now, let me ask you. If there was a big truck heading their way, would you run out into the road to save them?" Duh. Yes. Of course. No doubts about that.

"Would you give your life to save theirs?" Yes.

"Would you stop doing something that was harming them even if it would be difficult for you to stop doing that thing?" Yes.

"As an example, if I told you that if you kept smoking you would *kill* this person or dramatically shorten their life and drastically decrease the quality of their existence... If you knew that you and only you had the power to stop the negative impact of your behavior for this person right now, this very second, would you be willing to put yourself through the discomfort and pain of change? Would you make the changes in your behavior so that you could make their life better?"

Duh. *Yes, yes, yes.* What is the point here? Then this question followed: "So why won't you do it for *you*?!"

Bam! It hit me like a truck!

Why was it that I was doing this to myself? Why wasn't *I* worth it? Why couldn't I do this for *me*? Why was everyone else more important than me? This was BS. I had had enough of my own shenanigans.

The insights I got by reading this article started a journey where *I* was the primary driver for change in my own life. My love for myself became the number one reason why I stopped doing the very things that were literally killing me. I became the reason for quitting those things that were keeping me from a life that my soul craved to experience.

I quit drinking, which was not only destroying my life and keeping me from looking and feeling sexy in my own skin but was also destroying my chances at ever having and keeping a happy, healthy, and loving relationship with an amazing man. I went into in-depth therapy and coaching in order to find out why I was doing this in the first place. I went on a quest to discover what I was numbing and how to create more healthy coping mechanisms for the unresolved feelings of anger, sadness, and pain that had been under the surface for most of my life.

I started changing the things that I put into and onto my body. I changed who I allowed into my life. Finally, I turned my home into my own magazine-layout version of beauty and heaven on earth, one I had envisioned for years but never made time to actually create. Literally *everything* changed.

I have been sober and cigarette-free from the very single moment that I realized that *I* was the reason I was going to change, that *I* was worth it, and that *I* deserve everything I crave and will stop at nothing to make my dreams a reality because I deserve it damn it!

You are worth it. You deserve everything you desire. This belief is my passionate mission. Sharing it with you is my intention for this book.

Here is the thing: if you won't do it for *you*, you will never have any of the things that your soul craves. Nope, there is no workaround for this. OK, I already hear your "Yeah, but…"

"Yeah, but my friend smokes, and she is madly in love. She has the best life ever…." Well, I call BS. You cannot treat your body like crap *and* have everything you want. You cannot put everyone else before you *and* have an epic version of happily ever after.

"Yeah, but… I *love* putting other people first. It feeds my soul." Bullshit. You love it until a certain point, and then it becomes toxic to you. You begin to resent others. As long as you are never first on your own priority list, you will never have what you want. Ever. Never. It is impossible. It's not going to happen.

Sure, you may be successful by societal definitions. You may make loads of money, buy a dream house, and drive a badass car. You may live a luxurious lifestyle, find the perfect lover, or have the smartest kids. Even if you do, you won't be able to enjoy any of it, because nothing will ever be enough. If you do not believe *you* are enough, then nothing will ever be enough. Not ever. Never, ever. No chance in hell.

I know, I am a bit direct and harsh. I write these things with love. I share this message with the intention of actually getting you what *you* want. If you are looking for a book that is going to empower you to stay in Victimville, to remain hopeless, and to keep a masterfully crafted list of an endless abundance of reasons as to why you will never get what you want, then you should put this book down right now and walk away.

If you are in a state where you are unwilling to take *full* responsibility for the fact that you do not have the life that you love living or if you are not ready to accept that *you* have the full power to make all your dreams come true, then this book will rock your world. But not in a good way. If any of these things are true, you will hate me the entire time you are reading this. You will MF me the whole time and, no, by MF I do not mean "Morgan Field." You will rationalize other people's epic existences as a complete anomaly and persist in saying, "Yeah, that works for other people, but not for me." The cursed "Yeah, but" syndrome will rear its ugly head.

If, however, you are ready to create a foundation to a "pinch me, am I dreaming?" kind of life, then this book is going to change you at the core of who you are. This book will rock your world in the best way imaginable. You will gain free access to epic code-breaking secrets that lead you straight to epic breakthroughs.

When you journey with me, you will discover how to move forward and in the direction of every single thing your soul craves. You will learn how to have the most epic love affair of all time – a love affair with *yourself.* From this moment forward, whatever you choose, just know that it is a choice. And *you* are the one in control of said choices.

For those of you who are on board, let's do this thaang. Up first: you've got to know what you want, girl. Let's take step one of four simple steps to Epic Sexy You.

Create the Ultimate Love Affair with Yourself

Step 1: Know What You Want

Know What You Want

What do you want?

How the hell are you ever going to get what you want if you don't know what you want?

A lot of people are afraid to say what they want.
That's why they don't get what they want.

Madonna

There is a quote that I particularly love. I am not sure who it even originated from, but the quote goes like this: "*Sometimes people around you won't understand your journey. They don't need to. It's not for them.*" This feels so true for the journey to Epic Sexy You. So many times in life, we find ourselves questioning our own sanity when we realize that we are the *only* person who feels a certain way, especially when we feel we are going against the grain of what is expected of us by some agreed-upon societal standard.

In those moments, quickly remind yourself that there is in fact a possibility that maybe *you* are the one who has it figured out and society has it wrong. Either way, as far as I am concerned, society can take its "shoulds" and "ought tos" and stick 'em where the sun don't shine!

Let me be very clear. The *only* person in your life that your decisions, actions, behaviors, visions, and leaps of faith need to

48

make sense to is *you*! Period. End of story. The sooner you can get to this kind of existence, the sooner you can have *all* your soul craves. This topic is critical in the foundation of creating a life you absolutely *love* living.

Without knowing what it is you really want, it is absolutely impossible to fall in love with yourself, to create a life you love living, to create your very own epic love story, or to truly find the work that ignites your soul. So, let's jump right in, shall we?

The Epic Battle Between Your Head and Your Heart

You are never going to figure out what *you* want until you learn how to control the battle between your head and heart. Until you learn to connect with your intuition first, searching for and finding the answers *inside you* instead of constantly searching for external validation, you can't make real progress toward your own version of an Epic Sexy Life.

There are two opposite ends of the spectrum from which you can operate as you navigate your way through this world. Each of these two approaches yields wildly different results and outcomes. In this section, we will take a look at the vast differences between epic overload and effortless, euphoric flow in your life. Let's look at the particulars of operating from each end of the spectrum: Headspace Overload and Heartspace Immersion.

Headspace: Epic Overload

On one end of the spectrum you have Headspace Overload. Headspace Overload occurs when you are *over*thinking, *over*analyzing, and *over*complicating things. It happens when you are trying to force a solution, stuck in analysis paralysis, or feeling under pressure to get something done. Simply put, it's not an enjoyable place to be. It is also not productive, and you do not have any access to your heart and intuition while you are operating in Headspace Overload.

In Headspace Overload, our hearts and feelings get shut down. Because you are operating from such a heavy thinking component, you do not have full access to all of yourself, heart and intuition included. You know on a deeper level that you can't actually trust yourself *fully* to make a decision that will be guided and supported, a decision that will yield the results and outcomes you deeply desire for yourself and others.

In Headspace Overload, you keep thinking that, if you keep thinking more and hit the problem from every angle, you will eventually get it "right." Yet, without any access to your heart and intuition, you will only have a very narrow field of possibilities, solutions, and options available to you. When you are operating solely from Headspace Overload, you will inevitably be left feeling depleted, exhausted, and drained. You will be frustrated, hopeless, and without the capability to be divinely guided in any way.

✦ *Telltale Signs of Headspace Overload* ✦

Headspace Overload results in a situation that makes it virtually impossible to yield the outcomes you desire for yourself or others. Here are some of the signs of Headspace Overload:

- ✓ Complexity
- ✓ Complication
- ✓ Restriction / Constriction
- ✓ Hammer / Force
- ✓ Struggle / Depletion

✦ *The Headspace Overload Navigation System* ✦

This navigation system is preprogramed with the conditioning to "Survive." This system is based on external factors, and it does not allow us access to our intuition and divine guidance. The Headspace Overload Navigation System is the default system passed down through the generations.

Heartspace: Effortless, Euphoric Flow

On the other end of the spectrum is Heartspace Immersion, which leads to effortless and euphoric flow. In Heartspace Immersion, you have access to your intuition in tandem with the *brilliance* and *sheer geniusrty* of the mind! (Yes, that is a made up word and I love it. Geniustry! Feel free to use it! You're welcome!)

In Heartspace Immersion, you have full-blown access to your divine guidance, to your intuition, and to your soul's wisdom. Heartspace Immersion is a place where you have an abundance of free-flowing limitless options, possibilities, and solutions available to you. This state allows for an effortless flow and ease. Instead of feeling you have to *force* a solution as you do in Headspace Overload, there is a quality of openness.

When you are immersed in your Heartspace, rather than stuck in familiar Headspace Overload, you are still accessing the mental capacity of your Headspace. You are just doing so in a completely different manner than you have previously been conditioned to do. You still get to use your mind in Heartspace Immersion, but you do so with full expansiveness, full clarity, and the optimal ability to create and put into action the most epic of strategies.

In Heartspace Immersion, you know you are meant to have *everything* that you desire *and* have a ton of fun while doing it *all*. When you are in Heartspace Immersion, you have full access to every fiber of your being. You are able to make informed decisions from the divine guidance you receive, and you enjoy the full integration of mind, body, and soul.

✦ *Telltale Signs of Heartspace Immersion* ✦

Heartspace Immersion is a state in which you trust yourself fully, eliminate self doubt, and get the results for yourself and others as you desire. Here are some of the markers and signs that you are in Heartspace Immersion:

- ✓ Open Mind
- ✓ Open Heart
- ✓ Connection and Activation
- ✓ Clarity
- ✓ Momentum
- ✓ Effortless Flow
- ✓ Action with Ease

✦ *Heartspace GPS: Goddess Power Source* ✦

Your Heartspace Navigation System is already preprogrammed to "Thrive." Everything you need to know is within you. You have all the answers. You have the full power and authority to create your own happiness and to make your dreams a reality. You are fully connected to your intuition, divine wisdom, and guidance.

You are fierce, fearless, and free when you are tuned in to your GPS and tapped in to your epic Goddess Power Source. You are unstoppable. From this state of Heartspace Immersion, there is not a single thing you could possibly do that would be "wrong." To kick-start the navigation of this journey of expansion, let's explore what it looks like when you are *not* utilizing your inner Heartspace GPS or Goddess Power Source to navigate your way through life.

Don't worry. If any of these hit home, I will share some *Epic Sexy Thrival Tips* so you can make changes that will yield new outcomes and results for you. I've got you girl!

If you catch yourself saying the following as you are seeking to make a decision, you are *not* tuned in to your Heartspace GPS and your Goddess Power Source is *not* activated:

✓ *What do you think?*
✓ *What should I do?*
✓ *What would you do if you were in my shoes?*

That last one drives me the most crazy of all, *especially* when in a romantic love scenario. I always hear people say, "Well, so-and-so said I should end the relationship." Here is the thing, so-and-so is not in your shoes. Even if they were, it is 99.99% likely that he or she would not follow their own advice.

So why the hell would you? I digress...

A big telltale sign that your Heartspace GPS is off is when you have a difficult time making decisions. For example, I was out to eat the other day with a girlfriend and she asked the waiter, "What is your favorite thing on the menu?" He responded with his selection, and she ordered the item.

Sure, maybe you are at a new place, and you are looking for someone to give you insights on what is most popular. Maybe you just want to know what is delicious and yummy, and you are looking for ideas to take them into consideration. Perhaps, when you are ordering, you ask to ensure you are going to get the chef's best. Sure.

But then there are the other people, such as my friend in this case, who asks the same question every single time and *always* gets what the other person recommends. No, she is not being adventurous and playing some kind of playful game. No, she is not experimenting, having fun, and trying new things. No.

She has a hard time making decisions, so she relies on the waiter to make the decision for her. That way, if it sucks, she doesn't have to bear the responsibility of the decision. How do I know for sure? I am an energy reader. I can feel indecision. Also, I brought it up to her and she said, "I know, I am working on it." This was followed by, "How can I get better at being decisive?" I've got you girl!

The number one telltale sign that you are *not* tuned in to your Heartspace GPS, that your Goddess Power Source is not activated, and that you are instead utilizing your Headspace Overload Navigation System is that you are experiencing one or all of the following symptoms:

- ✓ You feel lost and tired.
- ✓ You feel lonely.
- ✓ You feel agitated or frustrated.

✓ You feel angry, sad, or overwhelmed.
✓ You feel like something is missing.

I can go on and on with this list, which basically includes any feeling that is draining or otherwise undesired. You can easily tell how tuned in to your Heartspace GPS you are by answering the following question:

On a scale of 1 to 10, with 1 being "never" and 10 being "always," how often are you immersed in a state of complete euphoric bliss? Really consider this question.

The more tuned in you are, the higher your number will be when you answer this question. This journey we are on together, right here, right now, will offer you options for *how* you can increase the number you chose when you answered this question. I will show you how to improve the quality of your connection to yourself and your Heartspace GPS and activate your Goddess Power Source.

In the pages that follow, I'll give you some scenarios which will help you determine the areas of your life where you are operating from your Heartspace GPS and those areas of your life where you do *not* have access to your Heartspace at all and are rather utilizing your Headspace Overload Navigation System. For the sake of ease and simplicity, I am going to refer to these two opposite states as Headspace Overload, which describes your experience when you are *not* tuned in to your heart at all, and

Heartspace Immersion, which is when your inner GPS, your Goddess Power Source, is on fire!

✦ *Headspace Overload: A Closer Look* ✦

Let me be clear: Before we jump into discussing Headspace Overload, know that what we are about to cover is merely the shadow side of Headspace. There are two sides of Headspace and utilizing the mind. One is the light side. The light side of Headspace has to do with strategizing, putting things into action, and building epic momentum to make your dreams come true.

The other side of Headspace, the shadow side, is the more common version most of us are conditioned to operate from and is based on what we have learned from prior generations. This less-desired experience includes *over*thinking and *over*analyzing. It involves endless mind chatter and analysis paralysis. In this book, you will learn how you can reprogram yourself into the light side of Headspace and move out of the shadow side. Having these insights will support you as you create a life that you truly *love* living and be a version of you that you *love* being, inside and out.

YOUR HEADSPACE OVERLOAD CHECKLIST

Explore and consider where in your life you are...

- ✓ Experiencing a lot of **fear**? Fear can also show up as worry, anxiety, or nervousness.

- ✓ Feeling as if you are **pushing yourself forward** as opposed to being pulled forward with ease?

✓ Hearing yourself give a lot of **reasons why** you can't do something, and / or can't have whatever it is that you want?

✓ Replaying **regrets** and what ifs from the past?

✓ Experiencing **doubts**?

✓ Seeking **external validation**?

SPOTLIGHT EXAMPLE #1. You experience something and feel the need to talk to other people to find out if what you are feeling and experiencing is normal or crazy, real or imagined, good or bad.

SPOTLIGHT EXAMPLE #2. You feel someone has wronged you and you share it with other people so you can find out for sure whether the other person is in the wrong.

SPOTLIGHT EXAMPLE #3. Someone says something about you that you totally do not believe is true, but it is throwing you for a loop. As a result, you reach out to others to see if maybe there is some truth in what was said.

SPOTLIGHT EXAMPLE #4. You start off thinking you look pretty damn good in your brand new outfit, but then no one says anything. You start to doubt how you were originally feeling. You start to question and tell yourself, "If no one tells me how good I look, then maybe I don't look that good."

SPOTLIGHT EXAMPLE #5. Wanting to be liked by others, you do things you don't want to do, because you are afraid others won't like you if you don't. Or, conversely, you don't do things that you do actually want to do, because you are afraid others will not like you or "get you" if you do said things. For example, you say, "Yes" when you want to say, "No." Or you say, "No" when you actually want to say "Hell yes!"

More from the Headspace Overload Checklist . . .

✓ Experiencing **consuming thoughts**?

✓ Giving up your own **opinions** to the "shoulds" and "ought tos" of others? Putting the opinions, thoughts, ideas, and advice of others above your own inner desires?

✓ Playing by **other people's rules**?

✓ Putting **others' needs** and wants above your own?

✓ Experiencing **guilt**?

✓ Finding yourself in **someone else's control**?

✓ **Blaming** others for your unhappiness? Consider where you are blaming others in the areas of work, relationships, and family.

✓ Seeking to **control other people**, events and circumstances, or situations and processes?

✓ Discovering you are not where you want to be or feeling as if you **cannot control** where you are?

✓ Feeling **lost** in the problem?

✓ **Judging** others?

SPOTLIGHT EXAMPLE #1. Feeling as if someone else is doing something "wrong" or believing you have a better way for them.

SPOTLIGHT EXAMPLE #2. Feeling as if someone else should be doing something in a different way than the way they are choosing to do something. Or believing that they should behave in a different way. Or *be* someone different than who they are being.

✓ **Comparing** yourself to others?

✓ Beating yourself up with **negative self-talk** or self-criticism?

✓ Focused on a mentality of **lack**? You may think, for example, that you do not have enough money, enough education, enough quality choices in your dating pool, or enough time.

✓ Feeling you are **just surviving** or getting through the day?

✓ Feeling **resentful**, angry, or overwhelmed?

✓ **Short of breath**?

✓ **Over-thinking** your way through a situation? So afraid of being "wrong" that you are stuck in analysis paralysis, replaying endless "what ifs"?

✓ **Doing things** you don't necessarily want to do? Or not doing things that you totally want to do, all because you have convinced yourself you are being "responsible"?

Headspace Overload feels exhausting. Even doing that exercise might have felt draining if you are caught up in overload. I promise the next exercise feels a whole lot better. I'll help you figure out how to decrease that damn drain, so stay with me here! Headspace Overload literally drains your entire body of energy. It drains your mind. It drains your emotional energy bank. It sucks your soul.

Headspace Overload leads you into living life on other people's terms. It leads you into patterns of people-pleasing, mind-reading, and care-taking. You tend to others' feelings above your own. Often times, when you are in Headspace Overload, you are nowhere to be found on your own priority list. We were taught that to make ourselves a priority was "selfish." Sigh. Oh man, it is so not selfish.

In fact, if everyone on this planet were to put themselves higher on their own priority list and embrace a life of Heartspace Immersion, we would be having soooo much more fun here, people! It is selfish to not put yourself on your own priority list, because when you are not on your own list of priorities, you are emotionally, mentally, and physically exhausted and drained.

Perpetual existence in such a state leaves you burnt-out, short-tempered, and unpleasant to be around. It leads you to all things negative or to living in the past or the future, neither of which is here and now. You will wind up trying to be something that you aren't just so that others will like you or not be upset by who you are. It will have you running around and taking care of others while unconsciously and unintentionally disempowering them.

Let's redefine the word "selfish" in a way that extends beyond the limitations of the past generations. What if it was "selfish" to deprive the world of you and your epic, awesome self in your full-blown authenticity? What if it was "selfish" to deprive your soulmate of the opportunity to find you because you are running around like a chicken with your head cut off, trying to be everything to everyone, trying to be everything but you!

What if you saw that it was selfish to deprive your children of being themselves, knowing they learn how to be based on what they see you do. That's right, not what you tell them to do, but actually what they see you do. Guuurrrllll, they are going to do it too. They will try to be someone they are not and become a chameleon, fitting in instead of being unapologetically themselves and letting the world see their true colors.

Let's stop passing this on from generation to generation. What if you stopped being what you are calling "selfish" and started just being you, unapologetically and authentically you? What if you broke the cycle and chose you?

Epic Sexy Q&A

Let's do a little exercise. Take out a piece of paper, and ask yourself the following questions.

✦ **Where in your life** are you experiencing the qualities on the Headspace Overload Checklist? Be as specific as you possibly can.

✦ **Where are you** when this characteristic of Headspace Overload shows up?

✦ **Who are you with** when you experience this particular effect of Headspace Overload?

✦ **What are you doing** when you feel this way?

Go one by one and explore. Be brutally honest with yourself. You are the only one who will even see your answers, and you can burn them later if you want. And guurll, if you can't be honest with *yourself*, then how the hell are you ever going to honest with others about what you want so that you can receive it all?

Let's do this!

Heartspace Immersion: A Closer Look

Each individual's Heartspace Immersion experience will be totally unique. It will look wildly different from one person to the next, because we all have different things that speak to our souls. We each have certain things that ignite us, that make us feel alive, that make us feel loved, inspired, and passionate! That is the beauty about us. We are each different. Each one of us has so much to offer one another as a result. It makes this place more interesting. Woo!

I am well aware that *my* own version of Heartspace Immersion, which I am about to share with you, may sound a little woo-woo or La La Land to some folks. It may perhaps seem inaccessible or not real. It may seem unattainable, intangible, or even somewhat imaginary. I personally love me some good woo-wooness, and I *love* letting my imagination run wild and free, so that makes perfect sense that I can come off that way at times.

Listen, I spent thirty years of my life angry as all hell, numbing and suppressing my true self. Now that I let my true self out of the cage, I let her run as wild and free as she wants to be. I am aware that she can be over the top. I *love* her for that! I love *me*.

I'll guide you through an exercise to help you figure out what *your* Heartspace Immersion looks and feels like. But, first, I will give you a little glimpse into my personal experience of Heartspace Immersion. This list will give you a start. Perhaps it will spark some ideas. For me, Heartspace Immersion is:

- ✓ Clouds parting, the sun shining, and angels singing
- ✓ Rainbows and sunshine

63

✓ Puppies and kittens

✓ Skipping playfully and running carefree

✓ Connecting with my favorite souls in the entire universe

✓ Fun, adventure, and play

✓ Growth, metamorphosis, and transformation

✓ Love, connection, and complete euphoric bliss

✓ The freedom to be unapologetically me

✓ A hug on my leg from my four-year-old nephew

✓ A child's giggle

✓ A cartwheel

✓ Experiencing anything new for the first time

✓ A walk on the beach

✓ Listening to the waves crash on the shore

✓ Snuggling up with my love

✓ Passionate kisses, holding my man's hand, making love

✓ Writing

✓ Jumping out of airplanes or off cliffs

✓ Running with my dog

✓ Facing a fear

✓ Life coaching with my Epic Sexy clients

✓ Driving in a convertible with the top down

✓ Being surrounded by epic, beautiful views of nature

✓ Seeing and connecting with animals of all kinds

✓ Laughing

✓ Seeing another human being smile

✓ Reading a good book

✓ Learning something new

✓ Making furniture

✓ Painting

- ✓ Going on lady dates with my soul sisters
- ✓ Getting a massage
- ✓ Dancing to my favorite jams
- ✓ Turning the music up in my car, singing at the top of my lungs while dancing in my seat, and amusing fellow drivers with their front-row seats to the concert of me
- ✓ Arts and crafts
- ✓ Decorating a house
- ✓ Putting together a smoking-hot outfit or playing dress up
- ✓ Designer gowns
- ✓ Dreaming up wildly vivid dreams of epic proportions
- ✓ Going to a live music concert
- ✓ Immersing myself in another culture and traveling the world
- ✓ Defying perceived limitations
- ✓ Stretching myself and expanding my comfort zone
- ✓ Taking leaps of faith and baby steps of growth
- ✓ Hosting an Epic Sexy Adventure Retreat
- ✓ Laying out in the sun or on a raft in a pool
- ✓ Jumping on a trampoline
- ✓ Making new memories with family, friends, and my love
- ✓ Connecting with kindred souls
- ✓ Channeling spirit guides
- ✓ Playing board games
- ✓ Building out coaching content that will blow people's minds and sustainably change their worlds forever

Now that you've had a mini-glimpse into my Heartspace Immersion ideal, take a second to think about *your* version. I *know* in every single fiber of my being that we each can absolutely create our very own Heaven on Earth. It happens when we embrace a Heartspace Immersion existence! Oooo, Heartspace, how I love thee!

Let's get you one step closer to YOUR very own Heartspace Immersion and Heaven on Earth, shall we? First, take a look at the qualities of Heartspace Immersion that follow.

YOUR HEARTSPACE IMMERSION CHECKLIST

Explore and consider where in your life you are...

✓ Feeling **drawn to life**, pulled effortlessly and joyfully forward, and immersed in a beautiful, momentous flow?

✓ Celebrating your **awesomeness**? Taking time to celebrate a breakthrough, achievement, or promotion, an Aha moment, a project finished, or a goal set and accomplished?

✓ Making **decisions** based on what you want?

✓ **Investing** your time and energy exploring your limitless possibilities and the opportunities available to you?

In a Headspace Overload state, you are caught up in *over*thinking, *over*analyzing, and think, think, thinking your way through as you navigate the complexities of the situation. Contrast this to the state of Heartspace Immersion, where you truly do have an overflowing and abundant source of creative solutions and possibilities available to you.

When you are in Heartspace Immersion, you take the time to explore options, capture them, play with them, and put them into action. You invest your time and energy in all things that are within your control, rather than wasting time wishing things, situations, events, and / or people were different. In Heartspace Immersion, you focus on the solution and not the problem.

You focus on your desires, your soul's cravings, and your want-tos instead of the perceived shoulds or ought-tos. You let your imagination run wild and free as you conjure up visions of your future that are so grand that others, and sometimes even yourself, think you are delusional. Then, you allow space and time to make those things happen!

More from Your Heartspace Immersion Checklist . . .

✓ **Solution-focused?** Your immediate auto-pilot reaction is to go right past the "perceived problem" into the solution.

✓ **Positive self-talk?**

✓ Focused on a mentality of **endless abundance**? Feeling an abundance of time, resources, money, love, energy, and ideas.

✓ **Listening to your gut**? Taking action on what it says, even when your Headspace or others have wildly opposing views to your divine guidance?

✓ Feeling blissful? **Peaceful**? Carefree?

✓ Euphoric? **Excited**? Joyful? Happy? Playing?

✓ **Laughing** and having fun?

✓ Feeling **warm and fuzzy**? A hug from your niece or nephew, a smile or giggle from a baby, snuggling with a fur baby, taking a hot bath, or curling up with a comfy blanket for movie night.

✓ **Fully present?** Enjoying the moments as they come and being fully present to the magic and beauty of the moment, rather than feeling lost in the worry of the what ifs about the future or the regrets of the past.

✓ Feeling **gratitude**? Love? Passion?

✓ **Ignited** in the depths of your soul?

✓ Inspired, **energized**, and fueled? Alive?

✓ Feelings of **thriving**?

✓ **Trusting** yourself?

✓ **Getting intuitive hits?** A sense of knowingness, even though the head may not logically be able to understand it.

✓ **Breathing deeply**, with great pleasure and joy?

✓ Intentionally, purposefully, and consciously **making decisions** and choices and *creating* a life that you love living?

✓ Successfully feeling your way through a situation? Getting the **results** that you desired because you trusted your intuition and it led you to a beautiful outcome?

Epic Sexy Q&A

Take out a piece of paper. Ask yourself the following questions.

✦ What are ideas for *your* very own **Heaven on Earth**? What does it look like? What delights your eyes?

✦ What **activities** are you doing? What are you experiencing?

✦ **Who** are you spending time with?

✦ What does it **sound like**? What sounds make your ears do an epic happy dance of joy?

✦ What does it **taste like**? What tastes make you salivate?

✦ What does it **feel like**? Activate your emotions: What emotions, when you experience them, make you feel like you are in heaven? Activate your sense of physical touch: What sensations do you love feeling on your skin? The wind? A lover's touch? A soft blanket?

✦ What does it **smell like**? What smells drive you wild with excitement, bring you back to the fondest of memories, make you feel the way you crave to feel, relax you beyond belief, and or energize you?

✦ How is life **different** when you are experiencing Heartspace Immersion rather than Headspace Overload? Consider work, family relationships, friendships, and romantic relationships.

✦ Where in your life are you experiencing the qualities listed on the **Heartspace Immersion** Checklist? Go one by one and explore.

✦ Keep up that brutal honesty with yourself. Create a column next to your "Where is this showing up in my life?" that explores the question, "In what **area of my life** would I like this to show up?"

✦ Think of each area of your life in which these qualities come into play, along with specifics like who you are with when you experience each of these qualities. **Where are you?** What are you doing? Be as specific as you possibly can.

✦ *Celebrating You Now* ✦

Here's the thing: if you have a heavily-weighted experience of a Headspace Overload existence, then you may be tempted to beat yourself up. Knock that off right meow. (Meow. Haha. I am such a child sometimes. That gets me every time!) No, seriously, knock that off. Pronto! Hold up, and let's take a second to acknowledge and validate that you are using your Heartspace Immersion right now, this very second.

You have this book in your possession right now at this *very* moment. It is a book you chose to buy based on your Heartspace desires, and it is a guide that will give you a plethora of options for *how* you can change your life. It will give you tools that will invite the pain and heaviness you are experiencing in your day-to-day life to take a hike. Actually, if you think about it, this book is *exactly* where it should be, at *exactly* the right time in your life, *exactly* what you need, and all because *you* tapped into your Heartspace Immersion GPS, and activated your Goddess Power Source. You manifested this through *your* desire to change *your* life. Ummm, hellooo Heartspace. You are already doing it! Look at you!!

So that means that *you rock*. Yeah, you are pretty damn badass. Take a second, and give yourself one of the following: 1) a pat on the back, 2) a high five, 3) a hug. Go ahead, take your time. I'll wait. Seriously. Amuse me. Pick *one* of the above, and just *do* it. I told you this book's intention is to create a habit of *doing*, and the act of *doing* is what is going to change your life. It's your choice. Do it! Woo!!

Insert anything you'd like. Me? I'm taking a break from the writing and giving myself a lovingly smug hug with a huge shit-eating grin on my face. Oh, that feels soooo nice. OK, I'll be honest. I followed that hug up with a pat on the back and a couple of high fives too. Don't judge me. Haha. Wooo!! Alrighty then, let's move on.

Epic Sexy Q&A

Take a moment to explore the following questions. To practice the habit of doing, write your answers down.

✦ How would my life be **different** if I immersed myself more in my Heartspace existence? Explore how each area of your life would change: Love. Health. Career. Relationships. Everyday Experience. Now, go back and compare your Headspace Overload and your Heartspace Immersion lists. Look for patterns. Write those bad boys down!

✦ What activities, people, things, situations, locations, and thoughts **add value** to my life and make me feel energized, invigorated, ignited, and alive?

✦ What activities, people, things, situations, locations, and thoughts **drain me** or suck the life out of me?

✦ **What can I do** now, today, to start experiencing more Heartspace Immersion in my life? *Today*, not tomorrow. How can I start right now?

We are not a tribe of waiters. We are a tribe of Epic Sexy doers! Take some time and think, "How can I experience Heartspace Immersion starting now?" You don't have to wait to feel Heaven on Earth. Start creating it and experiencing it today. Write out a list of ideas to get your creative juices flowing. Then, pick one and make it happen.

SPOTLIGHT EXAMPLE. You might pick up a book you've been wanting to read. Perhaps you'll keep reading this epically expansive one because it's so super awesome, why would you ever want to put it down? Right? Preach. You could share your smile with everyone you encounter, call a loved one to connect, or turn on your favorite music and dance. You might take a hot bath, journal, do a few yoga poses, or download the Duo Lingo app to learn that language you've always wanted to learn.

What can you do right this minute to start creating your very own Heaven on Earth?

Here's Your Wake-Up Call: Guurrll, You Better Wake Up and Love Yourself!

Now, I am not saying that using your head or thinking are bad necessarily. But I do believe that there is a better way to use the mind than the historically-conditioned, generationally-inherited way that I've observed that we utilize it today. Guuurrrl, living a Headspace Overload existence shuts off your Heartspace Immersion GPS, leaving you with no access to your Goddess Power Source whatsoever. It's basically like packing up your inner compass, with all of it's divine guidance and wisdom, putting it in a box, and stocking it on the shelf to be utilized at a later date.

Trust me, I *know* this because that was me for the first thirty years of my life. Let me tell you what that Headspace existence looked like for me. Here are the results I was getting:

- ✓ I suffered from the **Epic Disease to Please**. No matter how badly I *reaaally* wanted to, I never said "No" to *anyone*. I thought it was selfish to do things any other way.

- ✓ I couldn't **make a decision** to save my life. One time I even had to ask my bestie to come over to my place and see the color I had painted my second bedroom to see if *she* liked it. That was the only way I could give myself permission to like it too. Or to paint it another color if she didn't like it. Yeah, that happened. Not my best work.

✓ My word to others was more important than **my word to myself**, which meant that I *never* kept promises to myself, *ever*. This also meant that I did not trust myself, at all. Who would trust someone who never kept her word? Right? How the hell could I trust myself when I was the Queen of Empty Promises?

✓ I was *nowhere* **to be found on my own priority list**, and I most definitely thought that it would be selfish if I even had a desire to be on my own list.

✓ **I drank.** A lot. Like alcoholic beast-mode status. I was a master number. I was highly functioning in my career and incredibly successful by society's definition, so I never thought it was a problem. I could not form and keep a healthy relationship as a direct result, because I would bottle things up and communicate in the form of epic meltdowns that took some liquid courage. It wasn't pretty.

✓ I dated incredibly *toxic* assclowns, **picking life partners who were emotionally unavailable** and usually an addict of some form. Then, once I broke that pattern, I dated a guy who was awesome. Well, on paper he was awesome. And by awesome I mean awesome for someone else. According to everyone else *except* me, he was *the* guy for me. I just didn't have that epic, sexy, want-to-rip-your-clothes-off kind of chemistry with him, and I wanted that in a relationship. I *knew* something was missing, and I even told my loved ones, but they kept telling me I was wrong. They said that the chemistry would come with time. I ignored my own desires, feelings, and inner knowing. I ignored my gut and stayed with him because my Headspace had a *long* list of reasons that I would be *crazy* if I left such an amazing man. And my Heartspace sat back down on the bench and sighed as it was yet again being ignored and not allowed in the game.

✓ I **chain-smoked** cigarettes.

✓ My **nutritional lifestyle** consisted of pizza, Oreo shakes, Big Macs, mozzarella sticks, hamburgers, and other fast food, mostly consumed while hungover, couch surfing, and wasting the day away.

✓ **I didn't think I was enough**. I felt I was not pretty enough, not worthy of the love I wanted, not lovable, and not thin enough. I believed I was never successful enough, even when I had paid off all of my debt, bought a condo and a car, had a ton of money in the bank, and was at the highest level in the company. It was never enough.

✓ I never treated myself to anything too extravagant. I **saved all my money**, because I believed that was the "responsible" thing to do. I never enjoyed my money or appreciated and honored my ability to create financial abundance. In other words, I made a ton of money, but never treated myself to a damn thing. I saved it all and had so much fear and guilt around spending my own hard-earned money, unless of course it was spent on someone else.

✓ For the first four years I lived in my condo, I had my bedroom setup in the small room of my place while I had the **master bedroom *empty***. I used it as a storage space for boxes, so that I could figure out how to furnish the most baller bedroom in *my* place as a room where guests could enjoy themselves when they came over. You know, because I was *nowhere* to be found on my own priority list. Yeah.

Epic Rewards You Can Expect

Through the years, I've dedicated myself to the path of self-discovery, growth, and exploration to become the woman that I am today. For an idea of the epic rewards you can expect on your own journey, let me share what happened as a result of my own consistent focus and *action* of immersing myself in a Heartspace Existence.

The picture on the left was taken while I was working in my office, which is where I spent my workaholic existence prior to my awakening. I spent more hours in that office than I did in my own home. When I wasn't working, I was often found in a bar, chain-smoking cigarettes, stuffing my face with pizza, and masterfully numbing myself with alcohol. The picture on the right was taken post-awakening, 35+ pounds lighter, four sizes smaller, and eight months into my journey to Epic Sexy Me. When I let go of all of the emotional shit that had been weighing me down for years, the pounds literally just melted off.

✓ **I lost 35+ pounds** and cellulite diminished.

✓ **I fell in love with myself**, mind, *body*, and soul. It was the first time in my life that I *loved* the skin I was in.

SPOTLIGHT EXAMPLE. When I was 20 years old I was incredibly thin and beautiful, and yet I never felt sexy. I used to hide myself. Literally. I remember living in Florida and going to the beach, and *always* keeping my legs covered. I was the girl who would bring the wrap or towel with me to the edge of the pool, drop it, and jump in as quickly as I could before people could see me!

Then, I would not get out of the pool without my safety blanket that could hide me. I remember wishing desperately to be the girl that could strut her stuff around the pool, feeling confident, radiant, and *sexy* in her own skin. I *am* that girl now. Sure, it helps that I look like a million bucks now, but I was hot and sexy at twenty years old too. I just didn't *feel* that way at all back then.

Sexy is a mindset, and a Self Love regimen makes all the difference in the world. Back when I was twenty years old, I was taking diet pills, not eating much, hiding, and feeling not enough. I was living in a Headspace Overload existence. Now, Heartspace Immersion has me all in love with myself – my body, my mind, my heart, my soul, *and* my life!

✓ **I broke free from the pattern** of dating toxic assclowns. I refused to date people who everyone else thought were great for me when I knew I would never fall super, madly, deeply, passionately in love with them. I found a man that was everything I was looking for and more. I fell madly, deeply in love *and* had that epic, sexy, want-to-rip-your-clothes-off kind of passion. I found it all, including a healthy, loving, exciting relationship where I feel *on fire*! I have a relationship with a man who inspires me to be a better woman, and I inspire him to be a better man. I am intellectually stimulated, emotionally supported, and unapologetically me. I am fully present in each moment. Fearless. Fierce. The best part? This epic love story is just the icing on the cake of an already euphoric existence.

✓ After first saying, "Yes," I gave myself **permission to change my mind** and be true to myself.

SPOTLIGHT EXAMPLE. I changed my mind, followed my heart, and walked away from an opportunity to be the sole spearheading creative contributor to build out and run an international group coaching program for a world-renowned life coach who I worked closely with for over a year. Most people around me thought it was *crazy* for me to pass up the opportunity. But I had a sense of *knowing* in the depths of my soul that I had my own mission to fulfill.

I was listening to my soul's cravings, which were loud and clear. I chose the freedom to be who I am, to do what I want, whenever I want and from wherever in the world I wanted to do it. I chose to create endless epic adventures for myself and my tribe so that we can all *experience* and *feel* that growth and expansion doesn't have to be so serious-pants and heavy. I chose the experience of feeling liberated, free, wild, crazy, and *fun*!

I wanted to travel the world and share this Heartspace mission with the entire universe. I wanted to take time to connect with each and every single person that I work with, whether one-on-one or in the intimate, group coaching environments created at the retreats and events I host. I craved to be able to integrate my intuitive spiritual gifts and not have to hold back or fit into someone else's idea of who I should and shouldn't be.

I craved creating a business with love as a primary foundation, one that was rooted in a connective principle and philosophy. I craved sharing all of the pattern-breaking information that I had collected over the years through experiences of breaking free from all the junk that weighs us down, instead of memorizing someone else's content and it not coming from my own heart and soul. Basically, no matter who the offer was coming from, it was clear to me that I couldn't play full out in honoring *my* values, my heart, my intuition, and my soul if I worked for anyone else but *me*.

After listening to my Headspace *Overload* and the gazillion reasons it made logical sense to say, "Yes!" to this opportunity to build out this international coaching program, I eventually took some time to be radically honest with myself. Then I walked away from the opportunity. After doing so, I went full speed ahead with my own Heartspace Immersion business.

I listened to my soul's fire, found my calling, and started to focus full-time on my own business and pursue my purpose. As a result, I have grown my very own wildly successful global coaching practice, winning in a Heartspace Immersion existence! Woo!!

Here are a few more things that happened for me...

✓ I moved my Epic Sexy Self into my **epic master bedroom** and swagged it out per my inner goddess's every desire. I gave myself permission to spend money on myself. Now, I treat myself, pamper myself, spoil myself, and celebrate myself, because I am abundantly, epically awesome!

✓ **I bet on me!** Taking an epic leap of faith, I quit my incredibly lucrative corporate job to focus full-time on my soul's passionate mission: to ignite souls worldwide to live from a "Hell Yes" space. I set out to create an empowered tribe of fearless individuals who set the world on fire by living a limitless life they love unapologetically.

I know in every single fiber of my being that we were put here to PLAY, *have* FUN, THRIVE, *experience endless* ADVENTURES, *and be immersed in a pure* HEARTSPACE *Immersion existence of boundless* EUPHORIA.

✓ I embraced the intuitive knowingness that **I came here on a mission** to show others that you *can* have it all. I fully accepted that I have been equipped with the kickass, code-breaking skills to help others unleash that ferocious, *unstoppable* power within.

✓ I embraced my **spiritual gifts**. The more I have leaned into these gifts, the more incredibly powerful they have become. I am an energy reader, which allows me to look for and see deeply ingrained energetic patterns that hold people back from the very things their souls crave. I also get intuitive downloads while I am coaching my clients as I channel their higher self and their spirit guides. It's funny, because sometimes people love what I say, and I'm all, "That is not me; that is *you*. Your higher self said that, not me. Own your power!" Sure, some people who are *not* a part of my tribe may judge me and think I am weird as all can be. Some people may call me "woo woo." Yet I have **embraced these gifts**, and I will touch billions of lives as a result.

It's a disservice to humanity when you don't live on purpose, embrace all you are, and intentionally tune into your Heartspace GPS, fully activating your Goddess Power Source, so that you can lean into your passion-filled mission, which will sustainably change the lives of all of those you encounter. Every example of expansion and uplevel in my own experience is similar to the outcomes and results I witness my clients experiencing when they journey into their Heartspace Immersion! You can have this too!!

• • • • •
THRIVAL PERSPECTIVE
• • • • •

When you tune into your own inner GPS {Goddess Power Source}, your Heartspace inevitably leads you to truly LOVING life and falling madly deeply in love with yourself!

If that is what is waiting for you on the other side, is there any reason that you wouldn't want to live a Heartspace existence? How are you ever going to get what you want if you are living a Headspace existence that is literally making it impossible for you to even know what it is that you want in the first place? You are an epically intuitive being, and you have an inner GPS there to guide you every single step of the way. I am going to show you how to tune into it so that you hear it loud and clear and claim all the desires that your soul craves.

EPIC SEXY THRIVAL TIPS

Let's move on to the fun stuff and the how-to. The remainder of this section is filled with different thaaangs that you can try, experiment with, play with, and have fun with as you explore your journey of how to find your inner voice, connect with your intuition, find out what you really want, and allow your heart and soul to be your GPS in life.

We will explore what you want, so you can program that destination of desire into your Heartspace GPS, activate your Goddess Power Source, and have your own customized roadmap to thriving. That map is actually waiting inside you. Once you find it, you'll never have to look external for love or happiness ever again.

Remember, pick one thing at a time and play with it for a week. Pay attention to how it makes you feel. If you experience an uplevel or insights, then keep doing it. Play, experiment, and have fun with it. Once you've got the hang of that thing, add another approach while sustaining the first thing. And repeat.

This is about laying one solid brick at a time to your foundation, and building upon each one, all the while having a ton of fun. These are not isolated, individual pieces, but rather many pieces to a whole. Let's go find your custom roadmap to a thriving existence!

Wake Up the Wild Wise Woman Within

These Thrival Tips are all about connecting with your intuition, and guiding you to finally answer the question, "What do *I* want?" Inside you, there is a woman who knows *exactly* what she wants. That woman is fierce, fearless, and free! Let's go find her, shall we?

✦ Questions to Get this Partaay Started! ✦

Get out a piece of paper and answer the questions in the following Epic Sexy Q&A. Don't judge or filter yourself. You are the only one who is going to read this, so just write down whatever comes to mind. Before you ask yourself these questions, let me remind you of something that will be an inevitable encounter for which you need to prepare yourself.

Do *not* count yourself out of the life you crave to live *before* you even give yourself the opportunity to dream it up and write it down. *Ignore* all your "Yeah, but" thoughts and fight against the voice of the "realist" in you. As my boy Will Smith says, "Being realistic is the most common path to mediocrity." And we are *not* settling for mediocrity anymore. That is precisely why you picked up this book! We are here to create a life you *love* living, not a life that is *realistic* based on someone else's limiting beliefs that keep *them* playing small and prevents *them* from thriving.

Epic Sexy Q&A

Take some time and write down your answers to the following questions. Before you get busy answering each question, take three deep breaths in and out. Breathe in to the count of 5, hold for the count of 5, breathe out to the count of 5, and hold for the count of 5. Then, read each question slowly. After reading each question, close your eyes and listen for whatever comes up. Then, pick up your pen and write it down. Work your way back to Epic Sexy You!

+ If **money and time** were in endless abundance, and if there were zero limitations, if you had all the resources, education, experience, intelligence, and connections that you already needed at your full disposal... What would you do with your life?

+ What are the **top three things** that your soul craves right now?

+ What is **one thing** that, if you dedicated your time, energy, focus, and consistent, intentional, purposeful action to that thing, would literally change your life?

+ Considering the above answer, what is the **one bold action** that you can do daily that will lead you to the life you desire?

+ What are **ten things** you want to accomplish this year?

✦ Which **one goal** of the above ten things, when you achieve that, will make the biggest shift in the trajectory towards the life your soul craves?

GET YOUR SHARE ON *#epicsexyyou*

✦ *Create Your Own Spoiled-Rotten, Pampered, Ninja Warrior Goddess Soul Cravings List* ✦

Literally just sit down and write out what your inner spoiled-rotten, pampered Ninja Warrior Goddess wants. *I want... I want... I want....* Repeat that over and over and over again until you run out of wants, and then repeat that some more. Woo! Do not hold back, and do not be "realistic." Just completely let your inner child unleash her epic imagination. Go wild and crazy and free, with absolutely no limitations. Ignore all the "Yeah, buts" that come up, and let your creativity run rampant.

We played with this at a speaking engagement that I did for a company and one woman was all about the llamas. Yes, that is right, I said llamas. She was a doctor, and yet her inner desire was to own a llama farm. Get it girl! Go on with your bad self! Don't judge your inner desires, just let them come out and write it all down.

I want... I want... I want...

SPOTLIGHT EXAMPLE. Before my business was ever a reality, I created a list to explore what I wanted. Here's my list:

✓ I want financial **abundance**.

✓ I want **endless adventures**.

✓ I want to **travel** this playground that is our world.

✓ I want **complete freedom**: in my life, my day, my decisions, and my actions; in who I am, in what I do, in how I do it, and in when I do it.

✓ I want to create **a sisterhood movement** that empowers women to own their power and create a life that they love living on their own terms.

✓ I want to embrace and use the **spiritual gifts** that have been bestowed upon me.

✓ I want to **change lives**.

✓ I want to help women **find love**.

✓ I want to help women **fall back in love** with themselves. I want to help them feel sexy in their own skin.

✓ I want to help women get where they want to go **faster** than how long it took me to get where I wanted to go and to experience less pain than what I went through.

✓ I want to **help female entrepreneurs** build Epic
Sexy Empires.

✓ I want to help people **find their purpose** in life.

I wrote my list, and then I created my business from that list of soul cravings. Not the other way around. I did *not* limit myself to some kind of cookie-cutter framework or stick to the so-called rules. I let my soul's cravings be the directional compass to the creation of the business, and those desires were *dead on* to the Epic Sexy You business and brand that exists today.

Let me give you an idea of some of the more random things that I want. These aren't even necessarily specific to my business. They are just general desires of my soul's playful cravings. Unfiltered, uninhibited, and running totally wild, rampant, and free, here are some of my desires:

✓ I want make random unsuspecting peoples **dreams
come true** for an *entire* year!

✓ I want my own awe-inspiring and **uplifting TV
show** that touches billions of lives and moves souls
beyond what is even currently fathomable! A show
that ignites people's fires within, inspires them to
know that they can have it all, that we are here to
have fun, that we are limitless beings, and that
anything is possible! A television show that
motivates others to create visions and dreams of
epic proportions, to fill their lives with epic

adventures, to lean into resistance, to challenge and stretch every perceived limit that they currently have, and to look and feel sexy while doing it all. Basically, I want a show where I bring an Epic Sexy Adventure Retreat into the homes of people around the globe! If you are reading this and can help make this dream happen, call me!

✓ I want a **backyard** where my dog can run around in circles, where we can both sunbathe like the sun goddesses that we are, and where I can work outside on beautiful days, reading, writing, and relaxing.

✓ I want a **pool**.

✓ I want a **hammock**. Plus, I want my man in a hammock of his own, next to me, holding my hand.

✓ I want a **house in a warm climate** *and* a house in my hometown. I want to spend winters in said warm climate like the epic snowbird that I am.

✓ I want to leave an **Oprah-like imprint** on the world, but in my own unique Epic Sexy way.

✓ I want to go **cage diving with sharks**. I want to base-jump. I want to repel a *tall* building. I want to hang-glide. I want to go skydiving again but this time with an epic view and a beach landing.

✓ I want to **learn how to fly** a plane.

✓ I want a **motorcycle**.

✓ I want to **travel first-class**, with access to first-class
   lounges in airports. I want to fly in private jets.

✓ I want an **underwater submarine** jet thingy that I
   can fly under the depths of the water in.

✓ I want to go to **outer space**. Come on, Richard
   Branson and team; as soon as you guys are offering
   it to the general public, I am on board that shuttle.

✓ **I want to meet** Elon Musk, Chelsea Handler,
   Richard Branson, Oprah, Marie Forleo, Danielle
   LaPorte, and Kris Carr. The last three are close
   friends and I want to take them on an epic adventure
   where I help them uplevel their already limitless
   and amazingly epic lives *and* have a ton of fun
   doing it. While I'm at it, I would like to bring
   Oprah, Gayle, and Chelsea Handler! OMG the six
   women that I just mentioned, all together on the
   same expansive adventure, an adventure of a
   lifetime that can only be created by channeling all
   their Spirit Guides at once (which happens to be my
   exact specialty) and delivering the most Epic Soul
   Pow Wow of all time. I think I could die and go to

heaven. And Chelsea, before you hate on this idea,
just know that your spirit team is all about it! Call
me ladies! Let's do this!

You bet your ass that your very own list of playful and imaginative desires will help you create and customize your very own Epic Sexy Life that you *absolutely love* living. Make sure to revisit your desires frequently. Imagine if you read this list every single morning first thing while you are still in bed. How different would you feel starting your day with this list rather than grabbing your phone to check emails? Do you really want to wake up to an endless list of requests, demands, and to dos littered in your inbox?

And don't forget to check back in with yourself. Our wants change over time, so give yourself permission to change your mind. Give yourself permission to want even more. Uplevel to the highest degree. Get it girl!!

GET YOUR SHARE ON #epicsexyyou

✦ *Play the "What Do I Want" Game* ✦

Every single time you are in a situation where you catch yourself thinking about what someone else wants in that moment, stop. Whether you catch yourself practicing mind-reading skills or find yourself in the midst of straight-up asking them what they want, stop and immediately ask yourself: *What do I want?*

If you spent the same amount of time and energy on exploring what you want as you do mind-reading others' wants, you'd already know what you want and you'd probably already have a ton of it. Now, I'm not suggesting that you stop giving a shit about others and be a completely self-absorbed, narcissistic diva. I'm just saying think about your own desires and needs just as much as you think about others. "Me too!"

Soon, you'll begin to notice that you are happier. Your relationships with others will improve too. Well, at least your relationship with healthy peeps. No healthy person wants all of your energy directed at them. That is overwhelming and suffocating, and healthy people know how to ask you for what they want and need so that you don't have to read their mind.

Have fun with this game! Play it all the time! Be silly and playful. Do it everywhere you go. At the grocery store: "What do I want?" Waiting in line, driving in the car or stopped at a traffic light: "Hmmm. What do I want?" Get curious. Intentionally feed your mind this question all day every day. Let it run on autopilot.

✦ *No Means, NO!* ✦

Assign yourself a day every week where you just say "No" to everyone and anyone who asks for anything. Nope. No. Naw. Ain't Happenin'. It doesn't matter how you say it, but that day is all about you. All day long, this day is about asking yourself, "What do I want?" and then taking action to make it happen.

You can even let people know ahead of time if you want: "Saturday is my Me Day." Just know that there are people who are still going to ask you for things on that very day. I mean, come on, if you don't usually say no, they are likely used to you saying one thing and doing another. You have conditioned them to believe that they come first, even above your own needs, and that you are most certainly not going to actually say "No" to them, especially when they "reeeaaallly neeeeed" you.

The only way to recondition others (and more importantly yourself) to believe that what you say is for real is to show them. You have to follow through with actions that align with the words that come out of your mouth. Say, "No," and then show them that you are serious. Show them that "No" means no.

Tomorrow you can help them, but not today. Wait, before you even think about moving your "me day" to the following day so you can help them today and do you tomorrow. Know that every time you break your word to yourself (and yes, moving the day is breaking your word to yourself), you are just showing yourself and others that you are not a priority in your own life.

You are essentially demonstrating to them that your word means nothing. You are sending a strong energetic vibration to yourself, others, and the universe that you don't deserve the Epic Sexy Existence that you truly crave. Harsh, I know. Tough love, sister friend, because this is so true.

I know from my own experience, since I really struggled with this one for a very long time. If I am being honest, I still struggle with this at times. For example, it's hard to say no to a lover, family member, or a friend when they ask you to spend time with them on the day that you dedicated to you already. It's hard to say no when they reach out and need your help, your time, or your love.

But if you give them your time when you already promised it to yourself, you will begin to resent yourself and them. You may not even realize it consciously, but energetically it is there. Trust me, energy is my jam. I speak that language better than I speak English, and I see the energetic pattern of resentment constantly.

To protect the energetic current that runs between you and your loved ones, so that you can have epic and thriving relationships of all kinds, just let them know that you love them. Then, tell them that tomorrow you are all theirs. Today is for you and only you. The happier you are, the healthier the people that you will attract and retain in your life. What's more, the sooner you can master an epic relationship with yourself, the sooner you can have everything your soul craves. Everything!

Before we call it a wrap on this topic, I want to cover one more thing. There is a fine line between an excuse and a true reason for not pulling through on your "me day." The only person who is going to know the truth of which is which... is *you*! Part of this journey is getting really good at calling BS on yourself, honoring and loving yourself, and giving yourself permission to change course when true reasons arise.

For example, say you are a mom and you have a child that is projectile vomiting. (Yes, this is a legit thing that happens.) Well, let's just say that it would be understandable for you to postpone your "me day" until your child is feeling better. Or say your best friend calls you bawling because she just found out her husband is cheating on her. As long as this is not a common occurrence for said friend, it would be understandable to be flexible on that week's "Me Day." Or if a loved one is rushed to the hospital: understandable cause for a reschedule!

The purpose of telling you this up front is so that you are not tempted to beat yourself up when these things happen. There are always true reasons to be flexible and shift course accordingly. In these cases, you are most definitely not betraying yourself and should in no way feel bad, guilty, or ashamed for postponing your day. If you start to notice habitual rescheduling and postponing, then it's time to get curious. In such a situation, ask yourself what is really going on. This process requires raw honesty with yourself.

Finally, give yourself permission to customize this to what fits for your life. Remove all and any excuses that could get in your way of having scheduled time devoted to all things you. For example, if you are a busy mom, maybe you have a "Me Hour" instead of a full "Me Day" every single week. Remember, this is an ever-evolving process. Experiment with this. Play with it. Try new things, and experience for yourself firsthand what works for you!

Unleash your Heartspace GPS, Activate Your Goddess Power Source

It's time to learn to connect with yourself. It is time to hear what your inner voice is saying, to honor it, to love yourself in a new way, and to transform your life as a result. The *Epic Sexy Thrival Tips* in this section will help you tap in and tune in to all things YOU! ;) xoxo

✦ *Get Your Decision Making On!* ✦

As I said earlier, I've noticed a pattern of epic indecisiveness with my goddesses who aren't tuned in to what they *want*! The good news is that if you are experiencing indecision, this means that you are actually still somewhat accessing your Heartspace or else you would just do whatever everyone else wanted to do and you wouldn't even feel torn in the first place. So, actually, that is means for celebration. Yaaay!!

Now we just need to play with turning the Headspace Overload down a few notches and turning the Heartspace Immersion up a few notches. From there, we can start making some decisions with more grace and ease. Woo!! Resist the temptation to judge yourself for being indecisive. You are merely out of practice with playing in your Heartspace, and that is what we are here to do. We want to move you more and more toward the end of the spectrum where you have access to your Heartspace Immersion GPS. We want your Goddess Power Source to be loud and clear.

From your Heartspace, decisions are made with full clarity, confidence, and an unwavering self-trust. How else do you get good at something other than practicing at it, right? So let's play with this. And let's have some fun, shall we?

First, it's important to meet yourself where you are. Some people are incredibly indecisive, which was where I was once upon a time. Back then, I never even gave myself a millisecond of time or energy to think about what *I* could possibly want, which made decisions *very* hard because I had no clue what I wanted. So, if that is where you are, start making *tiny* decisions like what to eat for lunch instead of asking the waiter to make the decision for you.

✓ Play with making *at least* **one extra decision** a day.

✓ Accompany each decision with an **intentional and purposeful action** and follow through to solidify the decision you've made.

✓ Take a **lesson** from each and every single decision you make. As you progress, implement the lessons learned from past choices. Incorporate these lessons in decisions you make moving forward.

✓ Pay attention to the **differences** between those times you make a decision from your Heartspace GPS as opposed to those times you make a decision from Headspace Overload. Notice where you operate on a "should," a fear, or what you think another wanted you to do. Look at differences in outcomes.

It's all just a learning process! Yes, at the beginning it will feel super uncomfy. You will be stretching yourself, but I assure you that it will feel easier as you do it more. One day soon you will feel so incredibly empowered by your ability to be make decisions and do so with ease, confidence, and rapid speed.

You learn from every decision you make, so the more decisions you make the more you learn. There is no "right" way. There is just the way that feels right to you. So play with this. Have fun, and, if you feel like you've made a "bad" decision, celebrate! Yes, that's right, I said celebrate. Awareness is the breeding ground for new choices, and with new choices come new opportunities for you to finally experience your desired outcomes.

Epic Sexy Q&A

Get curious and ask yourself:

✓ What was it that made that a **"bad" decision**?

✓ Which **navigation system** was I utilizing when I made that decision?

✓ What are **all of the clues** I can gather and use for next time to know when I am utilizing the Heartspace GPS, where no "bad" decisions are even possible?

✓ How can I **learn from this** and prevent a situation where I feel this way again?

✦ *Stop, Meditate, and Listen!* ✦

It's like if Vanilla Ice was to name this *Epic Sexy Thrival Tip*, that is what he'd call it. Yeah, let that one sink in and then try not to sing the song and get your dance on. I digress. There are different forms of meditating and tuning into your inner voice. Get started with a few of my faves.

✓ **Lie down or sit**, whatever is most comfortable to you.

✓ **Just breathe.** Close your eyes. Quiet mind chatter.

✓ Ask yourself **questions** and see what pops up.

✓ Meditate while repeating a **mantra or affirmation** you would like to ingrain deeper into the fiber of your being.

✓ Find **guided meditations** that will walk you through to the relaxation and / or focus you on an intention that you are craving to keep top of mind. (YouTube is an awesome source for freebies.)

✓ Focus on **thoughts of gratitude**, love, laughter, and happiness.

✓ **Yoga** can also be a form of meditation. Your mat. Your practice. Connecting with yourself, getting into the body and out of the mind, and focusing on a physical energetic flow that calms the chatter of the mind.

✓ Even **breath work** can be meditative. Sitting and just taking intentional deep breaths in and out for a few minutes time. Breathing into the tummy for a fully oxygenating experience!

✓ For some, it can even be incredibly meditative and therapeutic to **journal** as your form of releasing and meditating. Just free flow whatever comes up. Or you can write out a question and then write down whatever answers follow!

To each their own! Play with these and find out which one works for YOU! ;) xoxo

✦ *Treat Yo-Self!* ✦

✓ Take yourself out, and / or **buy yourself something
  nice**. Be loving and gentle and kind to yourself: with
  your thoughts, words, actions, and behavior. Give
  yourself the thoughtfulness you so easily give others.
  If you do not hesitate to buy something when you see
  something little you think a loved one will appreciate,
  do the same for yourself. When you see something
  you like, gift it to you!

✓ Pamper yourself with a **massage** or a **mani / pedi**.
  You can even do the mani and pedi at home if your
  budget is tight. Don't let money become an excuse.
  Ask, "What are the free or budget-friendly ways that I
  can treat myself today?"

✓ Take yourself to a **movie** you've been dying to see.

✓ Go out to a **nice dinner** and bring that favorite book
  that you've been dying to jump into but haven't made
  the time for yet. This book makes an epic date
  companion... captivating, soul awakening, bold, sexy,
  zesty, spunky, fun, life-changing, or as Kat O'Heir
  puts it, "dreaming big and dancing with your demons
  with a sense of adventure and lots of laughter..."
  BEST date ever!

✓ Take a **long walk** and observe the beauty around you.

✓ Go to the park and have a **picnic**.

✓ Sign up for a **class** you've been dying to take.

✓ Finally **go on that trip** you've been craving to take.

✓ Take yourself on an **adventure**! It can even be a local adventure. Try something new for the first time: a new dish, a new restaurant, going to the zoo or a museum on their free days. Get creative and think of ways not to let money or time become an excuse that gets in the way of you being the Master Creator of your own epic adventures.

Think about what *you* want. Write a list. Pick one at a time and make it happen. Woo yourself! Date yourself! Treat yo-self like the Epic Sexy Goddess that you are, and others will follow suit.

✦ *Trust Yo-Self* ✦

What's the quickest way to replenish self-trust? Keep promises to yourself! Think about it this way: if you were in a relationship with someone who promised you things but then never followed through, how long do you think that things would last before it all went terribly wrong? Now imagine you are *both* people in that scenario. You are the one making the promises to you, and you are the one breaking those promises. You are also the one who is losing all faith in you because you never follow through. So how the hell can you trust you when your word is worth nothing?

It's all about self-trust. Girl, if you cannot trust yourself, how the hell are you ever going to be able to trust anyone else? You can't trust anyone when you don't even trust yourself. Sure, you will masterfully project onto others your own lack of trust in yourself. You will make it so that you either drive yourself or your healthy lovers crazy with your endless insecurities and lack of trust in them (even when really it's rooted unconsciously in your lack of trust in self). Or you will do what I did for the longest time, which is to date incredibly unhealthy, toxic people who legitimately are *not* trustworthy, just so that you can prove to yourself that your own story that "no one can be trusted" is true.

Write a list of things that you have been promising yourself you'd do for a while now. Think about all of the things that come to mind when I ask you these questions.

✓ What **books** have you been wanting to read?

✓ What things have you wanted to **learn**?

✓ What **classes** have you wanted to take?

✓ What have you been wanting to change in your eating or **workout** regimen?

✓ What **projects** have you been promising yourself you would get to around the house?

✓ What have you been promising yourself that you would do for the **past week**?

✓ What have you been promising yourself that you would do for the **past month**?

✓ What have you been promising yourself that you would do for the **past year**?

✓ What have you been promising yourself that you would do for the **past five years**?

First of all, go back and look at your list. Cross off anything that is a "should" do. Second, once you've got a yummy list of purely soul-craving, desire-based thaaangs, pick *one thing* and DO it. This has a powerful energetic clearing component and will help you develop a stronger bond with yourself. Taking action increases the volume and clarity of your inner Heartspace GPS, activates your Goddess Power Source, and keeps you on your Epic Sexy path.

Embrace Your Divine Power

When you tap in to your inner GPS, you will hear that guiding whisper so much more clearly than ever before. The following *Epic Sexy Thrival Tips* will help you to recognize your distinct inner voice and separate it from the chatter of other's voices, from your own self-doubt, your self-sabotage Headspace voice, and from the voices and whispers of societal confines and limitations.

✦ *Create an Intuition Log* ✦

The Intuition Log is a playful exploration for uncovering your intuition. It will help you discover what your intuition sounds like, what it feels like, and how it typically guides you. Intuition is similar to the uniqueness of our fingerprints. No one's intuition operates in exactly the same way as the next person's intuition. So get playful, have fun, and come up with a way that feels good to you. There is no possible way to get this wrong. Below are some examples to get your creative juices flowing.

✓ **Make a note** about those times you hear that whisper that comes to you with information, insights, or knowledge.

✓ Capture **what the voice said**, what you did, and the result of listening or not listening to it. What did it cost you if your inner voice was right but you didn't listen? What did you gain as a result of listening when it was dead on?

✓ Pay attention to when you get **"gut" hits**.

✓ Notice when you see **red flags**.

✓ Pay attention when you have a **sense of knowing**.

✓ Notice when you have that **initial instinct**.

In the notes section on my phone, I capture intuitive hits I get. Later, I go back and notice when those intuitive hits are validated. This allows me to extrapolate clues that confirm that my intuition is indeed speaking to me. It helps me to know that what I might otherwise dismiss as Headspace Overload in the works is actually my true inner voice.

Through your consistent logging of these intuitive hits, you can look for patterns over time. These patterns reveal what your intuition feels like, sounds like, and all the ways it likes to guide you. You can look for the patterns that signal you are experiencing Headspace Overload too. This is a great tool to help you differentiate between the two states. Here are a few examples from my Intuition Log that highlight how my intuition speaks to me.

SPOTLIGHT EXAMPLE #1. I pulled out a pair of jeans from my closet that still had the tag on them. A whisper said, "Try the jeans on before you pull the tag off." I didn't listen. I tore the tags off and put the jeans on. Cameltoe. TMI? That is not pretty. LOL. Should have listened to that voice. Not listening to it cost me $80.

SPOTLIGHT EXAMPLE #2. My boyfriend asked me if I wanted to change our originally agreed upon plans and head downtown instead of sticking local. Every single fiber of my being said "No, stick with the original plan." Yet, my Heasdspace Overload said, "Be the cool girlfriend. Be spontaneous and go downtown." So I said "Sure." This decision resulted in me spending about an hour and a half in rush hour traffic, stuck in the hustle and bustle of the city's energy, which overstimulates me.

Then I drove around looking for parking for more than twenty minutes, all the while in the dead winter of CHIBERIA (the Antarctic freezingness that is the Chicago winter. I'm a Sun Goddess, not an Eskimo. *My* body was made for 90-degree weather.). I finally get to the place, and apparently we got our signals crossed, because he was at another location of what was apparently a chain of restaurants in our area. We had no idea there were multiple locations. Clearly.

Epic Meltdown ensued. I am talking temper tantrum to rival those displayed by my four-year-old nephew. It wasn't my best work. Oooo, look at how cool of a girlfriend you are now with your temper tantrum and tears! Baahhahahhaha. This cost me time, energy, and a completely unnecessary meltdown with my man. Headspace Overload, you are a sneaky son of a…

SPOTLIGHT EXAMPLE #3. I made plans to have a lunch date with my girlfriend. We were going to meet in the middle. Then she asked me to come to her house. We live about thirty minutes away from one another. My gut said no. My Headspace said, "Be a good friend, and don't make a big deal out of it. Just go over there." So I did. Lesson learned. Next time I will just go with my original gut instinct and just tell her how I feel. This cost me time, energy, and damage to my relationship with myself, because I am not honoring what *I* want and I am not speaking up for myself!

SPOTLIGHT EXAMPLE #4. When I was with a friend once I kept seeing a yellow sweater, a football field, and cheerleaders with an energetic vibe tied to Homecoming. Finally, I asked what that was about. She shared that she was crowned Homecoming

Queen in high school, on the football field, and cheerleaders were on the sidelines wearing the school color in the fashion of yellow sweaters. This allowed me to further validate that my visions are real and to be even more trusting of my spiritual gifts. Now, I freely share what I hear Spirit saying or showing me. As a result, I'm even more powerful in my one-on-one life coaching sessions. I often share, completely unfiltered, what I hear and see from their spirit guides, who come through to provide them with invaluable messages. Often times what I see and hear makes absolutely no sense to me, and it doesn't need to. The only person it needs to make sense to is the one receiving the message! Winning!!

✦ *Leverage the Past* ✦

I was having a convo with a client who was telling me about a man that she had been dating for several months. She said that a couple months ago, "Something in my gut was telling me that something was off…" As it turned out, he was married.

My immediate question was, "When you play the Sixth Sense Movie Game with yourself now, what was the very first red flag you saw?" You know, when you find out the cold, hard truth and then you look back at all of the red flags you saw. You look back and see it all, wondering how it never reeeeaaaally sunk in as to what was actually happening the whole time until the very end.

Her response, "Well, I guess it was at the *very beginning* when..." No need to even finish that sentence, because here is the thing, sister friend. You are a strong, powerful, fierce force of intuition with an epic inner Heartspace GPS guiding you, nudging you, whispering to you, sometimes *screaming* at you. Just play with *listening* to it. Resist the urge to judge yourself, beat yourself up, blame yourself, or feel an ounce of guilt or shame.

Release yourself from the potential energetic pattern of "I should have known." Don't utter the words, "I feel bad because I knew it, and I didn't do anything about it." Instead, celebrate the fact that you did, in fact, know something was off. That is some exciting stuff, sister.

That means you are more connected to your intuition than you may have thought you were in the first place. Your intuition is on point, and this exercise will help you learn to trust it. In time, it will support you in taking action on those intuitive nudges a lot sooner. That means you can spend more time living a limitless life and being Epic Sexy limitless you! Woo!!

✦ *Go Retro* ✦

For this exercise, go back into the past to search for golden nuggets of intuitive info.

- ✓ Think of a time **when something went wrong**
  in your life. Maybe it was a perceived failure in a
  relationship or with a project you were working
  on once upon a time.

- ✓ Write down all the **red flags** you saw before the
  final straw that broke the camel's back.

- ✓ See how your **intuition** is on point! You are already
  half way there. You see things. Now, intentionally
  listen to it and take action on what it is telling you.

Play with taking action from this new place of awareness. As you move forward, even taking action one red flag earlier than you may have in the past will change your life forever. Get it girl!

✦ *Get Your Heart On!* ✦

Go back to your notes on Headspace and Heartspace, and start being consciously aware of when you are experiencing each of these in your every day life. Become a student of Headspace and Heartspace. Notice what each one feels like. Start to pay attention when you are experiencing each one.

Play with intentionally creating more Heartspace Immersion in your life. If you are focusing on a problem from your Headspace, ask your Heartspace: "What are some possible solutions?" If you find yourself saying, "Why is this happening to me?" ask, "What if this was happening *for* me? What might be the lessons I could learn from this? What are the blessings I am receiving through this situation?"

This is not at all about *never* spending time in Headspace. Your head is with you for a reason. It is a *powerful* resource to help you strategize and put into action what is necessary to make your dreams a reality. I encourage you to dream and vision from your Heartspace, where literally *anything* you desire is possible and you will find a way to make it happen. Then, call upon your Headspace to execute those thaangs through consistent focus and action.

Heartstorming Thrival Tips

The set of *Epic Sexy Thrival Tips* that follows will explore ways to reinforce your deepest desires and visions. These tips will give you a deeper understanding of what you want and turn up the volume of your GPS, all while improving the clarity of your built-in signal.

Heartstorming is like brainstorming, but instead of using your brain you use your heart. Remember: dream from the heart and soul, then execute and implement with the brilliance of your brain. Don't let "logic" get in the way of what your soul desires.

Soulstorming. Heartstorming. Dreamstorming. Call it whatever you want. Just try and avoid "brainstorming" as you embark on the following thaangs, because Headspace is no place for visions and dreams of epic proportions.

As you partake in the following *Epic Sexy Thrival Tips*, be sure to unleash your deepest burning desires and dream as big as you possibly can. When you think you are dreaming big, dream even bigger. Stretch your heart's imagination as far as it can possibly go, and then stretch it a little further.

Woo!! Get it!

✦ *Create a Vision Board* ✦

Think about each area of your life and what you want it to look and feel like. Cut out words and pictures from magazines. You can even print stuff off from online. Make sure you put it front and center for you to see it. I framed my vision in an 8x10 frame I keep on my desk. I see it all day every day while I am working. Here are some questions to help you create your Vision Board:

✓ **Love.** What words or images would you like to use to best describe your ideal love life? What is your dream lover like? Physically? Mentally? Emotionally? Spiritually? How would you like he or she to make you feel?

✓ **Career.** In your dream vision what would you love to be doing for your career that feeds your soul? How much money do you crave to make? What would you love to spend your money on? What do you want to spend your time doing?

✓ **Body.** How do you desire each body part to look. How do you want to feel? What activities do you want to participate in regularly? How do you want to dress?

✓ **Home.** What would you like your house to look like? Describe each room individually. What is your style?

✓ **Travel.** What adventures would you like to experience? What places are you craving to visit and explore? Places to go? Things to do? People to see?

✦ *Make Magical Dream Jars* ✦

✓ **Get two mason jars** and decorate them to your liking.
I use a clear, see-through jar and write on colored,
neon paper. Make it something that feels good to *you*.

✓ Write short **"Dear Universe, I want…"** notes. Place
your written desires in your Dear Universe Jar.

✓ Pull them out and **read them often**. Remind
yourself what you want. Keep it top of mind.

✓ When they come true, switch them to the **"The
Universe Rocks and Delivers My Wishes"** Jar.

✓ On the days you are looking for more hope, **go to
both jars.** The first reminds you to focus on what
you want, not what you don't want. The second
reminds you that the Universe *does* deliver as long
as you ask clearly for what you want.

SPOTLIGHT EXAMPLE #1. "Dear Spirit Team, Please deliver a
baby to a client whose ultimate dream is to be a mom. Then, let me
meet that little angel nugget of love! Xoxox You guys rock! Thank
you!!"

SPOTLIGHT EXAMPLE #2. "Dear Spirit Team, I would like to
fall madly, deeply, head-over-heels in love with someone who is a
healthy, funny, loving, intelligent kickass man and have that epic,

sexy, want-to-rip-your-clothes-off kind of attraction to him. Thank you! Woo!! Xoxo"

SPOTLIGHT EXAMPLE #3. "Dear Universe / MVP Spirit Team, best f'in team of all time, I want to go to a client's wedding. This client, who was single when we first started working together, is now madly deeply in love and walkin' down that aisle!! WOO!!"

SPOTLIGHT EXAMPLE #4. "Dear Epic Sexy Spirit Team, I want to be a published author. Let's do this!"

✦ *Keep the Dream Alive* ✦

Once you start to get an idea of what you want, it's important to have reminders of those visions, soul cravings, and desires everywhere. I mean, you don't just read a set of directions that route you to your desired destination and then never look at the map again, right?! Unless you are Elon Musk. (P.S. I would love to interview that man and share his inspirational insights with the world in a way that no one else has yet to capture and bring to light. He is brilliantly limitless: a true Epic Sexy Soul. Hey, I have to walk the talk and ask for what I want, right?! Elon, call me!)

Where were we? Ah, yes. How do you know where you are going if you've never been there before? It's important to ensure that the destination is in front of you the whole time. Make sure to have beautiful, awe-inspiring visual reminders of your desires and soul cravings everywhere you go. Put reminders on your desk or workspace, in your car, on your phone screen, on your computer screen, in your purse, on your fridge, and all over your house. Put them in the bathroom, kitchen, and bedroom.

Each visual will act as a beautiful reminder of your desires. Find quotes that light you up. Paint your walls with colors that ignite you. Cut out pictures from magazines that inspire you. Print out pictures of loved ones that move you. Think art, paintings, sculptures, and pictures of places you want to travel. Create a vision board. Collect mementos that remind you of how loved, awesome, beautiful, badass, unstoppable, fierce, fearless, and free you are. You truly are such an Epic Sexy Goddess!

• • • • •
THRIVAL PERSPECTIVE
• • • • •

Decorate all of your most frequented spaces with visuals that remind you of your deepest desires, soul cravings, wants, and dreams.

Make these visions aesthetically pleasing and totally soul-moving. The intention is to inspire you, ignite you, and fill you with joy. Let these reminders touch your soul, move you, and draw you to them. Feel magnetized and effortlessly pulled forward toward your dreams. Make sure that each visual you create comes from a place of *desire*, not a place of a "should" or obligation.

Another thing that has worked incredibly well for some of the women I have worked with is to have an item of jewelry that you can wear every single day to remind you of something specific that you crave. For example, decide which soul craving you'd like to make your *main* focus, then purchase a bracelet and give a meaning to said bracelet. Let the bracelet be a constant reminder to make that particular dream, intention, or soul cravings come true. It's a reminder to constantly ask yourself, "Is what I am doing right now feeding my dream, or prolonging it?'

Epic Sexy Standards

In love, relationships, friendships, business, and all aspects of life, you get what you tolerate. People follow *your* lead. You and only you set the bar for what others will think about you and how others will treat you. You set those standards by what *you* think of yourself, and how you treat you. The *Epic Sexy Thrival Tips* in this section will help you think more highly of yourself and explore ways to set your bar higher. They will also help you integrate your desires on a cellular level so you can have everything that your soul craves, rather effortlessly. WOO!

✦ *Never Forget That You're Worth It* ✦

Create an affirmation or mantra that reminds you that you are worth it! Start with focusing on the Number One thing that you want to work on shifting, expanding, growing, and manifesting. Then, make signs with that mantra and or affirmation, and post them everywhere in your house. This is about living on purpose, and with full intention.

SPOTLIGHT EXAMPLE. When I first started out on my own journey, I realized that I never said "No" mainly because *I* was nowhere to be found on my own priority list. As a result, everything that everyone else wanted or needed from me was more important than what *I* wanted and needed for myself. So I made signs that said, "I am a Priority." I hung them up everywhere in my house: on my kitchen cabinets, fridge, and bathroom mirrors; even on the front door. (On the inside of course, haha.)

Eventually, I was able to change the affirmation signs to say, "I am #1." This new affirmation was to help me realize that it's OK to experience "Me First" when my soul is craving it so that I can reconnect with myself, rejuvenate, relax, restore, and then go back out into the world and share the best of me with others from a true soulful desire to do so. Funny side note: I had a date come over once, and I forgot that I had those up. He saw them and asked about them. I was mortified and mumbled my way through an incoherent explanation. After the date I never heard from him again. LOL. Whatever. His loss! Haha. Woo!!

I only share that with you as a playful reminder that if you are going to invite a date over, just remember those affirmations are there. I tell you this so that you can't be pissed off and say, "This was the worst idea ever" and give up if something like this happens to you. If I am being totally honest, I forgot a second time and had the exact same experience with another date too! Haha.

And look, now I have funny stories, and you and I can laugh about it together. You can laugh with me or at me. Either way you are laughing and that is a huge win! I tell you this so that you don't use this as an excuse *not* to put the signs up, but merely as a reminder to be aware that they are there. If you have company over and you don't want that company to see them, then you can put them in a drawer for the time they are there and immediately put them back up when they leave.

Seriously though, at the beginning these signs were incredibly uncomfortable to see, because they shocked my system. I didn't believe them, so my whole being aggressively resisted these signs. Over time, I started to believe it, and now it's just who I am. Whenever I need a little sprinkle of the magical "Me First" experience I take it. Unapologetically!

This doesn't mean that I don't give to others, because that is the core of my life's mission. It just means that I give from a place of complete bliss and fullness of self. I make sure that I am complete and whole. This allows me to give to others from that blissful place instead of giving to them from a burnt-out, half-assed, no-energy, depleted space of exhaustion.

✦ *Set That Bar High, Sister Friend!* ✦

Early in 2014, I did what most of us would call "taking a leap of faith." I personally like to call it "betting on me." I put in my notice at work. I started the convo with something most corporate employers don't often hear. I said, "I have been doing some soul searching..." And then I quit my lucrative full-time job to go full-time with my business instead of doing it part-time as I had been doing for the years prior.

I had decided to finally say, "Yes!" to me and shift over to the side of the spectrum where Heartspace Immersion exists. I decided to give every ounce of my being to the very thing that was calling to me and feeds my soul beyond anything I've ever experienced before – my life coaching business, Epic Sexy You. I live, eat, breathe, and sleep my passion every single moment of every single day, and I could not be more in love with this business and life that I have created. I am going to share with you something simple that will help you do the same thing for yourself.

In that first year after quitting my corporate job and going full-time with all things Heartspace Immersion, I built a thriving business. I created a life where I often was all, "Pinch me! Am I dreaming? Ahhh. I loooove life!" I also fell madly, deeply in love with an amazing man, fell even more in love with myself, traveled the globe, met sooooo many Epic Sexy Souls, and had more Epic Adventures and fun than I had ever even thought was possible. I would like for you to be able to intentionally create this kind of life for yourself too by living life on purpose and setting an intention.

So, let's play with this! In 2014, I set an intention. My number one focus was to fill my life with endless adventures. I wanted to make 2014 the most fun year of my life. My mantra became: *Just Have Fun!* I asked myself constantly, "Is this going to be fun?" If the answer was "No," I didn't do it. I was always on the hunt for fun. And more fun! Fun, fun, fun. One of my life's mottos is, "If it's not fun, why do it?" As a result of setting this intention and keeping it top of mind, I had the most fun year of my entire life!

In 2015, I decided to reevaluate for a new intention. After looking at what I wanted to feel more of, be more of, experience more of, and achieve more of in the upcoming year, I realized that the mantra that was going to suit me best to get me what my soul was craving was, *Play Full Out.* OMG, did that create an Epic Uplevel and a massive shift in my energy. I made intentional and purposeful decisions and took actions from the very moment that I set the new intention.

Every single decision that I made, I asked myself my Top of Mind Question (that's when you constantly and intentionally feed your brain a question that will propel you toward your desired outcomes). My question was, "Am I playing full out?" If the answer was "No," then I challenged myself to think bigger and stretch myself beyond any zone I'd ever played in. If the answer was "Yes" and there was any resistance, then I explored further.

For example, when I asked myself if I was playing full out in deciding to go to a retreat in Fiji where I'd be a participant for my own growth, evolution, and expansion and the answer was a resounding "Yes," I still noticed myself feeling incredibly resistant to going. I realized it was going to be right after I hosted an Epic Sexy Adventure Retreat in Mexico, and I'd be away from home for almost a month if I went to Fiji too. I also realized it would be close to thirty hours of travel door-to-door. I was met with Epic Resistance from myself.

I decided to lean into that resistance, as I have trained myself to do. I realized that I was giving myself a ton of "reasons" that I "can't" go. This showed me Fiji was definitely a "must" for me. I felt that I would come out the other end a stronger, smarter, and more enlightened being, and I most certainly did. Not to mention that I made some new soul connections and friends for life!

When I intentionally created the new Top of Mind Question for myself, "Am I playing full-out?!" the immediate months that followed were filled with more living than some people experience in a lifetime. I hosted an Epic Sexy Adventure Retreat in Mexico. We swam with whale sharks. We zip-lined over the jungle. We went off-roading with ATVs in the rain and the muddy wonderland of the jungle. We climbed wobbly tall poles, one higher than the next, and then took the terrifying leap of faith from the highest one.

We got our rock climbing on. We climbed bridges in the treetops. We became a human roller coaster (most EPIC roller coaster ride of all time; in fact, I am ruined for regular roller coasters from now on because they will never be as cool ever again.) We flew in Superman fashion over the jungle. We got our pamper on and treated ourselves to massages and body scrubs.

Then I went to Fiji. There, I rode some incredibly powerful and beautiful horses. I rode a jet ski in the waters surrounding the island of Fiji. I went water-skiing. I jumped on a trampoline in the ocean and challenged myself to revisit my younger years as a gymnast, getting my flips on. I paddle-boarded for the first time. I went snorkeling. I went scuba diving for the first time ever!

I volunteered to go first to climb a single pole, several stories high, and then jumped off that bad boy. I came back down and helped coach everyone else how to overcome their fears and climb to the top to experience the victory that was rightfully theirs for the taking. I met the most amazing souls and kindred spirits, and I now have a massive amount of new friends for life.

Then I said yes to playing the 2015 IPEC Coaches Cup. From among more than sixteen years of IPEC Life Coaching Certification graduates, I was among the 300+ coaches nominated to play in the Coaches Cup. Over the course of four months, I played full out and had an absolute blast. I learned a ton about my own self-mastery and took my coaching mastery to the next level. I fell even more in love with the IPEC coaching program, their employees, and the entire community of coaches. Then, I took home the trophy and won the whole thaang!

I wrote this book. I went on a family adventure to South Carolina. I threw an unleash your inner child, reverse aging par-tay on the same playground where I had played in elementary school. Think kickball, kids toys as prizes, hula hoops, a spy game, and sooo much fun!

All of this in just the four months following setting that intention, and all because I had one constant question or mantra on my mind: "Am I playing full out?" I was constantly asking, "What are *all* the ways that I can play full out?" and, "How can I raise my bar even higher and push myself even further to play full out?" Woo!! This was all on a consciously created replay loop all day every day. I was intentionally feeding my brain the Top of Mind Question that fueled my deepest desires and wildest dreams.

In prepping for 2016, after doing some soul searching, the new intentional Top of Mind Question became, "What the Hell are you Waiting For? Make it Happen!" This is sure to lead to 365 days of an epic, limitless me! Boom! #WTHAYWF

*Now, let's look at how you can create your **Best Year Ever**. In the next exercise, I share insights that led me to my mantra so that you can get a clear picture of how to create your own!*

Before we begin, do not let a limited perception of "There's not enough time," or "There's too much time already wasted, and it's too late," or any other limiting perceptions of age, missed chances, and no more time get in the way of you dreaming big and making your dreams real. Remember, in Headspace Overload, time is distorted and moves at a blinding pace.

It's like you wake up and go, "Where did all the time go?" You get lost in the "busy," but never truly feel as if there's time for your desires and soul cravings. There never seems to be enough time and you are always swimming in an endless list of to dos, so how the hell are you ever going to have "time" to get to these frivolous luxuries that you call "dreams," eh?

In contrast, time as it exists in Heartspace Immersion has an effortless rhythmic flow and miraculous ease and speed. Whatever you want is yours for the taking. *You* are the master creator of time. It's like having access to Super Human Time.

It is *never* too late for anything, and you have plenty of time for every single thing that your soul craves. If you didn't have enough "time," you wouldn't have that soul craving in the first place. That is the magic of Heartspace, intuition, and divine guidance from your spirit guides! They have brilliantly and masterfully created those very desires inside of you to act as clues and signals of what direction to go in life so you can stay on your path toward optimal thriving which leads to limitless and Epic Sexy You. So let those cravings be proof that you've got plenty of time to make it happen!

So, what the hell are *you* waiting for? Make it happen! #WTHAYWF

Epic, Sexy Q&A

Take out a pen and paper, and write down what comes up for you. Remember, answer these questions as Epic Limitless You. You have unlimited time, unlimited resources, unlimited access to contacts that you'll need, unlimited knowledge and information at your disposal as the needs arise, and unlimited energy. You are completely limitless! Now, go!!

✓ What do I want to *feel* more of this year? Examples: Even more love for myself. Even more love for and with my man. More fun and connection with my family. More alive. More carefree. More euphoria. More bliss. More unconditional love.

✓ What do I want to *be* more of? Examples: Sculpted like a piece of art work. Tight and toned. Even more ignited. More fearless. More powerful.

✓ What do I want to *experience* more of? Examples: More exhilaration. More self-mastery. More adventures. More travels to see even more of the world. Connect with more kindred souls. Find more of my tribe. More exhilaration. More time outside my already expansive "comfort zone." More time with Self Love activities and loving myself up in relaxation, rejuvenation, pampering, and spoiling.

✓ What do I want to *achieve* more of? Examples: Take my business to the next level. Touch more lives. Push myself beyond any zone I have ever experienced in my entire life. Take my body to the next level. Take my relationships to the next level. More financial mastery. More coaching mastery. More self mastery.

✓ What would I like to ***do*** to take my life to new heights? Examples: Stretch myself beyond anything I've experienced before. Do more speaking engagements so that I can touch more lives and spread the love, light, and joy that I emanate. Say yes *only* when it is a, "Hell Yes!" Only do the things that are moving me forward toward my soul's fulfillment to spread ignition in people's souls like wildfire. I want to leave this place brighter than what any of us can even fathom right now.

The minute that you get clear on where you want to go in life and the minute you declare what you want out of life, your Heartspace GPS automatically loads the maps that show you how to get you there. Get clear on the what, and surrender to the magical journey of the how. If you hold yourself back and put limits on unleashing your soul's cravings or on dreaming wild and free, then there is no map, because there is no true destination!

You must first get clear on the destination of where you want to go and then fuel the Heartspace GPS with desire! Obligation, on the other hand, is like an empty gas tank. You'll be left either sitting still, taking a long walk to try and find a gas station in the middle of nowhere, or getting out and pushing your car. Hello exhaustion, depletion, burn out, and the whole journey feeling like heaping loads of work. Do yourself a favor. Tell obligation to take a hike, and fuel your journey with your deepest desires.

I realized that the destination I desired to go in 2015 required a mantra that was going to suit me best, to get me what my soul was craving, and that was, "Play Full Out!" I was constantly asking myself the following questions:

✓ Am I playing *full out*?

✓ What are *all* the ways that I can play full out?

✓ How can I raise my bar *even higher* and push myself even further to play full out?

What is your mantra? What's your new Top of Mind Question? Write it down! Tell peeps about it. Then, go have the best year *ever*, living life on purpose! #WTHAYWF

GET YOUR SHARE ON *#epicsexyyou*

OK. Now that you have some clarity around your WHAT, let's take step two of four simple steps to Epic Sexy You.

*Create the Ultimate
Love Affair with Yourself*

**Step 2: Step Out and Put
Your Best Self Forward**

Step Out and Put Your Best Self Forward

*Are you ready to
present you to the world?*

*Give a girl the right shoes
and she can conquer the world.*

Marilyn Monroe

I just love this quote! Here is the thing: it's not even really about the shoes. I know, I know, some shoe lovers I know will adamantly disagree with me and say it *is* about the shoes! The thing is, this is about more than just what you are wearing. It's about how you *feel* when you are wearing it, and it is about how *you* show up in this world differently as a result of the energy you put into presenting yourself.

You can either present yourself intentionally and purposefully to the world or unconsciously and haphazardly. Which do you choose?

In helping thousands of women over the years to break free from the shit that weighs them down and explore what holds them back from the love and fulfillment their soul craves, there is something that inevitably comes to the surface every single time.

When you aren't getting what you want, the common denominator is *always* you.

Yeah. You. *Always.*

When you are not getting the outcomes you crave, it's usually because you are experiencing life from the Headspace Overload perspective rather than from Heartspace Immersion. The good news is that this means that all you have to do is tweak something on your end and shift yourself to experience life from more of a Heartspace Immersion perspective. Once you do, your desired outcomes follow right along with it.

This book is chock-full of opportunities to make tweaks that feel good to you. So why stop now? Am I right? Amen, sister friend! Let's do this!! In the first section of this book you found out what you wanted. Now it's time to play with how you actually want to express yourself out there in the world. You cannot have the *Ultimate Love Affair* if you are not putting your best foot forward. Let's go get you everythaaang your soul craves, shall we?

Yoga Pants Pandemic Sweeps the Nation

I remember when I was in the depths of my darkest phase. My morning routine was to hit snooze and roll out of bed. Yep. That's about it. OK, I'm exaggerating. I would usually brush my teeth if I was going out in public. Ok, now that's it. Everyone reading this has either been there, is there, or knows someone who is there.

It is now socially acceptable to wear Yoga Pants and other pajama-like outfits in public. Yes, I most definitely participate in this comfy phenomenon as well. So, let me just start by saying, this is not about being glammed out to the nines every single time you step outside to so much as grab your mail, walk your dog, or run a quick errand. But it is important to be honest with yourself about how you are showing up on a day-to-day basis. It's important to be aware of which version of yourself you are bringing with you as you embark on each new day in this world.

Awareness is the key to consciously creating a life you love living, based on intentionally and purposefully being a who that you love being.

Hot Ass Mess

Imagine yourself on the days where you give zero shits (and not in a good kind of way). I'm talking about the days where it's more of the, "I don't care enough to give myself a single ounce of energy in prepping myself for the world I am about to encounter."

That is not consciously what you are saying to yourself per say, but it is often the underlying energetic vibration you are experiencing and sending out to the world. You know, the days where you roll out of bed, put your hair in a messy ponytail or maybe even put a hat on, brush your teeth (and if we are being *reeeaaally* honest here, brushing your teeth is more for other people's sake than your own on said days), and leave home to run an errand in your PJs.

Whether it's that you're too busy, you don't give a shit, or you have no energy, you are literally in the very same clothes that you slept in the night before, now masterfully masked as "workout gear." Thank you Yoga Pants Pandemic! It's a total *who cares* and *why bother* kind of day. Now imagine, on this very day, a total hottie looks your way. What goes through your mind?

Let me give you a live example of this. One day when I rolled out of bed, I got lost in the love and passion that I have for my business and worked all day. Then my dog came over and gave me that look that seems to say, "Listen lady, how many times do I have to tell you that I need to go to the bathroom before you get off your rump and take me?! Rar."

Actually, maybe that is me projecting my Spicy McChicken Avatar personality onto her. More on Spicy McChicken later. If my dog could talk, she is more likely to say, "Excuse me, Mommy. If you don't mind, I *reeeaaaally* need to potty. Can you *puh-leeeze* take me?" So I finally took a much-needed break that day and went outside to walk her. Thank God for my fur baby or I think I would never see the daylight!

I don't even think I brushed my teeth that day. I most certainly did not do a damn thing with my hair, and I was looking a hot wild messy mess. My thought process was, "Whatever. Who cares. I am just taking my dog for a walk. Who the hell am I going to run into that it would even matter what I look like?" Am I right ladies? We can walk around in our PJs and look a hot mess and still be confident! Who needs makeup and fancy clothes anyways?

Well, sure, that female empowerment tune of "I can be a hot mess if I want to, and it shouldn't change the way people treat me" is fine and dandy until... As I was rounding the corner, on the final block of my walk, I saw a man who I had had the most epic crush on for *years* and who had happened, serendipitously, to move into my building in the recent months.

Thank you universe for him moving in. But WTF universe for me being a complete and utter hot mess! See how I just blamed the universe for what was fully *my* doing? This is a powerful example of how blaming can block you from your power and ability to be a Master Creator of your life and your fulfillment. OK, so I had been dying to run into him so he could see me, spend time with me, be wowed by my charm, my wit, my intellect, and my humor, and fall madly deeply in love with me. Duh! Best game plan ever!!

As I was walking towards him with my heart doing an epic happy dance of euphoric joy, I immediately stopped dead in my tracks and gently reminded myself of the version of me that I had chosen to put forth into the world on this very day. I stopped, and then I turned the other direction. I am not proud that I did this, and it isn't easy to admit to all of you, because I would like to believe that I am confident enough that I would behave the *exact* same way *regardless* of how I look.

I'd like to tell you that I believe that it doesn't matter what you look like, but, sister friend, it most certainly does matter. Stay with me here. It's not for the reasons that you may think. I am sharing my example with you so that can see how you may behave differently depending on the version of you you choose to bring to the world on any given day.

That is what matters: who *you* are. How *you* show up. Not what you look like, but how what you look like is impacting the who that you are. This isn't exclusive to just romantic love interests, by the way. How you show up is impacting your ability to make a shit ton of money, to win clients over, to get those promotions you crave, to make new friends, and to love yourself. Remember, people follow your lead. How you feel about yourself in any given moment will be what others feel about you too.

It's the law of energetic vibrations. So, are you having a lot of "crawl in a hole and hide" kind of moments like the one I just shared with you? If so, you are blocking yourself from the things your soul craves more than anything else. The good news: a higher vibration option is available, and it will allow you to finally get the results and outcomes you desire. That brings us to the alternative kind of day from the sloppy hot mess version of you.

Imagine yourself on a day where you love being you. You are on point. You have your hair styled in a fashion where you feel so connected with your inner goddess. You are practically purring like the epic sex kitten that you are. Your makeup is *flawless*. Your legs are shaved. Yeah, you know what I'm talking about. You've even put on lotion. Yeah, it's that kind of day, and, girlfriend, you are feeling silky smooth.

Your eyebrows are shaped perfectly. You have an outfit on that you absolutely positively *love*, and you are accessorized to perfection. Your nails are done, and guuurrrl you are looking mighty *fine*! Maybe these things are projections of my idea of what it looks and feels like when I love being me. You'll have to create a vision of what your version looks and feels like. Do that now. Then, explore the following questions.

Epic Sexy Q&A

Get clear on what it looks and feels like on a day where you love to be you, then consider these questions. Maybe think of a specific day where you were actually being that version of you.

✦ What does it *feel* like to be you on these days?

✦ What do you **experience** on these days?

✦ How do those feelings and experiences **impact** what you do?

On those days, the lover you want, the career you want, the life you want, and the new friends you've been craving to meet and connect with… it's *all* yours for the taking. On the days where you love what it's like to be you, *everything* is yours for the taking! See, this all has *nothing* to do with *other* people. This is all about *you*! It's about how *you* feel. What *you* think. What level of risk *you* are willing to take.

It's about how *you* are willing to show up. How far *you* are willing to stretch yourself outside of your comfort zone to get everything that your soul craves. This is about intentionally creating versions of yourself every single day that have you stepping out of your door in the morning and heading into the world feeling exactly how *you* desire to feel on that given day.

I am as confident as they come, and I genuinely *love* what it feels like being me. When I intentionally *choose* to go in public without makeup, I know that I am physically just as sexy as when I am wearing makeup. There are those days where I go out in yoga clothes and no makeup, and I am still an epic powerhouse of awesomeness, like the total *Boss Babe that I am*!

But I've paid attention to the difference in how *I* show up on the days when I walk out of my house not having intentionally created a version of me that makes me feel however I am craving to feel that day — beautiful, sexy, playful, full of life — compared to the days when I am the Master Creator of my who and my inner goddess purrs with Epic Sexy delight.

When I *love* what it feels like being me, everything is effortless. I glide through my day like the Epic Sexy Goddess I am. I've noticed the difference in my thoughts, behaviors, choices, and actions. I've listened to the excuses that I tell myself when I get the double-take glance from a hottie or when I get ignored. Listen, I have a man, so it isn't about the attention. I am satisfied, pleased, fulfilled, and ignited. I only have eyes for my man. But how I intentionally or haphazardly create my who *does* change the story I tell myself as to why I get the look or why I don't.

Some stories chip away at our ability to be connected to our inner goddess and be fierce, fearless, wild, playful, and free. Consider the difference between those days when you are feeling like you are on point and those when you are not. On the days where you have intentionally created a *who* that you love being, someone could look in your direction because they are looking at the clock on the wall and you're all, "Damn, I know I am looking good, but take it easy checking me out. I am taken."

Now, consider the not-so-good days when you have put in *zero* effort and *zero* energy toward bringing a version of you that you love being to the party of life. You feel far less than the limitless awesomeness that you are. Put yourself in the same "person looking at the clock on the wall" situation that we discussed earlier. On those days, even if that person is in fact checking you out, you may not pay it any mind because you would assume they are checking for the time.

Here is the thing... confidence is *sexy*. Insecurities and a lack of self worth are *not*. Your level of confidence is in direct correlation to what you are capable of attracting and manifesting in your career, your love life, your finances, and your friendships.

Let me give you an example. Have you ever seen someone at work who keeps getting promoted when truth be told they aren't even the most qualified person for said promotions? The heightened version of this is in the movie "Office Space" where the main character Peter gets stuck in a hypnotic state that leaves him essentially not caring a single iota what people think of him.

Instantly, he has no filter. He does whatever he wants, including sleeping in and skipping work. He starts saying no to his boss. He starts telling the truth and speaking his mind. He does *not* care at all! The two consultants the company hired to assess the efficiencies of the organization just *love* his confidence, and Peter soon finds himself in their boys' club, rewarded for his new state of confidence. *Nothing* changed other than his state of confidence.

There are two other employees in Peter's office who try so hard to get the consultants to like them to no avail. Think about it, often times when people try so hard to get us to like them, it actually pushes us away further, right? Have you ever met someone who tries too hard? They want *desperately* for you to like them and you can *feel* it! How does that make you feel? As a result of how that makes you feel, how do you end up feeling about that person? How do you act around that person as a result of their insecurity?

Conversely, think about someone who you know who has a *lot* of confidence. Do you think that person would truly care if you didn't like them? Do you think they would doubt themselves if you didn't agree with them? Do you think they would care if you didn't like what they were wearing?

In fact, some people who wear the wildest outfits, the *very* thing that makes or breaks the outfit is if they *own* it and if *they* love it. It's about intentionally creating versions of yourself that you love being. It's about feeling free in your own skin, loving the hell out of yourself, and caring about you from a "Me First" perspective. What do *I* think about this outfit? How do *I* feel in it? Me First.

When you love who you are, you give others permission to do the same. Think coworkers, friends, family, lovers. Give yourself permission to be you, unapologetically, because this whole journey is about creating the unshakable foundation to do so. It doesn't even really matter if another person is or isn't looking at you.

• • • • •
THRIVAL PERSPECTIVE
• • • • •

Your perspective creates your reality.

Creating an epic existence is contingent upon you bringing your best you, everywhere you go. Or, rather, it is about you creating a version of yourself that you love being in that given moment. There are limitless versions of yourself that you can create, which we will explore throughout this book. The key to all of this is to be consciously awakened to which version you are choosing to be in any given moment, to choose intentionally, and to love your choice in that moment so that you can get the outcomes and results that your soul is craving!

You can feel the difference when you are creating your versions of yourself from an external focus, which is the Headspace Overload experience. You may feel insecure. You may find yourself comparing yourself to others. You may start worrying about if you're getting it "right" or "wrong" or thinking there is a better way to do it. You may also start worrying about what others may think.

You may become indecisive, doubt yourself, or wonder how you "should" do it. Insert each of the items from the Headspace Overload checklist in the first section of the book here. The great thing about finding yourself doing and or experiencing any of these things is that, moving forward, you can choose to use these as new signals to help trigger you to choose Heartspace Immersion!

When you create your version of you from a Heartspace it is desire-based. It boils down to you. How do you want to feel being you? It's about leveraging the Me First existence. You do it for you, not for others.

How do you want to feel about yourself? And why do you want to feel that way about yourself? What are the limitless possibilities of what you can do, experience, achieve, and accomplish when you feel that way about yourself? How can you contribute to the world and those around you in a more expansive way when you are out there in the world loving being yourself, loving life, and glowing from the inside out?

There are so many ways to bring the best you everywhere you go — even beyond fashion, makeup, hair, and accessories — all of which we will cover in this section's *Epic Sexy Thrival Tips*.

So, let's get it girl!

Wake-up Call: Wake Up! You Matter!!

The truth is, if you're half-assing in the presentation of yourself department, people assume you half-ass in other areas of your life. That means you are not on the top of anyone's mind for career advancements. Nor will you be asked out for a hot date. Truth! If you look sloppy or if you look like you don't care and if you aren't putting in any effort, attention, or energy into how you show up, then it will be impossible to attract someone awesome. Quite frankly, it will be impossible to have the self-esteem required for an awesome relationship with yourself, let alone another person.

You *are* what you attract. End of story. "Yeah, but..." Shut it. End of story. You cannot attract a total hottie who is healthy mind, body, and soul... You cannot attract someone who is confident, fashionable, and presentable, who has impeccable style, grooming, and hygiene, who has the body of a well-sculpted Greek God (my projections here), and who has the energy to spoil you like the Goddess that you are if you are not putting the effort and energy into your own self *first*. Me First. Your relationship with you is the leading indicator of how your relationship with others will be. Period. End of story.

People follow *your* lead. If you don't give enough of a shit about you to take time in the morning to intentionally and purposefully put your best you into the world... If you don't believe you are worth that effort and energy, and act accordingly... Well then, honey, you are most definitely going to find lovers that treat you the same. Lovers. Friends. Coworkers. Family. Even your bank account!

They all follow your lead. It ALL starts with you. You own the power. You get to decide what roles you create and play.

You make your own rules for each role you want to play. There truly are no limits. Showing up fully in each role may look wildly different for each one, and yet each is wildly authentically you. You are *limitless*! You get to be *whoever* you want to be in each moment. There is no "right" way to do this, and there is *nothing* that you could ever possibly even do "wrong" when you are being true to yourself.

When you are accessing your *full* self – your Heartspace as well as the brilliant cerebral functioning and capability of your Headspace, life flows effortlessly. Create your who from a Heartspace Immersion place, where the possibilities available to you are truly limitless. It's about knowing how you want to feel and then acting accordingly. It's about giving yourself permission to change your mind as you go and to feel your way through life.

If you don't feel good, then let that be a brilliant signal that you may be a bit too far on the end of the spectrum of Headspace. Let this be a signal to you to take a step towards Heartspace, back to a more expansive you where you *feel* how you desire to feel. When you step into the role of being a Conscious Creator, you are the true architect of your life, and everything you crave is yours for the taking.

• • • • •
THRIVAL PERSPECTIVE
• • • • •

The mastery of your WHO gets you the WOO!

A New Possibility for "Comfy"

Having an uber crush on a man who lived in my building, who I could potentially run into even when I was merely taking the trash out, ignited me enough that it changed the version of me that I intentionally put out into the world every single day. It paid off too, because it upleveled the ever-living shit out of my life. I always intentionally created and brought the best me everywhere I went. Even to the dumpster. In the end, I got the man and the Woo!

What's the Woo? The "Woo" as in the love and affection of the man my heart and soul had been crushin' on. The "Woo" as in the wooing. You know: the flowers, the love notes, the dates, the epic adventures, the thoughtfulness, the brightening of the bad days, the taking care of me when I am sick, the having my back, and the being on my team. The "Woo" as in the excitement and passion in life that I have created. Woo!

Listen, I'm not saying that I never hang out super casual with no makeup when my man is with me (that is plentiful), but I have mastered the art of intentionally and strategically selecting my who for each scenario in life to get the results I am craving in that moment! It's all about how I want to feel. For example, when I want to unleash my inner sex kitten I put on some sexy lingerie. When I want to feel super feminine, I wear a flowy dress. When I want to feel super sexy on a night out, I tend to wear skin-tight clothes that hug my curves and a bright, bold lipstick color that makes me feel extra super hot! If I want to feel a certain way, I dress the part.

For the first two days of a week-long retreat that I guest-hosted, I wore bright-colored, long and flowy, backless dresses with my hair down and curly. On the third day, I showed up wearing skin-tight, black and white, Aztec-patterned pants with a black top and my hair in a bun. I was looking and feeling all badass rocker and edgy. One of the attendees walked up to me and said, "Wow, I had your style all wrong! I totally thought you were like bohemian chic and super fem."

Here is the thing: I am those things when I feel like that is who I want to be. Then there are days where I am feeling like I want to connect with my Uber Badass Rocker Avatar. She likes blue nail polish, black leather, funky hairstyles, and smoky eyes. It's all about being intentional with who you are sending out into the world so that you can get the outcomes that you crave.

Shit, I even hang out in my lingerie at home, by myself, just for me! I'll be sitting in front of my computer working away while I'm all sex-kittened out in my epic sexy lingerie.

Just because. Just for me. Me First.

Why the F* not?! Or maybe, like right this very moment, I'll hang out in a bra and underwear with a silk robe on, feeling that silky smooth material on my skin. This reminds me that I am one sexy mofo. It allows me to embrace the skin that I am in, and love being me that much more. Remember, if you are hiding your body when it's just you, it's going to be hard to share your body and feel sexy when you're with anyone else. Period. It all comes down to you. Me First.

You see, when you are dating: it is not about "finding a partner who loves you as you are" on those days when you are a hot mess, with zero effort or intention to the creation of your who.

It reaches a level deeper than that. The goal is to find all the different versions of you that you love being from a Heartspace, desire-based, "Me First" foundation. And doing it all intentionally, fully awakened to the Master Creator that you are!!

Maybe you are thinking, "People shouldn't make judgments based on outer appearance." Or the age-old "Don't judge a book by its cover" is coming to mind. Well, they do, but who cares what they think, anyway? That's all Headspace Overload junk, right? What is most important is this: How do you feel? Energetically, how are you showing up based on what version of *you* you created that day. You hold all of the power, and you hold the key to the destiny of your soul's cravings. Truth.

Oh man, when you intentionally decide how you want to feel and show up in each moment, when you consciously create and bring your best you everywhere you go, purposefully selecting the version of you that is the best fit for that scenario and your soul's cravings in that specific area of your life, things start to change in a big way. I remember talking to a friend once about all of this. After some reflection she said, "How come no one told me I had become a slob and let myself go?"

She had a realization that after getting married she had gotten "comfy." It's quite a normal pattern that I observe. A lot, actually. A woman presents one version of herself at the beginning of the relationship for the benefit of the other person. Then, a few years in, she stops being intentional about the who that she is sending out into the world. I mean, who does she have to impress, right? She's already got the person she wanted. And when you live with your lover, get in a habit of staying in, and that person loves you just as you are, "slob" and all, why bother, right? Wrong.

You bother because if you are not intentional about your who, then your energy follows, and you become comfy in every area of your life. Comfy is not where thriving happens. It's not about pleasing anyone else. This is about doing it for you! Since "comfy" is not where thriving is even possible, let's talk about that word for a minute: "comfy." Sometimes we use that word, as an excuse to be a slob, and an excuse to escape the Headspace Overload that we may be operating from and experiencing in life at that moment.

There is another way to do "comfy"… from your Heartspace.

Let's call the Headspace Overload, escapism, numbing version of "comfy" **Comfy Slob**, *and let's call the Heartspace Immersion version of the word "comfy"* **Comfort Goddess**.

Let's walk through a few examples of a new possibility to create luxurious and empowering comfort in our lives. You will notice that we still get the desired *feeling* we want. We just do it in a new way that is actually energizing, loving, intentional, and purposeful!

Am I a "Comfy Slob?" Or a "Comfort Goddess?"

Comfy Slob

The energetic pattern of escaping life's overwhelming responsibilities and demands, distracting yourself from having to deal with anything, and totally numbing out!

vs.

Comfort Goddess

The energetic pattern of honoring yourself, listening to your body, knowing when to take a break, and treating yourself to some luxurious, intentional, and purposeful R&R and pampering!

Comfy Slob
Avoiding. Ignoring.

vs.

Comfort Goddess
Igniting. Fueling.

Comfy Slob
Zombie. Physically present, but protesting the use of mind, body, or soul.

vs.

Comfort Goddess
Intentional and purposeful, alive, thriving, and experiencing yourself fully.

Comfy Slob
Meh. Whatever. Blah. Why Bother.

vs.

Comfort Goddess
Hell Yes! Generous Goddess and Queen
of Luxurious Comfort.

Comfy Slob
I am way too tired or exhausted to even be
in the damn game, so please leave me alone,
I can't adult right now.

vs.

Comfort Goddess
I'm currently unavailable to you because
I am consciously creating and experiencing my intentional
Me First existence, so take a number. I'll get back to you
when I'm rejuvenated and can share myself with you and
the world from a fully expansive place.

With these new possibilities, you are now empowered with new options for making clear choices in how you create and honor your desire for comfort in your days. One of the coolest parts about this newfound awareness is that when you find yourself chasing "comfy," you can ask yourself again, "Am I being a comfy slob or a comfy goddess?"

If you are honest with yourself and the answer is that you are being a "Comfy Slob," it's usually a brilliantly magical signal that you are operating in a Headspace Overload existence where you have been give, give, giving to others and are overloaded with others' needs, desires, and requests. You are likely people-pleasing and not taking space and time for yourself. This is an epically beautiful clue that your soul is craving some good ol' sparkly sprinkles of Me First.

This is your invitation to tap into your Heartspace and ask, "What do I want? How do I want to feel? How can I honor that craving as a Comfort Goddess?" (Name your Comfort Goddess whatever *feels* good to you!) Every single time you catch yourself being a "Comfy Slob," celebrate. Awareness brings new options, possibilities, and choices for intentional living, empowering you to be the Life Architect you are and to create your life on purpose!

When you are intentional about the who that you send out into the world, you will experience an increase in your Thrival Factor in the following areas of your life: Love Life, Work Life, Friendships, Familyships (family relationships), and Finances. Most importantly, above all else, your relationship with yourself, which truly is the ultimate love affair of all time, will come alive!

Let's face it, you are with you 24/7. Who better to fall madly, deeply in love with than the one person who will be with you all the time? When you are intentional with yourself, you show yourself that *You Matter*. On the contrary, when you are not intentional, well, unfortunately, you are unconsciously sending an energetic vibe to yourself that you don't matter. When you do that, that will wreak havoc in your life without you even being consciously aware it's going down.

Really, there are zero downsides and nothing but massive upsides to intentionally creating the best version of yourself in every given moment! Go on with your badass self, sister friend! It's time to get that Limitless Woo that you deserve!!

EPIC SEXY THRIVAL TIPS

The remainder of this section is filled with *Epic Sexy Thrival Tips* that will help you learn how to intentionally create versions of you that you love being!

Remember, pick one thing at a time and play with it for a week. Pay attention to how it makes you feel. If you experience an uplevel or insights, then keep doing it. Play, experiment, and have fun with it. Once you've got the hang of that thing, add another approach while sustaining the first thing. And repeat.

This is about laying one solid brick at a time to your foundation and building upon each one, all the while having a ton of fun. These are not isolated, individual pieces, but rather many pieces to a whole. Let's go find your custom roadmap to a thriving existence!

Role Play

As you create your epic and Limitless Life, you will notice that you have an unlimited abundance of whos or what I refer to as "Avatars." These avatars represent all the different versions of you that you experience yourself as being in this limitless world. Each comes with infinite facets and expressions of your soul's core essence. Every who or "avatar" you have ever created or that you will ever create is encoded with its own magically divine set of lessons, blessings, and gifts!

As you play the following game of awareness, start thinking about what versions of you and avatars you have already created in your life. Consider which ones you want to create. Get specific. Be playful. Name them! Gather as many specifics about each one as possible. Have pictures taken of yourself that show you what you look like as you are being each one! The more playful you get, and the more specifics that you collect, the more able you are to recognize which one you are expressing in any given moment. This will support you in deciding with clarity which one may be an even better fit to get you the outcomes and results that your soul craves as you live your life on purpose!

✦ *Play The Awareness Game for Each Who* ✦

Let's start with exploring how you show up different on the days when you have the "roll out of bed hot mess look" versus the "dolled up, glammed out, Epic Sexy You look."

Epic Sexy Q&A

Pull out that journal and your pen. Explore the differences in yourself on those days you are calling forth Epic Sexy You:

✦ How do you **stand** different?

✦ How do you **breathe** different?

✦ How do you **talk** different? Consider the words you use. Consider the tone, clarity, and volume of your voice and the speed of your communication.

✦ How is your **level of risk** and boldness different?

✦ How are your **interactions** with people different?

✦ How are your **thoughts** different?

✦ What are the **stories** you tell yourself when someone looks at you? How do these stories differ when someone doesn't look at you based on a different *who* you've brought into your day?

SPOTLIGHT EXAMPLE #1. We were at a concert in the park one day when I noticed a guy who kept staring at me. I was all, "Oh man, please stop checking me out. You are making me uncomfortable! And how rude, my man is sitting here right next to me!! Control yourself, for God's sake!!!" The guy stood up and walked over to us. I was certain he was about to embarrass himself as I was going to have to turn him down right in front of everyone. And then he said, "Can you guys please keep it down? We are having a hard time hearing the music while you guys are talking so loud." Oh. Hahaha. Here is the thing though, is it ever going to hurt you to walk through the world thinking you rock?

SPOTLIGHT EXAMPLE #2. Waaaay back in the day, I used to present an Avatar my man affectionately refers to as "Spicy

McChicken." I was a hot mess of complete *spice*. Here are some specifics on this particular avatar. I was always drinking and always looking for someone to fight with. I was an angry ball of fire. That was the who that I was sending out into the world, rather unconsciously at the time. Running wild, rampant, and free.

I had a girlfriend who had an Avatar that was more like "Little Miss Sunshine" with rainbows and sunshine in her forecast all day every day. One day, my friend literally had a person call her a bitch to her face. Her response was to look behind her to see who this person was talking to. I kid you not.

This girl's most active avatar was one that refused to see anything negative with the world. Spicy McChicken and Little Miss Sunshine were in the car one day and a woman that Little Miss Sunshine cut off made a certain hand gesture. Little Miss Sunshine said excitedly, "Aww, that was so nice."

I, Spicy McChicken, was confused. I was like, "Wait, what did *you* see?" Little Miss Sunshine said the woman gave her the thumbs up. As Spicy McChicken, I, on the other hand, was one hundred percent certain I saw the middle finger.

Who knows what the woman in the other car actually gestured. My programming as my hot-headed, angry, feisty Spicy McChicken self was looking for a fight. Little Miss Sunshine was looking for the love. We both always found what we were looking for. That day, even in the exact same situation, we had two completely different perceptions of what happened, because we had two wildly opposing whos.

Remember, looks aren't the only thing that are going to determine the who that you send out into the world. The most common things you think, say, and do, will shape your who too. So be mindful of all of these pieces.

Be *intentional* with them. Live your life on *purpose*. Create your who masterfully. Don't allow it to create you.

Be playful! Create Avatars that will get you the results that you crave. If you notice that you are being a particular Avatar that is holding you back from the results and outcomes you crave, celebrate that awareness. With awareness comes new possibilities that were otherwise unavailable to you.

The *who* that you send out is going to determine *what* you see, because the ego is on the hunt to prove you right. Are you looking for people who are waving at you or for people who are flipping the bird? Whatever you are looking for is what you are going to find. Be intentional with the whos you create. Play with this.

• • • • •
THRIVAL PERSPECTIVE
• • • • •

Our Avatars are our vehicles that create the lens through which we view the world.

Really, test this out. Try on different characters and see how *you* show up different accordingly. Name each avatar you create! Notice how each who stands different, talks different, has a different level of risk and boldness, and interacts with people in a different manner. Don't forget to capture and celebrate your Aha moments so you can get where you want to go faster! The more curious you become and the more you capture whatever it is that you are witnessing while you are in the moment of experiencing it, the more that you will ingrain shifts that will propel you into a new, more powerful, unstoppable, fierce, and fab *you.*

✦ *Consciously Create Avatars* ✦

If you don't step into each avatar, consciously creating your who as you navigate your life, you may end up haphazardly and unconsciously sabotaging yourself. You may keep yourself from the results and desires that you crave. That being said, let's play with how you can use your avatars to live life more on purpose.

Let me give you an example. One of the versions of me that I experience myself as being in this world is named "Crazy, Sexy, Fun, Wild, and Free." She is all of those things. She is the Avatar expression of me who appears on the front cover of this book. She doesn't care much about anything other than experiencing new things, going on adventures, going fast, jumping out of planes, swimming with sharks, traveling the globe, pampering herself, having more fun than what others even think is humanly possible, and pushing every single fun-limiting barrier that exists in life.

For the first year of the relationship with my man, she was the Avatar fully present when I was with him. I wasn't consciously creating her as the Avatar at the time. I just got lucky that somehow she was the one that showed up in the relationship and, as a result, it was pretty damn awesome! Crazy, Sexy, Fun, Wild, and Free doesn't care much about defining things. She lives fully immersed in the present moment, and she could care less about the future, because she takes each day as it comes. She honors freedom in herself and in others, so my relationship was magically delicious as we enjoyed every single moment together.

For that whole first year of the relationship, my Crazy, Sexy, Fun, Wild, and Free Avatar was *also* running my business, but I did *not* consciously realize that at the time either. The business was thriving. I was having so much *fun*, and the Epic Sexy Adventure Retreats were mind-blowing because of her desire to push limits which truly stretched people into a new zone in their life. I was able, with the help of this Avatar, to take people to a place where sustainable change is limitless!

But there were no systems in place that could truly build the most epic of empires, because this particular Avatar didn't care much about planning for the future. Or doing anything that wasn't fun, things such as creating systems that would make tracking financials easier than, "Oh, crap. It's tax time, and now I have to spend *days* on end doing it all at once! Rar."

Then one day, I took emotional stock and noticed that I had been feeling super irritated and frustrated on and off for about a month straight, which was incredibly rare for me. So I dug deeper. After some exploration, I experienced an Aha moment that changed my relationship, my business, and my life forever! I realized that a new Avatar had been running rampant in my relationship for the entirety of that month of frustration.

I had experienced firsthand what happens when you haphazardly and unconsciously utilize Avatars in your life. Or rather, when *they* use you!

Enter "Power House Boss Babe," the kickass, unstoppable, plan-in-detail, future-focused, get shit done, conquer the world, *make* shit happen, *create* your own destiny, and *do whatever it takes to get the results you desire* kind of girl. She's the one who is on the back cover of this book next to my bio. Yeah, *that* girl had taken over my love life, and I had no conscious idea it had even happened! She literally came out of nowhere and decided that my relationship was where she belonged.

Oy-Vey!

Can you imagine how confused my man must have been? Look at the girl on the front cover, who he had been with for a year, who was all "Live in the moment. Where is our next adventure? Let's have fun!" And then, bam, out of nowhere the girl on the back of the book shows up and is all, "What's your plan son? What are your intentions here?"

I remember finding out about Power House Boss Babes's presence when I was talking to a friend about how frustrated I was in my relationship. I must have been trying to come up with a game plan to *make* things change (aka make *my man* change, because of course if I wasn't happy it must be *his* fault, right?). This is what thoughts sound like when you are experiencing life from a limited existence of Headspace Overload.

You believe that your happiness is contingent upon what others do and do not do instead of realizing that you are a limitless being. You suddenly forget that you have full power and authority to create your own happiness, which all starts from the inside out. As I was coming up with a plan of action to improve my love life, my friend interrupted me and said, "Morgan, this isn't a business review."

Bam. Aha moment! Power House Boss Babe, you sneaky beeyotch. You see, Power House Boss Babe had been banned from the roster. She was once the star player, always in the game, and now she was a permanent fixture on the bench.

Why? Because when she was in charge of my career, she worked me to death. Literally. I was completely exhausted all day, *every* day. To say that I was "burned out" is an understatement. I was seeing a doctor for treatment of ongoing fatigue. Sure, Power House Boss Babe kicked major ass with one promotion after the next, climbing the corporate ladder, money galore. But I was never happy when she was in charge. No time for anything other than work, work, work, WORK! I was a workaholic for *years*.

Unbeknownst to me at the time, she was in constant pursuit of the wrong thing. She was chasing the need to be *significant*. To prove herself to the world! To *be* somebody that would make up for the lack and the emptiness I felt inside. As long as those were her intentions, she would singlehandedly destroy everything good that I would ever build in my life.

Because of all the destruction she had caused through the years, I was afraid to put her back in the game. As you can imagine, though, that awesome badass ninja warrior goddess does not settle for sitting on the bench. So she slipped in through the back door, as Avatars often do when you are not paying close attention. She put herself back in the game in an area that I had *not* intentionally blocked her from, because who the hell thought that she would ever get in my relationship. Aaahhhhh!

With this newfound awareness, I decided to make an epic change to the roster. I moved Power House Boss Babe to the spot of CEO of Epic Sexy You. With one, life-altering shift that was the biggest game-changer of all time, I gave her a new intention:

growth and contribution through my business. She is now chasing growth and leaving a legacy of contribution everywhere she goes.

She is honestly the most powerful force I have encountered. Ever. I now unleash her in all things business, from coaching sessions, events, and retreats to writing and producing this book. She builds impactful, life-altering, mind-blowing programs. She is a beast of epic proportions with an unrivaled passion to live a Limitless Life and help inspire every single soul she encounters to do the same. This shift of her focus on growth and contribution instead of needing to prove herself in attempts to feel significant allowed her to get even *stronger*, stronger beyond my wildest dreams. It unlocked something that had always been there that I just hadn't ever allowed to be front and center: my energy reading capabilities *skyrocketed*.

My ability to receive spiritual intuitive downloads became even more effortless than anything I had ever experienced before. It's almost overwhelming the amount that comes through now! It's as if I opened a portal. Or rather blew one open with a massive stick of dynamite! It propelled me into experiencing more *fun* than I have ever had playing with my spiritual gifts — channeling, connecting with spirits, reading energy, and life coaching. Even better, I get stronger and stronger every single day!

Meanwhile Miss Crazy, Sexy, Fun, Wild, and Free was all, "Oooooo Puhhlllleeeeeze put me back in the relationship, that area of your life was sooooo much more fun when I was there!" So I did just that. And bam! Back to a *fun*, in-the-flow relationship, where I was completely immersed in the moments and in the joy of connection, love, bliss, and adventure and everything *but* business! It was as simple as that. Back to Euphoric Bliss.

Crazy, Sexy, Fun, Wild, and Free is now an acting member on the board of Epic Sexy You, sprinkling in all of her yummy delicious magical fun and limit-pushing, adventurous ideas to help people experience the life-altering breakthroughs that get them the results they crave and desire.

Here is the beauty of it all: Power House lost her serious-pants attitude once I changed her intention to that of growth and contribution instead of her original intention, which was needing to prove that she was significant. What has been bred as a result, at an even higher level than anything I have experienced in my entire life, is an epic momentum in tandem with complete, in-the-flow, euphoric bliss and ease in *all* areas of my life. I have become an Epic and Limitless me, living an Epic and Limitless Life!

You are not here to be ONE thing. You can be anything that your heart desires! Are you ready for your own epic, LIMITLESS LIFE?

Epic Sexy Q&A

My challenge to you: take out your pen and journal. Let's *do* this! Ask yourself the following questions.

✦ What and who do I **desire to be**?

✦ What are all of the **versions** of me that I *love* being?

✦ Who are my **favorite avatars** that I've already created? What do I love about each of them?

✦ Get creative! **Make up avatars** based on what you want to feel, be, and experience more of.

✦ Which avatars **feel heavy** or are no fun?

✦ Which avatars are the ones that can be **given new intentions** that would be game-changers for me?

✦ Don't forget to **name them!** Be as specific as possible about what each one is like so that you will know who is who. Naming your avatars will help you use them effectively especially when asking yourself, "Who would be the MVP for this particular play?"

✦ Which avatars make me feel **more alive**?

✦ Which avatars make me feel the **most excited** to be me? I *love* being me when (fill in the blank)?

✦ Think of each area of your life. Which avatars are the **main players** for each? Is there potentially a better fit that will give me better chances for getting the desired results and outcomes I am craving?

✦ If I could make some **changes to the roster**, shift avatars to new positions, or put brand new players in the game, what would be the most epic layout possible to get me what my soul is yearning and craving for in each area of my life?

Make sure to write down what comes up. Aha moments, when written down, have a far higher chance of being integrated into the essence of your being than if you just "think" about them. We are not just "thinking" here. We are *doing*. We are making things happen, and we are on the path to doing that as quickly as we can.

Are you with me?

Once you have assessed which roster changes need to be made for optimal performance and fulfillment, put those swaps at the forefront of your mind and implement the changes necessary to get what you want! As an example, bringing your sex kitten to work and your business woman to the bedroom may not be your best bet to get the most out of those areas of your life. That is unless those roles actually suit you in each area and, in that case, go on with your bad self! This is about doing things *your* way, whatever way *feels* best for *you*!

The point is, be conscious of the who that you bring to every encounter that you have in life. This way, you can live a life on purpose instead of manifesting things haphazardly. You've got access to limitless possibilities and choices. Play with this. Have fun! Let your imagination run wild and free. Try different avatars on in different areas of your life and feel out which ones are the best for *you* in each desired moment. I want you to experience the outcomes and results that your soul is craving!

You've got this!! Get it girl!!!

GET YOUR SHARE ON *#epicsexyyou*

✦ *Feminize, Sexify, and Get Your Power On* ✦

Different costumes elicit different avatars and expressions of you. You can intentionally create different avatars through the use of costumes and then send them out into the world. Doing so sets you up to experience the limitless expressions of yourself that this world has to offer you. You are not here to be one thing, or to be the same thing over time. Unless you *want* to be. You grow. You evolve. You transform — mentally, emotionally, physically, and spiritually. At each moment in life, you experience yourself and the world in new and different ways. Look at all of the ways you have already changed, and allow yourself the opportunity to be playful and free as you step into the conscious elicitation of desired feelings through playing dress up with your avatars.

Epic Sexy Q&A

Write down the answer to each of these questions:

✦ What do I want to feel more of **at work**?
   What do I want to be more of? Experience more of?

✦ What do I want to feel more of **in my love life**?
   What do I want to be more of? Experience more of?

✦ What do I want to feel more of **in my friendships**?
   What do I want to be more of? Experience more of?

✦ What avatar can I **create intentionally** to elicit those
   feelings in that area of my life?

Replicate this with whatever areas of your life are a main priority to you and would be impactful to explore (family, spirituality, finances, or health, for example).

SPOTLIGHT EXAMPLE #1. Sexy in Love. Want to feel sexier and create more attraction, desire, and passionate fire in your love life? What avatar can you use to intentionally create those feelings in that area of your life? How can you *be* her, even when you are just at home lounging around? How can you try her on for size and get super comfy in her skin before you share her with a lover? Hint: try lingerie lounging at home. Literally, I even do my hair, put on smoky eyes, get all dolled up and sexified, and it's just for me to sit and be her and immerse myself in her sex kitten energy! If you try lingerie lounging and it feels awkward when you are alone, celebrate that! That means that there is a potential energetic block to share her with a lover, which may be blocking you from the love and intimacy that you crave. Practice being her *for you*. This will afford you the opportunity to embrace what it's like to be her in your own skin before you share her with someone else.

SPOTLIGHT EXAMPLE #2. Powerhouse Boss Babe @ Work. Let's say you want to be more powerful and bold at work. What avatars do you already have access to or which ones could you create that will allow you to be that? There are sooo many ways that you can experience being more powerful and bold. The key is to find which ways are a big fat "Hell Yes!" for *you*!

What do you want your avatar to dress like that would make *you* feel powerful and bold? What posture would your avatar take on that would make you feel like a Power House? What way would your avatar interact with others that would make you feel powerful and bold? What kind of a makeup look would make you feel powerful? What kind of colors would make you feel how you desire to feel?

For example, my Power House Boss Babe stands out. She makes sure that she is seen and heard! She wears bright colors, bold patterns, and she isn't afraid to embrace her femininity in the workplace, because she knows that her femininity is a powerful gift and not something that she needs to hide in order to be taken seriously.

What is the power outfit that your avatar could wear that makes you feel unstoppable? Would she wear a suit? Or does she wear a Power Dress and knock everyone's socks off, turn heads, get noticed, and be put on the radar for the promotion and or raise that she craves? When I started wearing power dresses to the office when I worked in the corporate world, I upleveled *my* energetic power big time. Everyone at work noticed. My energy screamed, "I am an epic powerhouse. I'm a fierce, feminine, and fab force of awesomeness. You'd be crazy not to beg me to come work for you, because I not only look like a million bucks but I am worth it too. You won't regret hiring me! In fact, I really am the *only* choice for this damn position. Where do I sign?" People followed my lead.

The key here is to explore and discover what works best for *you*! There is no universal "right" answer to what works.

You'll know what works for you by how you feel! Do you feel more of what you want to feel? If the answer is yes, do more of whatever you are doing! If the answer is no, stop doing it!

SPOTLIGHT EXAMPLE #3. Feminine Goddess Gets Her Masculine Lover. You want to attract a masculine lover?! Guuurrrlll, then you have to unleash the feminine divine goddess within. Feminize the avatar you are putting out into the world. Not tapping your feminine energy is such a common pattern that I see, and I myself even used to experience this dilemma. If you desire to create attraction with super masculine lovers but instead you keep attracting feminine ones, it is often because the current avatar that you are utilizing in your love life has a *lot* of masculine energy. Which is usually the same avatar that you are utilizing in your career, typically with great success in that area of your life. This often leaves you confused about why the same avatar can't lead you to epic success in other areas of your life too.

Often times, you are merely lacking the conscious awareness or the knowledge about how to utilize avatars effectively in order to get the results you crave and desire. The great news is you are in the right place. Woo! Feminine attracts masculine, and masculine attracts feminine. Don't believe me? Give it a *try*. Unleash a feminine avatar and let me know how it goes.

I went through this experience myself. I feminized my energy, my wardrobe, and my avatars, and it radically shifted the people who were drawn in and magnetized to me. Here is the key to this: you've got to *create* the character, and then *be* it. You've got to *Act As If.* Act as if you already *are* that character. Step into it. Play full out! See how each one feels, and intentionally *be* the ones that work best for *you*. Remember, focus on how *you* want to feel. How does this avatar feel for me?

Creating avatars is a Me First, desire-based, Heartspace Immersion process. You *feel* your way through it. Notice and enjoy what *you* love about experiencing each avatar with all of your senses. Think about it this way: even if I never left my house, how would this avatar feel for me as I explore, discover, and step fully into being and experiencing it? You are the master creator of your limitless life. *You* decide which characters play the leading roles.

✦ *Honor, Capture, and Leverage Your Low-Vibe Avatars* ✦

If you feel that one of your avatars limits you in any way, that can be a clue to let you know what you *don't* want to feel like, what you *don't* want to experience, and what you *don't* want to be. Those same things then tell you what you *do* want to feel more of, experience more of, and *be* more of, which sets you up for a win.

Let's use Spicy McChicken as an example. Personally, I am not a fan of her work. I do not like being her. She is a heavy drinker, a compulsive number always looking for a fight. She is insecure and terrified of intimacy, so she dates unavailable men who she knows can never get close enough to authentically reject her. She feels tense, she is infinitely wound up, and she has little to no coping mechanisms available to her. She has epic outbursts and her go-to emotion is anger. I spent thirty years of my life being her, so I know *exactly* what she feels like and I do *not* love being me when I am her.

When she is hurt, she lashes out and then shuts down. Or shuts down and then lashes out. And then shuts down some more. When she is hurt, she will *not* look you in the eye. She will insist that you leave, even when she *really* wants you to stay and make it better. She pushes people away to see if they love her enough to stay.

Spicy McChicken was the inspiration for me to create a brand new avatar, because I was curious to experience what it felt like to be the complete opposite of her. Since I knew what I did *not* like about being her, I was able to play with creating everything that she wasn't. I didn't like the heavy drinking, so I created an avatar that was sober. I didn't like the anger outbursts or feeling tight and tensed, so I created a new avatar who is loving, peaceful, calm, and grounded — one who feels light, liberated, and free. I looked at every dislike and created an avatar that embodied the opposing energetic pattern.

Now, when Spicy McChicken surfaces, she is a brilliant signal to me that there is something deeper going on underneath the surface that I need to explore. It's usually some kind of boundary I am not honoring for myself unknowingly. It may be something that I am taking personally that has nothing to do with me. It may be that I am hinging my happiness on the reactions and opinions of others and handing my power away as a result.

When Spicy McChicken surfaces, it is a signal that I am operating from a lower vibration, one where I am limited. It is a sign that I am operating from my Headspace Overload Navigation System. Spicy McChicken signals to me that it's time for some Me First Heartspace, desire-based exploration and activities. This allows me to shift back over to the side of the spectrum where my new, opposing avatar lives in the land of Heartspace Immersion.

Here, in my Heartspace, is where all my epic and limitless avatar selections are accessible to me. From here, I can create and experience my Epic Limitless Life. I am so incredibly grateful for having been Spicy McChicken for so long. It was so constricting to be her, so limiting, so lifeless, and so painful, mentally, emotionally, physically, and spiritually. All of those experiences provided a reference point for where I used to be. They allowed me to acknowledge and celebrate how much I have grown.

After accessing and experiencing the limitless me, there is no way in hell that I will ever go back and allow Spicy to be a main character in my life's journey. She still sneaks in the back door every now and again, for shorter and shorter visits each time. Her existence provides the most epic fuel to remain on the spectrum of experiencing life where *everything* that I desire and crave is available to me here and now. See, even your most challenging Avatars have some blessings and divine guidance in them!

Leverage Your Goddess Alert System to Prevent the Not-So-Epic, Not-So-Sexy Life

Now, let's shift our focus to a maintenance routine for Epic Sexy You. We will begin to identify and implement your very own customized reminders that will activate your Goddess Alert System. These reminders are similar to the lights on the dashboard of your car, those simple, easy, automated reminders that tell you when your car needs maintenance. The light goes on, and you are instantly reminded that an oil change is needed within the next one hundred miles in order for your car to stay in its Thrival Zone!

A car will not run at optimal efficiency if you don't keep up with regular maintenance such as oil changes. In the same way, there are various maintenance actions that are unique to *you*. If you don't take care of these items, they jeopardize your ability to experience fully your Epic Sexy and Limitless Self. Your own customized activations for your Goddess Alert System will act as built-in, automated reminders of when you are in need of doing something to keep yourself in *your* unique Thrival Zone.

These activations for your Goddess Alert System act as gentle, loving reminders that it's time to take a look at what is going on around you and discover what you may need to do in order to get back into a "Me Too" Heartspace Immersion existence. They are a signal to you that it is time to sprinkle in some sparkly magical "Me First" as needed. Often times, when the Goddess Alert System signals you, it is an indicator that you have gone rogue and forgotten about yourself along the way. The great news is that these can act as beautiful reminders of opportunities to get back on your path. Often times, when your Goddess Alert System is going off, it is letting you know that there is a possibility that you are giving too much to everyone and everything else around you. It reminds you to stop and give back to yourself.

Remember, the better your relationship is with *you*, the more *thriving* existence you will be able to experience all around. So, when your Goddess Alert System is going off, it's also a reminder to celebrate. "Yessss! I have intentionally built a customized and automated way to remind myself to get back to *me*! Woo! I rock!"

Let me share a few examples of my activations for my Goddess Alert System to help you start the brainstorming for some thaaangs that *you* can use for yourself. Please remember that you need to find what works best for *you*!

SPOTLIGHT EXAMPLE #1. Nails. Guuurrrl, if my fingers and toes are not done up, then it's sirens going off that I am not taking time to spoil myself, give myself love, and be gentle, loving, and kind with myself. For example, right this very moment, as I am writing this, my nails are paintless. I have spent the weekend writing, prepping for retreats in Mexico, Fiji, and South Africa, spending time with my man, building my empire, and *not* giving any time to myself. Goddess Alert System has been activated! Wooo!! This is my reminder to give back to me. A heaping serving of Me First is coming right up. Woo!!

SPOTLIGHT EXAMPLE #2. My House. If my house is a mess, then *I* am a mess. This is a simple one for me. If I am not taking time to take care of my home, my beautiful luxurious haven sanctuary, then you best believe I am not taking care of me! This activates my Goddess Alert System! Wooo!! Time to get to some good ol' self lovin' in the form of some therapeutic cleansing of my home! Woo!

SPOTLIGHT EXAMPLE #3. Tanned Golden Goddess. I am a sun goddess. I feel better when I am tan. I look better when I am tan. I just *looove* basking in the sun. I love being me even more when I am tan. It's an epic Zen factor for me. If I am noticing myself getting all pale and pasty, my Goddess Alert System goes off! Wooo!! Thank you for that simple, easy, automated, built-in reminder that I am not taking time to do the things I love. Yaaaaayyy! An opportunity to start taking some time for myself.

Thank God for the Goddess Alert System. It prevents the overwhelm and burnout that I used to feel when I had *no* systems whatsoever in place. Back then, I never even knew there was an opportunity for me to hit the pause button waaaaayyy before burnout. If I had known, I could have refueled to experience my optimal self and stay in my Thrival Zone! Winning!

Other examples for me include things such as skin blemishes in the form of a big, fat, pus-filled, painful pimple. TMI? Those always tell me to take a deeper look at what is going on and explore *why* I got them in the first place. It's a signal for me to look at what I have been eating, so I can ensure that I am nourishing my temple and keeping my body looking and feeling sexy. Something unwanted, like that skin blemish, is an opportunity for me to explore how much sleep I am getting and ensure my body gets the rejuvenation it craves for optimal, Epic Sexy Thrival Factors. It's a prompter to look for opportunities to decrease stress. Woo! Goddess Alert System! Look at that, keeping me in my optimal sexy zone too! Woo!!

Also, the length of time in between haircuts, massages, or getting on my yoga mat are all activations for my Goddess Alert System. This signals to me that I am neglecting myself – mind, body, and soul. It reminds me to take some much needed Me First time! If I notice I am eating out a lot and have no groceries in the house, the Goddess Alert System goes off! I *love* having a plethora of yummy, healthy and deliciously nourishing foods to satisfy my limitless desire, so when the fridge is empty or I'm ordering in or going out a *lot* — Goddess Alert System! Woo!!

There are even certain foods that activate my Goddess Alert System. When I find myself picking up the phone to order pizza, Goddess Alert System! I have found that when I start craving pizza, it's because I am focusing too much on work and putting in too many hours. Yaaaayyy, Goddess Alert System!!! This Epic Sexy alert system lets you know what to look for and gives you new options and choices that lead you back to you. You can intentionally create your own preprogrammed signals that will activate your Goddess Alert System when you are nearing the exit of your Optimal Thrival Zone, which is where your divine Goddess Source Power resides.

You don't necessarily have to take action immediately when the system is alerted. Rather, the alert simply reminds you of the opportunity to explore a bit further to see what's *really* going on before any real damage is caused. Now, that is sexy! Consider the example with the oil change. When your Goddess Alert System goes off, you get the warning a hundred miles in advance. You don't necessarily need to take action *immediately*, but you do definitely need to start paying attention and scheduling whatever it is that you need to do to keep yourself in your optimal Thrival Zone. The Goddess Alert System is the *best*!

Epic Sexy Q&A

Take out that journal or piece of paper and a good ol' pen, and get to writing. What are some things that come to mind for you that you can use to activate your own Goddess Alert System?

✦ What are the things that you **love doing for yourself**? Consider those things that, if too much time lapses in between them, you know you are neglecting yourself and are off your path of intentionally and purposefully creating a life you love living and a *you* that you love being!

✦ What are the things you **love having done**?
Examples might include a massage, your nails, a
facial, your haircut, your eyebrows, or waxing.

✦ What will be the **signs that will let you know**
when you are on and off your path?

Remember, these things let you know when you are rocking
your Goddess connection too. For example, when my house is
clean, I've got groceries, and my nails are painted, it reminds me
that I am on my path and totally connected with and being guided
by my divine Goddess Power Source.

Write down your ideas of things that you can use. Test em' out!
Experiment and play. See what works for YOU!

GET YOUR SHARE ON *#epicsexyyou*

Channel Your Inner Goddess

Find a seat. Get comfy. Relax your body. Relax your mind.
OK. Now, close your eyes. Take a few deep breaths in, and connect
to the Goddess within you. Be patient. Tune in. Find her inside
you. Feel how she feels. Become her. When you are ready, ask her,
"How would you *love* to show up?" Ask a ton of questions and see
what comes up.

✦ How would you *love* to **look** physically? Hair?
Makeup? Nails? Outfit? Posture? Facial
Expressions?

✦ How would you *love* to **walk**?

✦ How would you *love* to **talk**?

✦ How would you *love* to **interact** with people?

✦ How do you *love* to **talk to yourself**?

✦ How would you *love* to **honor and love yourself**? What would that look like? What would that feel like?

✦ What do you **want**?

The list goes on and on. You will get visions or words that come through. Don't question them. Just write that magical beauty down. Capture it! Explore it. Play with it. Have fun with it! Then pick *one* thing, and take action on it!

If you don't already look the way that you envision, work on the things that you *can* do right now. Do *not* wait for a tomorrow that never comes. Then, you are just putting your Goddess back on the bench, and she is sitting on the sidelines watching you go through life without her. It would be sooooo much more fun, sexy, passionate, and fulfilling with her in the game *with* you!

SPOTLIGHT EXAMPLE. I did this one day when I was sitting in my car about to walk into a salon to get a haircut. I closed my eyes and took in a few deep breaths. I relaxed my body. Then I asked her, "What do you want to look like?" She gave me the clearest vision that I have ever seen! My hair was about twelve inches shorter in the back and about nine inches shorter in the front. It was an angled bob, clear as day. Then, she showed me exactly what I was wearing: a white tank top, jeans, and sneakers. My nails were painted a vibrant red.

She went on and on. She was lean, toned, and she felt like such an f'in badass. She was fierce, powerful, liberated, and unstoppable. I opened my eyes and said, "OK, when I am lean and toned I will make that happen, and I will get that haircut that she showed me." Then it hit me. I actually already looked the exact way she showed me. Even if I hadn't looked that way already, what I heard myself say loud and clear was, "I'll do it when...." Oh, you sneaky, "I'll do it when..." Syndrome. You rat bastard.

I hear this all the time from clients and I watch how it keeps them from living a life that they love *now*. It locks them into a continual holding pattern. They are *waiting* to live life. It shows up as "I'll work out when I am more fit..." or "I'll buy new clothes that I love and dress like my goddess wants when I lose weight..." or "I'll start living my life when I move to (insert wherever you plan on moving to)..." No. Stop that shit!

Do it *now*! You can always do *something* right now!

If I was being honest with myself, I had to call a big fat *bullshit* on me and my poo poo story. Yes, I said poo poo. Because that is what it was: a big, heaping, pile of shit! I realized just how much fear had its grip on me. I had a lot of fear about cutting my hair, because when I was 13 years old, I had a traumatizing experience tied to the world's worst haircut of all time. Haven't we all?!

My bad haircut experience coincided with a time where I played a little game with fate, danced on the ledge of life, and tried to end my existence. Yes, I am talking the "S" word.... Suicide. Spoiler alert: Fate won. That traumatizing experience was so powerfully strong in my current energetic field that I was literally reliving the past every single time I went to get my haircut. I hadn't changed my hair since then. That's right; I was holding myself hostage in a 20-year-long energetic holding pattern because of one bad experience. That was it! I had had enough.

"Not today," I said. I marched in there and I gave my goddess exactly what she asked for. That day, I broke free from something that had been weighing me down for what felt like two centuries. I walked out of there as sexy and sassy as I had ever been, feeling completely liberated and free. It was an incredible energetic liberation that opened the floodgates to me leaving shame and feeling unworthy behind me, all the while embracing feeling so f'in lovable and worth every single ounce of juiciness this life has to offer me.

My new energetic pattern screamed, "You bet your ass I am fucking worth it!" I went home, put on the very outfit my goddess had shown me and painted my nails red. With my makeup done to perfection, I hit the town to be seen by all! It was one of those days where you want the whole world to see you because you are that f'in awesome! It was an Epic Sexy Day for sure.

My goddess has been unleashed and she is the most powerful, lovable, divine, incredible source of guidance and love that I have ever experienced. I want nothing more than for you to feel that unshakable love, confidence, and power! Listen to your Goddess. She knows what she is talking about, ladies!

Unleash Your Inner Fashionista

Typically when I work with clients who want insights on how to unleash their inner fashionista we do home visits or Skype calls. The client brings me into her closet to walk me through her current outfit-building patterns. Through these experiences, I have come to realize that the majority of my clients build an outfit by starting with a top or a pair of pants and build from there. There are other ways of unleashing your inner fashionista that will allow you to not only upgrade your current wardrobe without having to buy a single piece of clothing but also support you as you pattern break wardrobe habits and routines that keep you feeling stuck. The big bonus? You will have more fun and look more fly as a result!

Here are some creative, out-of-the-box ideas for building an outfit that fits the who that you are trying to manifest for that given day. These ideas take you beyond doing the norm every day. They get you out of the routine and rut you are in, whether that is building an outfit around the shirts in your closet or starting with the common question, "What pair of pants am I going to wear today?" Energetically, when you break free from one rut, it opens doors to new possibilities in other areas of your life! So let's get creative and experiment with new thaangs.

Let's get your Sexy Swag on, shall we?

Nail Polish. *Build an outfit around a nail polish color!* Pick out a color of nail polish that is calling out to you. Ask yourself, "How do I want to feel this week?" Pick a color that will make you feel that way. For example, if you want to feel upbeat and happy, go with a bright yellow! Or perhaps you are feeling edgy and totally badass rocker. You might go with a bold blue, a grey, a dark blue, or a funky and edgy black. For the rest of the week, build outfits around that nail polish color! When it starts chipping, switch it up and start all over with a new color. No Limits. No Rules. WOO!

Lipstick. *Build an outfit around a lipstick color!* Ask yourself, "How do I want to feel today?" Then, pick a lipstick color that is going to set that tone and build your outfit around that color. For example, if you want to feel sexy, hot, and sassy, maybe you go with a bright red lipstick. Then, you plan your outfit, makeup, and accessories around that color.

Jewelry. *Build an outfit around a piece of jewelry!* For example, you can buy what I call a "statement" necklace. It's bold, chunky, radiant, beautiful, and it says "Bam! Check me out! I am fancy!" Haha. Or you can pick what you want your necklace to say when you wear it, so that you select the one that matches the who that you want to intentionally put out into the world that day. You start with the necklace and then you build the outfit around that! You can do this with a pair of earrings. You can do it with a funky, chunky, edgy, fun ring. You can do it with a bracelet or a cuff. The possibilities are endless when it comes to starting with accessories and then building an outfit around that!

Shoes. *For my shoe addicts out there, you know what I'm talkin' about!* Find the pair of shoes that speaks to your inner goddess. For some, the experience of finding just the right shoes could be compared to finding your soulmate. Shoe divas just "know" when they find the sole mate that they can't be without! Pick out a pair that makes you feel how you want to feel that day. Then, build an outfit around that! You can do this same thing with belts, jackets, and blazers, with purses and bags, with scarves, and even with eye shadow colors.

Think outside the box, and try something new. For a quick and cheap wardrobe makeover, instead of buying more clothes, buy a new nail polish color, lipstick, or some inexpensive, fun, and playful jewelry. Pick up a pair of shoes, a jacket or blazer, or a scarf. Choose some new makeup colors. Try on a new hairstyle. Buy a new belt. Get a complete wardrobe makeover without having to buy any new clothes!

Play with each of these and see what *feels* good to you. How do you want to *feel*? Create from that space of desire! Enter into that space of yearning and craving. What do you want to feel more of? Be more of? Experience more of? Experiment. Create. Play. Trust your gut reaction when you try things on. When you put something on, if it's not a "Hell Yes!" it is a "No." Do you *love* it? If not, you'd be settling, and settling is for suckers. Don't be a sucker. Put that thing in the no pile, and try again!

Beware of the "Yeah, buts...." That's when your immediate reaction is one of "Meh" but you try to talk yourself into it, anyway. I see this happen in dating too. Trust your initial gut instinct. If you get an immediate meh when it comes to choosing a new addition for your wardrobe, then that is an item that is going to sit and collect dust, then go into the donation pile years later with the tag still on it! Stop the cycle at the meh point. You are here to live an Epic Sexy Life. You deserve to create avatars that make you feel like a million bucks, so hold out, be patient, and find what truly is a "Hell Yes!" for you. Clothes, accessories, lovers, jobs, friends... the meh factor works ladies. Try it on for size.

Finally, the definition of insanity is doing the same things over and over, expecting different results, so make sure to step outside of your comfort zone. Try on new things, things that you've never tried on before. How do you know for sure if you're going to love it or hate it unless you get to experience yourself in it and feel it out? Bravely, boldly go where you've never gone before! Woo!!

• • • • •
THRIVAL PERSPECTIVE
• • • • •

Please do not let TIME or MONEY be an excuse. It's just that... an EXCUSE.

Epic Sexy Thrival Actions

✓ If you took 10 minutes in the morning, 5 minutes to put makeup on and 5 minutes to do your hair, you would feel wildly different than if you invested no time at all into yourself. The more **time and energy** you intentionally invest in yourself, with purpose,

179

the more you will reap the rewards and feel the difference as you navigate through your day!

✓ If you perpetually run late in the morning, get a **head start**. Pick out your outfit, shoes, and accessories the night before.

✓ If you don't have the money, shop at **discount retailers**. Ask around to see where people find epic deals on their shoes, accessories, blazers, jackets, and purses. You may be surprised just how many women around you who look like major Money Bags McGee Fashionistas are actually just divas who are getting style at a steal!

If there WAS a way you could make this happen, what might that way be?

Here is the thing: what you focus on grows. If you constantly look for a reason why you can't or find problems with every can, I can promise you, sister friend, you will *always* find those things. If, however, you constantly look for a solution, one will *always* be there waiting for you. And I do mean *always*!

It's your choice! Choosing to *not* have fun creating your who... well, sister friend, that is still a choice, and the choice is all yours for the making. Everything you want is yours for the taking!

Get Your Epic Sexy Posture On

Get up! Go find a full-length mirror and stand in front of it. If you do not have a full length mirror, go buy one so you can see, appreciate, and admire your beautiful self and all the Epic Sexy Avatars that you are creating as you unleash your inner fashionista!

Epic Sexy Q&A

Get out your journals and let's explore, discover, and play!

STEP 1: Hunch over. Explore the following questions.

+ What do you **notice**?

+ How does this posture **look**?

+ How does it make you **feel**?

+ If you saw someone standing like this, what are some **assumptions** you would make?

STEP 2: Stand up straight. Close your eyes, take a deep breath in, and channel your inner badass ninja warrior goddess.

+ **How does she stand?** Get into that position.

+ Now open your eyes. **What do you see?**

✦ How does she **look different** than the not-so-sexy hunchback of Notre Dame from a minute ago?

✦ How does this posture **feel**?

Write it down! Whatever you just noticed, capture that Aha moment. Nothing is too small of an observation to include. Life is about the little tweaks, and those little thaangs create the most epic shifts you can imagine. You can even step into different avatars to intentionally learn more about them and experience in a new and vividly conscious way what each one looks and feels like.

Go stand in front of the mirror, close your eyes, take a deep breath in, and channel a particular avatar that you would like to learn more about. Connect with her. Step into her. Then ask:

✓ **How does she stand?** Get into that position.

✓ Now open your eyes. **What do you see?**

✓ **How does she look different** than other avatars?
What do you notice? How does she look?

✓ How does she **make you feel**?

Write it down! Whatever you just noticed, capture that Aha moment. Nothing is too small of an observation to include.

✦ *Play the Awareness Game with Your Posture* ✦

Look at others around you. Explore what assumptions you make based on their posture. Look at who you are magnetized to and notice what their posture is like. Look at the women you admire, respect, adore, the ones you think are total powerhouses. What is their posture like? How do they carry themselves different than other women? What sets them apart?

Confident people take up space, so take what is yours. Pay attention to when you are taking up less space, and let that be a signal to activate your Goddess Alert System. Let it remind you to sit up tall, expand yourself, and take up more space. Do this from a feeling of desire. What kind of space feels great to you? What kind of space do you really want? Be true to yourself. If you want more space, it's yours! Truth be told, anything is yours for the taking.

Are you seeing a pattern yet in the shaping of the limitless Epic Sexy You? You *can* have it all. You can have *anything* you want. The possibilities are limitless! *No Limits. No Rules.*

Capture your insights and Aha moments as you play this game. You are a detective, on the hunt for an epic sexy limitless existence! Record your research, so you can finally create the life you *love* living and the you (or shall I say all the versions of you), that *you love* being!

Now that you are putting your best self forward, let's take step three of four simple steps to Epic Sexy You . . .

III

*Create the Ultimate
Love Affair with Yourself*

Step 3: Ditch the Baggage and Get the Love you Crave

Ditch the Baggage and Get the Love You Crave

Are you ready for a change?
Are you committed to change?

So many people live within unhappy circumstances and yet will not take the initiative to change their situation because they are conditioned to a life of security, conformity, and conservatism, all of which may appear to give one peace of mind, but in reality nothing is more dangerous to the adventurous spirit within a man than a secure future. The very basic core of a man's living spirit is his passion for adventure. The joy of life comes from our encounters with new experiences, and hence there is no greater joy than to have an endlessly changing horizon, for each new day to have a new and different sun.

Jon Krakauer, *Into the Wild*

If you are not already living an Epic and Limitless Life, then it is time for some changes. You can't be Epic Sexy You when the energetic crap that comes along with carrying other people's bags of shit weighs you down. This section is about intentionally creating space for *you.* It is too hard, and absolutely *no* fun, to try and squeeze your expansive self and your limitless desires into a suitcase filled to the brim with other people's crap.

We are preparing for *your* trip of a truly epic and limitless lifetime. This is about unpacking other people's crap and making room for all that *you* crave here and now! Others have their own suitcases. If they can't fit their crap into the space they have, then trust that they have their own work to do. Know that your choice to continue to carry their bags of shit prevents them from going on their own journey to create their own limitless life. They don't have anything weighing them down, because *you* are carrying it all for them! Do them *and* yourself a favor; ditch the baggage!

Guuurrrrllll, let me tell you this right now: if you think you are good at hiding what's going on underneath the surface, let's review. If you are still dealing with the pain, sadness, and anger, the past regrets and anxiety, go back to that Headspace Overload list in the first section of the book. Insert all of those things into the list provided. If you think that somehow you are masterfully pushing those things down and no one can see what's going on underneath your surface, think again, sister friend.

"I'm Fine" Is a Load of Crap

I used to have a coworker who would huff and puff and slam drawers. Yes, we *all* get it: you are having a bad day. When we would ask her if everything was OK, she would always say, "I'm fine." She was always "fine." OK, sister, not sure who you are fooling with this "I'm fine" BS.

Whatever was going on, it was clear that toxic thoughts were impacting her day, and she genuinely thought she was doing a good job of keeping those negative thoughts to herself. In actuality, being around her was like tip-toeing through a minefield of

186

negativity, never knowing when an explosion could be triggered. That explosion would surely impact anyone and everyone she came in contact with.

When I finally had a honest and candid convo with her about it all, she said she was having a hard time (which we all already knew, apparently even before she was able to admit that to herself). This is an incredibly common energetic occurrence, by the way. She said she had *no* idea that anyone could tell, and she definitely did not know that she was spreading negativity everywhere she went. She felt awful about it.

If I am being honest, *I* have been this person too! We have all been there at some point, right? We have all had an awful day, month, year, or decade. We have all felt super-stressed about something and found ourselves lost in the negative, downward thought spiral of a Headspace Overload existence. When people ask us, "Are you okay?" the answer we give is nearly always, "I'm fine." You aren't even really consciously lying to those around you, are you? You are lying to yourself more than anything, trying to contain whatever the hell it is that is going on inside you.

If you are living your life in the "I'm fine," "It's fine," "He's fine," "She's fine," "We are all fine" mode, well then, sister friend, you are lying to yourself. You are most certainly *not* fine. You are bringing that negative toxicity to every single person you interact with. When you are in this state, you are at the effect of life and not in the Creation Seat of it. In short, you are settling for mediocrity, and in the Epic Sexy You tribe we do not allow a soul sister to do that. We are for *thriving*, not just surviving. We are Epically Limitless, and settling is for suckers! Don't be a sucker!

• • • • •
THRIVAL PERSPECTIVE
• • • • •

We are Epically LIMITLESS.
There is no settling for mediocrity
in the Epic Sexy You tribe.

Pack Your Power!

The good news is that you have the power to change energetic patterns that run deep and are causing you to lie to yourself, be unknowingly toxic to yourself and to those around you, and settle for mediocrity. All the aforementioned things fall into the realm of "surviving." Sometimes surviving serves you. Like, "Oh shit, there's a bear. I should probably run." But *thriving*, when used as the foundation of your entire lifestyle, is the real game-changer.

When you are feeling as if life is happening to you and that you are not in control, you are operating from a very old energetic pattern that gets recycled and passed down from generation to generation. This is your default survival mode. When you are blaming other people or external circumstances for what you are experiencing in life, you are caught up in surviving.

Thrival mode, on the other hand, will lead to expressions such as "I love the life I am creating and choosing to live!" The key words here are love, creating, and choosing!

It's about never settling. We are continually stretching and evolving into a more expansive and limitless existence. When you are in thrival mode, you know in every fiber of your being that you are the Master Creator of your life! If your soul is craving something, then this craving is your divine signal that you already have everything that you need to make that thing happen. You are an Epically Limitless being, living a life of your desire and creation.

So, what we are going to do here is play with the energetic patterns of surviving and thriving. We want to turn down the survival mode instincts, which will still be there when you truly need them. Think of the bear example, a situation when you might need to "Get your run on sister!" Meanwhile, we'll turn up your Thrival Mode and empower you to claim every single thing your soul craves.

If there is one thing I know better than anything, it's energy. In fact, I can speak the language of energy even better than English. Truth be told, energy was my first language. I came into this realm knowing it. Energy is what I do best. It's my "It" Factor. It's my jam. It's my thaang. I am an Energy Reader. I can hear you now, "What does that even mean Morgan?" It means I can feel what you are feeling, and I can see energetic patterns that are underneath the surface of you, patterns that keep you feeling stuck.

Through my one-on-one coaching practice, the retreats and events that I host, online programs, my newsletter, blog posts, and this book, I share insights, tips, and tools to help you reprogram your energetic current. I help you create and operate from new energy patterns that allow you to find, finally, your missing pieces. These new patterns lead you to answers to questions that have been plaguing you for years. They help you break old patterns to get the things your soul craves.

When it comes to learning how to shift energetic patterns, a great place to start is with your thoughts. Your thoughts create your reality, which is why meditation, imagination, and visioning are so powerful. If you can see what you want in your mind, then your body can feel it and you can create it. Likewise, if you are intentional about how you spend your time and your energy, you can create an epic momentum of euphoric flow in your life. That flow will allow you to create whatever your heart desires in such an effortless state of ease and bliss.

Different thoughts carry different energy. Part of you *knows* this already. Let's play with, explore, and discover the magic in the power of the energetic vibration of your thoughts. Let's find out how you can use your thoughts to make your desires a reality. Visualization offers one great example of how you can intentionally use the best your Headspace has to offer to better focus your thoughts and intentionally harness the power your Heartspace desires.

Let me give you an example. When I was younger, I was a competitive gymnast. I was, and still am, quite a badass, if I do say so myself. What took others months to learn took me days. Once, when I was learning a difficult trick, my coach told me it would take weeks to learn. "Even the best gymnasts struggle with learning this trick," and I was "not going to be an exception to the rule," the coach warned me.

First of all, I am stubborn, and I do not like being told what to do, how to think, or that I am not an exception to a "rule." F you very much. I was quite fiery, even as a child. Maybe as a child it was more like, "Screw you, buddy, I'll show you what I'm made of!" I'm very fortunate to have a father who flamed that fire inside me. Early on in my gymnastics career he taught me to use the power of my mind to visualize myself doing the trick and to trust that my body would naturally follow.

I paired this visualization exercise with my screw you buddy fire. (That fire is now a higher vibration, as in, "Thank you for adding the fuel to my already epic fire.") I channeled that fire, began staring at the bar, and visualizing step by step the mount I was learning so I could successfully compete at the next level. As I was visualizing, I could feel my body trying to learn the muscle memory to help me get where I wanted to go. I would break it down step by step. As soon as I would master one piece of the puzzle, I would get on the bar and do that piece, just as I had in my mind. Then my body would help me find the next piece I needed to rework in the mind.

The partnership of my body and mind was a fierce, unstoppable pairing. In just a few days, I mastered the mount and defied the odds of the "rule of averages." Boom. On to the next level of competition for me. Like a boss. Yeah. Screw you, buddy, and thank you for adding fuel to my fire to prove you wrong.

EPIC SEXY THRIVAL TIPS

You can intentionally and purposefully harness the power of your thoughts, your words, your environment, and your peers to consciously release the energetic baggage that has you stuck, so that you can move forward and be the Master Creator of your own life. I truly believe that when you learn to tame a dark, unconscious mind, you will change your life forever. You will gain access to an existence beyond your wildest dreams.

The remainder of this section is filled with *Epic Sexy Thrival Tips* that will help you learn how to intentionally clear the clutter so you can make room for the limitless Epic Sexy You! With this set of *Epic Sexy Thrival Tips*, we'll be doing some spring cleaning. I'll give you a new thrival perspective, plus tips to ditch the junk, remove the clutter, and make room for the golden, sparkly, magical goddess goodies that ignite and fuel the fire inside you as you create a limitless life.

Remember, pick one thing at a time and play with it for a week. Pay attention to how it makes you feel. If you experience an uplevel or insights, then keep doing it. Play, experiment, have fun with it. Once you've got the hang of that thing, add another approach while sustaining the first thing. And repeat.

This is about laying one solid brick at a time to your foundation and building upon each one, all the while having a ton of fun. These are not isolated, individual pieces, but rather many pieces to a whole. Let's go find your custom roadmap to a thriving existence!

Ditch the Dogma: Stop Shoulding on Yourself and Ask, "But What If You Could?"

This section is about getting conscious clarity around what limits you are allowing to confine you and then breaking free from those limits once and for all. There is power in redefining what is true for you based on your own desires and giving birth to new choices and possibilities. We will explore new definitions and take a look at limiting language.

"Can't" and "should" are quite possibly the two most common limiting, destructive, debilitating, paralyzing, and toxic words in our vocabulary. When you set up your powerful Goddess Alert System, these words will become ones you begin to question adamantly rather than sprinkling them into your speech unknowingly and unconsciously accepting them. When you begin to do this, your life will change forever.

These two words, "can't" and "should," are signals for you to become a super ninja expert by leveraging them for change. Pack your power. Meet "can't" and "should" face-to-face. We will explore several ways you can set up your powerful Goddess Alert System to really challenge these limiting beliefs. Each pathway can lead you to a new energetic pattern that will empower you to break free from the limitations that currently weigh you down.

It all begins with listening.

✓ Listen for when you hear others say these words **about themselves**.

✓ Listen for when you hear others say these words **to you**, especially where they are being used in a way that feels limiting to you.

✓ Listen for when you hear yourself say these words **about yourself**.

✓ Listen for when **you speak these words to others**,
especially where they are being used in a way
that may potentially be limiting others.

Every single time you hear "can't" or "should" in any of the
scenarios above, activate your Goddess Alert System. Stop
immediately. Then, use your ninja skills to leverage a powerful line
of questioning to break free from limiting energetic patterns and
get yourself unstuck.

✦ *Break Free From Can't* ✦

Sometimes "I can't" is really just code for...

✓ "I'm scared that I can't do it."
✓ "I'm afraid that I will fail."
✓ "I'm afraid I'm not enough."
✓ "I do not think I am even capable of doing that."
✓ "I have no idea how to even do that."
✓ "How the hell is that even possible?"

These are the flavors of can't that are truly limiting you from
expansion. They force you to play small, to squeeze your limitless
self into some kind of illusionary box. As you bravely go where
you've never been before and stretch yourself outside of the
limitations of these flavors of can't, your world will wildly
transform. Woo!

Sometimes "I can't" translates to "I don't want to." In this
scenario, "I can't" is super low-vibe and creates unintentional
energetic limitations for you without you even knowing you are

placing those limitations on yourself! You are limitless, designed to create a high-vibe existence here, and there is a better way to say, "I don't want to" than using a low-vibe cop-out like "I can't."

This flavor of "can't" signals a clear opportunity for you to explore whether or not you are saying what you really mean. At the very least, it presents an opportunity to reframe the "can't" so you are not suppressed by it's energetic limitations. For example, if you are invited to a party that you do not want to attend, instead of saying, "Sorry, I can't make it," you might say, "I've already got plans. Thank you so much for the invite though, and I hope that you have the best party ever!"

On the other hand, sometimes "I can't" means, "I seriously wish I could but I have no energy or no time." This flavor of can't can be used to activate your Goddess Alert System and warn you that you may be giving too much to others and to the world around you. Leverage this and reframe it as an opportunity to reprioritize and make space for you to be able to do everything that you truly desire to do. "Me First" time!

Now, I do not mean to make space for saying yes to more obligations, more responsibilities, or more of whatever others need. This is about living a Hell Yes Life, one where you truly only say yes to things when they are a big fat huge, "Hell Yes!" and where you say no to opportunities that are anything less than that highest vibration of a yes. Explore places in your life where you are saying yes to things that are anything less than an absolute, desire-based "Hell Yes."

When you are living a truly Limitless Life, you will sometimes have so many epic "Hell Yes" opportunities flying your way that you will have to say no to some things to which you would love to say "Yes"! For example, you may be super pumped to attend a party you are invited to, but you already have another "Hell Yes" scheduled at that time. So you respond, "I've already got plans. Thank you so much for the invite though, and I hope that you have the best party ever!"

Notice this is the same way you would say no to the things that you do not want to do. It's a high-vibe way to say no, and it doesn't matter why you are saying no. How you say no creates the energetic vibration within yourself. Here's to the High-Vibe Life! Are you with me? Woo!!

Epic Sexy Q&A

In the event of the "can'ts" ask yourself the following:

+ What **flavor of "can't"** is this? What is this a signal for me to do more of, be more of, experience more of, and or feel more of?

+ How true is it really that you can't? **Based on what?** Why can't you?

+ **Says who?** Who says that you "can't" do it? Whose story is this? Whose "rule" is this?

+ Do I even **want to believe** this is true?

+ **What if this *is* possible?** What if I could? How might I be able to do that? What are the limitless ways I might be able to make this happen?

✦ What are the **reasons, stories, or beliefs** that hold
me back from turning this can't into a *can*?

✦ What am I **getting out of saying I can't?** What
are all of the possible ways that I may be able to
give myself that same thing in another way?

✦ What if "I can't," as in, "I can't but I really want
to," became a signal for **"I'll Find a Way"**?

✦ What if "I can't," as in, "I'm scared that I can't do
it," "I'm afraid that I will fail," "I'm afraid I'm
not enough," "I don't think I am even capable of
doing that," "I have no idea how to even do that,"
or "How the hell is that even possible, you must
be crazy?!" became signals for **"Here is an
opportunity for me to create my limitless Epic
Sexy Life!"** How would that change the way you
approached the situation?

SPOTLIGHT EXAMPLE. Someone asks you to speak in front of
a crowd of three hundred people. You have a fear of public
speaking, but you really want to be great at it. You know it would
take you to the next level in your business, which is something
your soul is craving. What if you heard yourself say, "I can't," and
you let it be a signal that that very thing is the *exact* thing you need
to do to grow into the fierce and fearless limitless being you crave
to be: Epic Sexy You. What if that "I can't" became your signal for

an "I must" and "I'll find a way!" If this is truly a desire-based "I must," because these are the standards for your Limitless Self, what are the creative ways you can make it happen?

Let's shift our attention and take a look at the "shoulds" that hold you back. We typically take action on "should" from a place of fear. We are afraid of not doing the perceived "should," so we just do it and keep on going. The thing is, when you follow the trail of "should," you'll see that the results you get perpetuate a cycle of mediocrity. You will see you are living life on other people's terms. "Shoulds" perpetuate a cycle of playing small. Essentially, you squeeze yourself into a box that it impossible for your Limitless Self to fit into. Since we typically approach should from an energetic pattern of fear, let's shift that right here and now.

Let's get playful! As you ask yourself the following questions, keep an open heart and mind. Think, "Well hello there 'should.' What are you serving up today?" Let's imagine we were ordering the "should" special off the menu at a restaurant. Let's find out what really comes with it, shall we?

Epic Sexy Q&A

In the event of the "shoulds" ask yourself the following:

✦ **Why** "should" I? Says who?

✦ Is that *really* **true**?

✦ Is this **someone else's** "should"? Whose might this be? Whose story is this? Whose "rule" is this?

198

✦ If I gave myself permission to **not care** about what anyone else would think, would I still *want* to do this?

✦ Is this a **Headspace** "should" or a Heartspace soul craving?

✦ What if I only have to do something if I really *want* to do it?

✦ **What do I want?** Do I *want* to do this? Play with the "Hell Yes" scale. From a 1 to 10, 1 being "Hell No," and 10 being "Hell Yes," what is my level of desire?

Don't be afraid of your shoulds. They are an *awesome* signal to activate your Goddess Alert System to explore further and uncover what you actually *want*! There is a fully expansive range of options available to you when you step outside of the should and explore what it's really all about. Connect with your Heartspace, get curious, and leverage your Headspace in a new way. Let it support you with an abundant flow of brilliant ideas. Remind yourself that words have powerful energy that can change the trajectory of the possibilities you have access to in your life. The possibilities are limitless when you allow yourself to explore what is truly available to you and step into the experience of your Limitless Self.

Become a word detective. Do *not* believe every word you or others say. Rewriting your script offers you opportunities for new possible outcomes that extend beyond the ones that you are currently experiencing and to which you have access today. When you change your word selection from a conscious, intentional, and purposeful space of creation, you change your life and expand the outcomes and possibilities available to you.

You can have it all. *Anything* you want is yours for the taking! Are you seeing a pattern here in all of this? YES you can have *anything* you want. *Anything*! Woo!!

GET YOUR SHARE ON *#epicsexyyou*

Unpack the Problems and Free Space for Solutions, Lessons, and Blessings

This is all about reframing and redirecting the energetic flow of your thought patterns so you can replace limiting thoughts with empowering thoughts. This is about swapping low vibes for high vibes, shifting you from Headspace Overload into harnessing the power of your Headspace in a way that allows you access to limitless possibilities, brilliance, and pure geniustry. You can have total access to your head *and* your heart at same time, where they're working together in divinely aligned intention.

The *Epic Sexy Thrival Tips* that follow are for when you feel "stuck" and are seeking to access *all* of you instead of just the limited portion you are experiencing in that moment. When you notice that you are consumed by thoughts of something that you are experiencing and it's *not* what you desire to be experiencing in that moment, let that be a signal to active your Goddess Alert System. Shift your energy and try something new! When you focus your energy on the problem and the things you do *not* want to experience, you inadvertently attract more of those things.

THRIVAL PERSPECTIVE

*When you feel stuck in low-vibe,
all-consuming thoughts, focus on what
you want. Focus on the SOLUTION.*

Epic Sexy Q&A

Ask yourself the following questions.

+ What is it I *do* **want to experience?** What do I *want*? What do I want to feel more of? Be more of? Do more of? If you are not sure, look at what you don't want and flip it to the opposite. If you are feeling sad, maybe you are craving to feel happy. If you are feeling exhausted, depleted, and fatigued, maybe you are longing to feel energized, ignited, alive, healthy, and full of vitality!

+ What are some **possible things that I can do**, in this very moment, to help me feel / be / do more of what I do want to feel / be / do more of right now, so I don't have to wait to experience what I want? What if I can have a little taste of that right now?

✦ What are some **possible things** I can do to help me experience what I want to feel more of, be more of, do more of in a more heightened and sustainable way? When your brain wants to go back to the problem, ask it again in a different way…

✦ OK, so **if I had to come up with an idea** and I didn't even necessarily have to implement it, what are some possible solutions to this problem?

✦ Become a **possibilitatrian.** Spend your time and energy on coming up with endless possibilities for how to resolve whatever perceived problem is in your path. Focus on the unlimited solutions. Get creative! Remember: what you focus on grows. Focus on coming up with solutions and an abundant flow of them will surely come your way!

✦ When you **find yourself stuck in the past…** You will know you are stuck there when you find yourself asking questions such as, "Why is this happening to me?!" Or "Can a girl just get a break?" Or "Whyyyyy???" Not the curiously playful kind of "Why?" More like: *Why did that happen? That shouldn't have happened like that. Why did I do that? I shouldn't have done that. Why did they do that? They shouldn't have done that.* All of these are flavors of energetic patterns that perpetuate the feeling of being lost, in the dark,

hopeless, helpless, and stuck in the past. Let these
be signals to activate your Goddess Alert System
and show you there is another way to playfully get
yourself back into the present moment and into your
Heartspace Immersion. There is no need for you to
suffer the wrath of Headspace Overload.

When you find yourself perpetuating any pattern that has you
feeling stuck, remind yourself to shift your focus and harness your
energy. Look for the lessons and blessings. Use the situation as an
opportunity to ask yourself the following questions.

✦ What were some of the **experiences in the past**
where I felt a similar way as I do in this moment and
then it turned out to be something that later I realized
happened *for* me? Explore as many as you can, so
you can see that sometimes time is the best healer
and revealer of all.

✦ What **lessons, blessings, or gifts** might I be
receiving from this experience?

✦ If I were to **remove myself from this situation** and
insert my best friend into the exact same experience,
what lessons, blessings, or gifts do I see that he or
she may be able to receive from this?

✦ When I **look back on this** a year from now, what
might I be grateful for in having experienced this?

✦ How might this be **happening *for* me** (*not to* me)?
What if this was actually happening *for* me?

✦ What are all of the **opportunities for growth**
I can find in this situation?

✦ *Stay Open to the "Blessons"* ✦

Even if you have no idea what the blessings and lessons are right now, just be open to them. Or as one of my absolute fave souls of all times, Miss Leecis Perry, calls them the "Blessons." Through the practice of trusting that at some point the Blessons will show themselves, you energetically shift the pattern you are experiencing and increase the vibrations you have access to instantly.

Just say "Yes" to blessings and lessons and remind yourself that you are an evolving being, here to learn. Opening up will lead to more blessons being revealed to you as you move forward on your journey. Stay open. Whenever you catch yourself focusing on the problems or stuck in the past, celebrate! You are expanding your consciousness and will expand what is available to you as you create a limitless Epic Sexy You. Remember: what you focus on grows. Intentionally focus on what you want to grow.

Maximize the Power and Energy of Words

It is important to bring your awareness to the power and energy of others' words. The words other people use give you insights into the possibilities that are available to them in that very moment that the words escape their lips. When you change your words, you change the energy that runs through every inch and fiber of your being. When your energy shifts, your life will change. You will intentionally create the kind of existence that your soul craves.

✦ *Be Quotable* ✦

Quotes are a powerful collaboration and co-creation of the brilliance of Headspace and the divine magic, ignition, and beauty of Heartspace. They are inspiring to the part of us that likes to think and they also tug at our hearts. They are powerful and moving because we believe them with our heads *and* our hearts.

Read through the following quotes. Circle those which move you. Which ones are *your* favorites? Which ones inspire you the most? Which ones touch your soul and appeal to the best of your Headspace *and* your Heartspace? What are the words in each that call to you, that speak to your soul, that move you?

> *You gain strength, courage, and confidence by every experience in which you really stop to look fear in the face. You are able to say to yourself, "I lived through this horror. I can take the next thing that comes along."*
>
> Eleanor Roosevelt

> *If you obey all the rules, you miss all the fun.*
>
> Katharine Hepburn

Imperfection is beauty, madness is genius, and it's better to be absolutely ridiculous than absolutely boring.

Marilyn Monroe

If you look at what you have in life, you'll always have more. If you look at what you don't have in life, you'll never have enough.

Oprah Winfrey

You may encounter many defeats, but you must not be defeated. In fact, it may be necessary to encounter the defeats, so you can know who you are, what you can rise from, how you can still come out of it.

Maya Angelou

I believe that anyone can conquer fear by doing the things he fears to do, provided he keeps doing them until he gets a record of successful experience behind him.

Eleanor Roosevelt

Your own words are the bricks and mortar of the dreams you want to realize. Your words are the greatest power you have. The words you choose and their use establish the life you experience.

Sonia Choquette

It's not your job to like me, it's mine.

Byron Katie

Epic Sexy Q&A

Everyone is quotable! Let's play with this right now to get you started on your journey of expansion as you explore and discover what are *your* simple beautiful truths are. It's time to get quotable. Consider the following questions.

✦ What are your life's foundational **unshakable truths** that you want to share? Get creative. Write down whatever comes up! Think about if you were on your deathbed and you were looking back at your life. What *really* mattered?

✦ What do you consider **keys to living a Limitless Life** that you would like to share with others?

✦ What can you share with others to help them create their very own **Heaven on Earth?**

✦ What are the **things that you say constantly**? Are those the things that you want to be known for? What *do* you want to be known for?

✦ As you move forward in your life, become more conscious of what you are saying. **Ask yourself**, "If someone quoted me saying this, would I *want* to be known for it?" If your answer is *no*, play with removing said things from your talk tracks!

People who are the world-shakers, pathfinders, trailblazers, and innovative souls who come here and sustainably change the world as we know it tend to be limitless in their own way. They think outside the box. They go against the grain. They color outside the lines.

When it comes to verbal communication, they use empowering words with full certainty and authority. Their language has a powerful, high energetic vibration. As a result, they experience an extraordinary life, a legendary life, and a truly epic and Limitless Life. They inspire individuals and groups around the globe and stand out from the crowd.

You can change your world too. Start by changing your words. Yes, *you*! Woo!!

Dispel Unconscious Negativity

This next piece is all about being aware of the energy behind your words *and* actions. For example, you may be saying you want one thing but *doing* something unconsciously that is totally sabotaging you from getting what you want. What's more, you may be completely unaware you are doing so. A lack of inner connection may lead you to spew negativity, often unconsciously, which is clearly a block to full thriving and a limitless life.

The goal is to *consciously* create your thoughts, words, energy, *and* actions, rather than being lost in a flow of unconscious creation. When you consciously choose and create your actions with considered words and clear expressions of your desires, you are able to create the results and outcomes that you crave. The power of limitless creation is in the alignment of actions and words. Yaaayy, limitless Epic Sexy You! Woo!!

✦ *Make It a Game and Have Fun* ✦

Pick a handful of friends and / or family members to do a little detective work with you. Choose people who will be up for a little fun and playful experimentation! Tell your players you are looking to grow and expand as a human being. Let them know you would like to ask them a few questions. Make it clear that you want the honest hard cold truth, delivered in raw, real, and loving fashion.

You want the full truth and nothing but the truth, with some sparkly sprinkles of love and light for good measure. Then, only if you feel you are prepared to fully deliver on this, promise them that you will *not* express anger toward them if they say something that is an uncomfortable surprise. This is bound to happen, so just remind yourself consciously that they are doing this *for* you. Their honest sharing is going to help you experience growth and uplevel your life so you can have all the things that your soul craves!

If you can't think of anyone to play this game with you, then play it with yourself! Be honest and raw and real with yourself! Do *not* let there be a single reason not to play this game! It is such a critical component to unpacking your baggage, and it will lead you into the ultimate love affair – you loving you!

When you are ready to begin, ask those supporting you with this game the following questions. Pay attention to the replies you receive. Look for common patterns and recurring themes as you compare the answers you collect from participants. As you play this game, record all of your goodies, keeping the information in one place, so you can easily cross-reference the information and spot the patterns when you've finished gathering the intel! Woo!!

Epic Sexy Q&A

Questions to ask those who have agreed to play with you.

✦ What are common **phrases** you hear me say?

✦ What are the common **positive, uplifting, inspiring, empowering phrases** you hear me say?

✦ What are the most common **words** you hear me use? Start with the sparkly magical yummy delicious goodies, and then work your way to explore the limiting ones too! Make a word buffet!! A few examples: *Awesome, Badass, Soul Sister, Yeah but, I can't, You should...*

✦ What are the common **disempowering or negative things** you hear me say about others and the world?

✦ What are **disempowering or negative things** you hear me say **about myself?** What's the negative self-talk you hear me spew out unconsciously?

✦ What are the **reasons I cite** for what's keeping me from doing things I've said I want to do? What are the most common excuses I make? Example: "I don't have enough time!" or "I can't afford that."

✦ On a scale of 1-10, with 1 being never and 10 being all the time, **how often do I complain?** Let me be very clear on this one. If it is a friend who will sugar-coat it (which is likely to happen because they love the ever-living shit out of you and, although you promised you wouldn't get mad and you said you wanted the truth, they still won't be 100% with you), do this: Take the number they give you. Add a few points to that, likely between 3 and 5 points. Unless they are direct, straight-shooting, truly honest, candid friends and family who have no filter. In this case you just need to add 1 to 2 points. The point is, those who love you often mistakenly think they are doing you a favor by sugar-coating the truth, so they can protect your fragility. In reality, they are only preventing you from the expansion that you crave. As such, you are going to need to be *really* honest with yourself here, and add a few points so that you can have the truth. Even your most honest friends may still go easy on the rating system. Let's face it though, sugar-coating is *not* going to help you expand and grow.

Sometimes the initial growth can be experienced as painful. What I can promise you is that it is a heck of a lot less painful to experience some temporary growing pains as you expand into your limitless and Epic Sexy Self than to settle for a lifetime of mediocrity. Remember, settling is for suckers! Don't be a sucker!! Haha. Woo! Growth, here we come!!

Epic Sexy Thrival Actions

OK, so we warmed up this game with all things words. Now, let's add *action* to the mix! This is a two-step process.

STEP #1: Share Your Top Three Soul Cravings. For example, your top three soul cravings might be: 1) Be madly, deeply in love, 2) Have a toned, epic, sexy body and be in the best shape of all time, and 3) Build the most epic empire of all time!

STEP #2: Ask This Question. What do you observe in my behavior that contradicts the things I have just shared? From your perspective how might I be blocking the very things my soul is craving the most in life with my choices and actions? Have those playing with you mirror back to you what you are saying or doing that is getting in your way of your epic sexy life.

SPOTLIGHT EXAMPLE: Soul Craving #1. You crave to be madly, deeply in love. Yet, you are dating someone you *know* you will *never* fall madly, deeply in love with. You tell yourself and others that you are just "killing time" and or "having fun." That comfort of having something that is "good enough" and "will do for now" will make you less likely to go out into the world to meet your madly, deeply in love person. Another example: You push away a man you are falling madly, deeply in love with because you are afraid to be hurt. You want to leave him before he has the chance to leave you. Yeah, you will never fall in love while that energetic pattern is running rampant in the currents below. The reality is you are going to have to spend some time and energy on working through that fear before you will be able to have what your soul craves. The first step is to stop blissfully ignoring what *you* are doing. Own what you are doing. Admit it's just fear. Admit that fear is keeping you from what you want, and then find someone who can help you break free from that fear and the energetic patterns that are running deep as a result of it. (I will continue to create content, programs, retreats, and goodies that will help you with this! So, visit the website, join the tribe, and continue to engage in all things growth. I've got you!)

SPOTLIGHT EXAMPLE: Soul Craving #2. You want to be in the best shape of your life, yet you are eating pizza, mozzarella sticks, burgers, and fries. You are *not* working out. If you are working out, it is only one day a week. Or maybe you work out every day, but you eat like shit. Umm... Yeah, that junk food is *not* going to get you what you want, so you are going to have to make some changes, sister friend.

SPOTLIGHT EXAMPLE: Soul Craving #3. You want to build the most epic empire of all time, and you quit your corporate job. You are "tired of working for all those years non-stop." You tell yourself you are just "taking some time to enjoy life" before you get your epic empire-building process started full force. This is a common pattern I have witnessed, and it is even something that I have experienced myself.

In fact, each of these examples are my raw, real, vulnerable experiences of incongruences in my own life from which I eventually broke free. Here is a little wake-up call: if you have this mentality of "taking a break before you jump right in," you are creating a habit of masterful avoidance. That avoidance will seep right into the cracks of your fledgling empire's foundation, and it will be very hard to clean it up. Totally possible to do so, but it will be easier to clean up the sooner you can put a stop to it.

More food for thought for budding entrepreneurs: yes, you do get to create your own hours. However, you still have to put in the time. No, you cannot sleep in till 3 p.m. *and* build an EPIC empire. Don't get me wrong, you can still build and run a "business" if you just put in a few hours a day, never do anything that is uncomfortable, and never really stretch too far out of your comfort zone. You can choose to put the rest of your time and energy into enjoying life, playing, and having fun. You just won't create a *thriving* business, and you most certainly will not create an epic, Oprah-like empire. So just be honest with yourself about what *you* want, and make sure that what you are *doing* is aligned with what you desire.

If this exercise has been helpful, tell your friends that you'd like to keep playing this game. Ask them to continue to point out when they hear you say something that sounds like an excuse. Request that they keep an eye out for ways you are limiting yourself from the things you say you want most in life.

At first this will possibly make you want to kill every single friend and family member who is playing this game with you. You may even want to scream, "I'm done. *This sucks!*" You may want to give up completely. Trust me; you will thank them and yourself when your life has changed dramatically. You will have nothing but gratitude when you see how you have broken free from the BS excuses you have been feeding yourself, out loud or through unconscious thoughts and behaviors for God knows how long!

Stop Complaining — That Shit Is Not Epic or Sexy

Complaining is low vibe, which as you know is a place where thriving cannot possibly exist. To catapult into an epic, sexy existence, we need to get you out of complaint mode and into high-vibe, thrive mode. This pattern shift that we are about to explore will raise the bar on your energetic vibration.

It's all good. You can use complaining as a signal to activate your Goddess Alert System and celebrate. Woo!!

What do you do when you feel like complaining? What can you do instead?

Have you discovered you complain a lot? Try this. Say to yourself, "Now that I realize I am complaining, I am consciously aware that I have been choosing to be in a low vibe. This limits me. Now that I am aware, I have new options available to me to *choose* a higher vibe!" It's time to ditch the excuses and stories and live full out.

Every single time I ask a client what they want and they tell me what they do *not* want, I know *immediately* why they don't have what they want: they don't actually know what that looks like in the first place! This one has been a *huge* piece of my own life's puzzle and a big part of my own growth and expansion journey.

When someone asks me what I want and I answer with what I want to *stop* happening, what I want less of, or what makes me mad, oh guuurrrl, then I *know* I've got some work to do.

Epic Sexy Thrival Challenge

I challenge you to do two things to be intentional with the energy you are putting out into the world. Try this:

✓ **Go a Full 24 Hours Without Complaining**. If you complain, start the clock over. If you play this game and you make it a whole 24 hours without complaining out loud, you will change your life. If that is too easy for you and you are looking for a harder version, I challenge you to go two days. Or three. Or a week. Or whatever is a stretch for *you*. If that game gets easy or if you begin to filter complaining thoughts and do not let them leave your lips for long periods of time, then extend this game to your thoughts. Go whatever period of time is a stretch for you to go without even *thinking* of a single complaint.

✓ **Tell Them What You Do Want!** For an entire week, every time you hear complaint thoughts in your mind or complaining words slip out of your mouth of the *"I don't want..."* nature, reframe them. This includes statements such as:

- *Why do you do that?*
- *I wish you didn't do that.*
- *I hate when you do that.*
- *You always do that.*
- *I wish you would stop doing that.*

Any time you hear these phrases, stop and reframe. Then, say what you *do* want. Stop communicating what you want someone to *stop* doing. Stop communicating what you *don't* like about them and their behavior, and start communicating in the language of what you *do* want.

Literally, even do this with your thoughts in your head. When you find yourself complaining about something, even if it's in your mind, ask yourself, "Right, but what *do* you want?"

●　●　●　●　●
THRIVAL PERSPECTIVE
●　●　●　●　●

If you complain or find yourself focusing on what you do not want, you will get more of what you do not want.

Choose You

One time my man called last minute to play a swithcerooski with our plans. I started thinking, "I *hate* this. It is rude and inconsiderate. I am sooooooo pissed. And hurt." So I cancelled the date all together. Then I had a huge, f'in meltdown. Yes. We *all* do it. We just don't talk about it. But how else do we learn and grow if we don't have a good laugh at ourselves and share our meltdowns? I am generous with sharing mine, so here we go.

I collapsed onto the floor like a small child in the most epic tantrum fit! I believe Spicy McChicken slipped in through the back door that day. She started working her magic, launching me into a downward spiral of hell. Oooo, Spicy McChicken, you are a real beeyotch sometimes! I could feel it coming on fast and furious, and I couldn't stop it. I could feel myself drowning in my own toxicity.

The thoughts started running rampant. "Why would he do this to me? He obviously doesn't care about me. If he did, he wouldn't have bailed on me last minute." Side note: he didn't actually bail. He was merely trying to weasel in a stop on our way that would potentially make us late to where we were going, in which case we would miss the fireworks. I thought to myself, "What the hell is the point of going if we are going to miss the fireworks... *again*!"

Oh yeah, because the other night he was running late and we missed the fireworks on the 4th of July. More angry thoughts: "He is sooooo selfish.... I don't want to be with a man that would bail on me last minute."

Side note: Notice I keep telling myself *he* bailed on me, when in actuality *I* was the one who cancelled on him. I could have just said no to the switcherooski in the first place. Or I could have told him how I was feeling instead of canceling, but nooo it was not that kind of day for me and Spicy McChicken doesn't use her words unless she uses them to lash out in anger.

My meltdown got bigger. "I hate him. He sucks at life sooooo bad. He is the worst person alive. Why am I with him? I want this feeling to stop. Ahhhh, whyyyyyy?! Whyyyy??!! WHYYYYYYY?"

Oh yeah, guurrl, we've all been there. No shame in my game. I'll own my trips to Meltdownvile if I can help you laugh at your own. Let's normalize those suckers. We all do it. But, here's the thing: there is another option I'd like to make available to you.

Here is what happened next for me. My Heartspace's inner coach voice came in to save the day. "Right," she said gently, "but what do you *want*?" Headspace butted in and answered, "I want a man who doesn't bail on me!" Heartspace wasn't giving up on me. "Right, so in a positive reframe, what is it that you actually *want*? In this moment? What do you want? How do you want to *feel*?"

Headspace considered and said: "I want to feel loved. I want to feel pampered and spoiled rotten. I want to feel like I am important and special. I want to feel like I matter! Raaarrrr."

"Great!" said Heartspace inner coach voice. "Then how can *you* create this feeling for yourself, right now, in this *very* moment?"

BOOM. Like a *boss* I stood up from the spilled mess on the floor I had become. I decided to take myself on a date. That's right, you heard me. In less than three minutes I had gone from Spicy McChicken in Meltdownville to Empowered Goddess on the way to the Thrival Life. Bam!

I checked in with the energetic current running behind my intention to take myself on a date, as that makes the biggest difference in the outcomes you will get in life. So I asked myself, "Why are you taking yourself on a date? Is it to punish him?" Nope. "Is it to teach him a lesson, or make him feel bad?" Nope. "Then why are you doing it?"

My answer to myself: "Because I am awesome, and I deserve to have everything I want, which includes feeling how I want to feel. I know that I am the owner of my own feelings. *I* have the control over whether I keep my power or hand it out, and I'll be damned if you think that I would give my power away like that."

Guess what happened? I had the best night ever! Took myself to a delicious dinner. Read a book I had been dying to read. Then went to see the Minions movie in 3D. Yeah, I felt pretty damn badass about choosing me that night. I carry that experience with me every single time my old energetic pattern creeps up and wants to blame others for how I feel. No chance in hell I am giving my power away like that. I choose how I feel. I go for what I want. Own that shit. Like a BOSS.

To intentionally *create* a life you *love*, the key is to become *conscious* of the energy you are putting out into the world. The next step is to explore the outcomes yielded by each energetic output and exchange. The next time that you notice yourself complaining or telling someone what you *don't* want or what you want them to *stop* doing, ask yourself, "What *do* I want?"

Honestly, unless you know what you want, you will never ever get it. That ties back to the first section of this book. Be sure to revisit the *Epic Sexy Thrival Tips* in that section to get back in touch with your inner wants voice. Give yourself permission to change your mind and revisit those wants as often as you desire. I've got you girl.

Pack In an Abundance of Gratitude

When you start to make gratitude a regular practice in your daily life, you are constantly loading up your suitcase with *high* vibes. Yaaay high vibes! High vibes make an epic and Limitless Life possible. If you were packing for an adventure of a lifetime, a dream trip that you've been waiting to experience your whole *entire* life, you wouldn't pack old crappy clothes that you absolutely hate. You would splurge and make sure that you've got the *best* clothes packed, right? This is the trip of a *lifetime*!!

Gratitude is like the accessory that you can wear with everything, and it looks killer. You look good in it. You feel good in it. It activates your magnetic energy field and attracts everything you crave. Oh, my God, the absolute POWER of gratitude....

I can't rave enough about how life-changing gratitude can be. It is one of the *fastest* ways to shift your energy from a negative to a positive, which, as we've been discussing, will dramatically and drastically shift the possibilities available to you at any given moment!

Epic Sexy Gratitude Tips

Here are some thaaangs you can do to use gratitude as an epic tool to create your very own Epic Sexy Existence:

The Reframe Game. When you feel yourself going down the downward spiral of hell, STOP. Take three deep breaths and ask yourself, "What are you grateful for?" What you focus on grows, so let's intentionally create more of what you love. Ask yourself that question and, for a minimum of three full minutes, just allow yourself to think about anything and everything you are grateful for! If you notice yourself focusing on the negative, reframe to the positive. Here's an example: If you are mad at someone for something they did or didn't do, ask yourself this: "What am I grateful for about this person? What is it that I like / love / respect / admire / adore about them? What are the good things about this person?"

Three Things. Before you go to bed each night, take three deep breaths. Intentionally feed your brain three things for which you are grateful. Put those bad boys on repeat in your head for 5+ minutes. Look for all the things that went *right* that day. What were the lessons learned? What were the blessings? Go back through your day and find the blessons. Where were the opportunities for growth? What are you proud of doing? What made you feel loved? Who or what touched your heart?

Gratitude Log. Turn each new day into a Gratitude Treasure Hunt. Every time you feel grateful for something, write it down! Keep a log on your phone or carry a miniature journal with you everywhere you go. Use it to keep a Gratitude Log for all the treasures you find along your journey!

Live Well. Give Well.
Create Energetic Bliss.

This energetic pattern shift is one that will increase your vibration and allow you to experience your expansion, abundance, and the effortless flow of *bliss!* When done from a place of true desire, not obligation, giving to others expands your energetic profile. It allows space for *more* of everything you crave.

The key here is to practice this from a space of true desire and without the "shoulds" and obligations. Practice only giving when you want to truly be generous to yourself and to others. Make sure to only give in whatever ways feels best to *you!* When you give well, living well effortlessly follows suit. The act of giving generously from a true Heartspace desire completely shifts your energetic patterns. There are limitless options of giving well available to you. Choose those that speak to your soul's desire.

Epic Sexy Thrival Giving Tips

Here are some ideas to get this Giving Par-Tay started!

- ✓ **Volunteer** your time for a cause you believe in.
- ✓ **Donate $** to a cause that speaks to your soul.
- ✓ **Donate clothes**, jewelry, shoes, books, or furniture.
- ✓ **Mentor** someone!

✓ Contribute by **sharing your knowledge** in a way
   that is accessible to anyone who wants or needs it.

✦ *Play the Giving Games* ✦

Here are a couple of playful ways that you can give well and
feed your soul at the same time. I invite you, on a *daily basis*, to
stretch beyond the traditional means of giving. This is the best way
I know to pack a love swag bag and rock the gratitude. Remember,
this is about giving because you *want* to, *not* because you feel like
you have to or it is what you should do. Play with what feels good
for you! If it feels good, do more of that. If it feels obligatory, kick
it to the curb. Let the giving games begin!

Only play a game if you genuinely feel called to do so in the
depths of your soul. The idea is to find something that ignites *you*.
This whole journey together is about discovering your own custom
ingredients to creating Epic Sexy You. Find something that touches
your heart and spreads love and joy to those around you, especially
the ones who need your love and light the most.

Yes, I realize I have said this about a million times already! I
do that because the energetic patterns we have collectively
inherited from the generations before us are strongly and deeply
rooted within us. Sometimes it helps to hear something over and
over again to remind us that there is another way available to us if
we would like to choose it! Yaaaay for giving games! Here we go.

GIVING GAME #1: Hand Out Those Dolla' Bills, Yo. Go on a
treasure hunt, round up some cash. Then, hand out single dollar
bills or loose change. I always make sure to have singles on me.
When I am driving and I see someone who is homeless, walking in

224

the middle of the street asking for money, I get sooo excited. I know this person is a part of my own treasure hunt. I am always on the lookout for someone to share my good fortune with. I want to find new ways to spread love, joy, hope, faith, and light.

I give them that dollar with the biggest smile I've got! Yes, I understand that some of those people may use the money for drugs. That's totally their decision, one that, quite frankly, doesn't concern me. I'm giving them more than a dollar when I play this game. I am giving them my energy. I am giving them my light and love. It's even more fun when I have the music jamming and I'm dancing. Or when I have a friend with me. We *all* win! We *all* get an energetic upgrade with that exchange.

You see, I have constructed a game where I am genuinely excited to see those who will benefit from my Giving Game. I cannot wait to give them the dollar and the light and love I hold in my heart. I'd rather be the one who *can* give and *does*, than the one who can't give or, even worse, the one who can give and does not.

I understand that, for some of you, this isn't going to be your game, and that is totally OK! It's about finding something that works for *you*! Find something that allows you to give to those in need *and* feed your soul at the same time. Get creative and play with different ideas of games you can play to open you up and allow you to give your light and love to someone who needs it most.

Maybe your game is to always greet the grumpy peeps with a smile and loads of light and love, no matter how much bitterness they send your way. Or maybe you'll join me in my game of sending waves, thumbs up, and smiles to those who have epic road rage, honk, and give you that special hand gesture.

Find what works for *you*. Then, share that game with others in our tribe so we can play too! Win, win!!

GIVING GAME #2: Pay It Forward. Another version of giving that you can try is the "Pay it Forward" game. I *love* this one! Essentially, you treat someone to something or do something for someone completely randomly and then you invite them to "pay it forward," meaning that, at some point in the future, they do a completely random act of kindness for a stranger they encounter. This creates an endless and epic domino effect of goodwill.

Before I started hosting my own life coaching retreats, I worked on a coaching team that hosted retreats for hundreds of women through weeklong experiences. On one of these retreats, I overheard a woman mention that she was going to have to go home to get ready in between the last day of coaching and our celebration dinner because she didn't have access to a room at the hotel. She seemed very stressed about that. I could tell she was going to have to rush around like a mad woman to make it back in time.

I immediately went to the front desk, had an extra key made, hunted her down in the room, and said, "This key will get you into the spa of this hotel which has the most luxurious, all-inclusive amenities. It has everything you will need to get ready here at the hotel. That way, you won't have to rush around tomorrow night before the celebration dinner."

Then I asked her if she knew what the "Pay It Forward" game was. I could tell by her perplexed look that she did not. I proceeded to fill her in and invited her to start playing with the women of the retreat. The game took off like wildfire! It started with one small but thoughtful gesture and the clear intention to spread the love and magic to everyone in the room.

I played this game at Starbucks one day. I had a couple dollars left on a gift card. I turned to the woman behind me and said, "Do you know about *Pay it Forward*?" She smiled huge and shook her head yes. I handed her the gift card with the remaining funds and walked out. This woman was a total stranger. I couldn't even point her out in a crowd if I ever ran into her again.

Truly, the only thing I even remember about that day was the overwhelming flood of pure euphoria that overcame me as I walked back to my car. To give to another being... just to give, for no other reason than that, is to know that a person's heart was touched. You know that you spread a little happiness and joy, and that that person will spread that feeling to someone else. See what can happen when you choose one small, simple act of kindness?

Wow. It's powerful. It can restore faith in someone's heart and soul. That someone might need a reminder of the good in the world on that day. It truly brings love, light, and bliss to everyone who plays. I literally cried tears of joy in my car that day when I left Starbucks. Yeah, I am a huge sap. I *love* this game.

News flash: life is about creating a ripple effect of love, joy, connection, unity, giving, and warmth to fellow souls alongside us on this journey of life!

GIVING GAME #3: Hand Out Compliments Like Candy. The Compliments Game not only makes someone else's day a little better; it makes yours better too! Play with being on a constant hunt for reasons to compliment someone. It can be anything: their hair, eyes, or teeth; their purse, shirt, or shoes; their posture or their sexy figure. This one is fun.

Seriously, you will see so many epic eyes out there that you never even noticed before. You will see some colors and sparkle that will rock your world. You will see the most beautiful smiles! You will see an endless sea of awesome and unique eyeglasses!!

If this feels weird, start by giving at least one compliment a day. Simply make sure it is genuine, and that you actually mean it. This isn't about making stuff up. It's about genuinely looking for the beauty in others, their uniqueness and the things that make them shine. It's about showing them that you see and you appreciate them for who they are. Each day, stretch yourself to give one more, and one more the next day than the day before. And one more the day after that. See how people respond to you.

Notice how the art of complimenting another person makes *you* feel different in your day-to-day experience. There is an endless sea of beauty out there, so many unique people with their own individual styles and expressions of self. Notice it all, and give people the gift of knowing that you *see* their beauty. Get your shine on, and let them know you see theirs too!

GIVING GAME #4: The Receiving Game. Whenever someone gives you a compliment, practice saying, "Thank you." Say it with me: "Thaaank You!" One more time. "Thaaaaank you..." Yep. That's it. Nothing more. You just take it, gurrrll!! Resist the urge to "Yeah, but..." the compliment. For example, if someone says to you, "Wow, I love your haircut!" and you respond with, "Thank you. She cut it a little shorter than I wanted...", you just poo-pooed on that compliment. Yes, I said poo-pooed. Yeah. Stick with "Thank you." Period. The end. Thank you! Thank you! Thank you!

Let me tell you something, the more you poo-poo on someone else's compliments to you, the more you condition people to *not* give you compliments. That is neither epic nor sexy, so knock that shit off! Say it with me: "THANK YOU!" Same goes when someone gives you a gift. Or wants to treat you! Just say, "Thank you!" That is it it. Avoid saying any of the following:

- *"You don't have to do that."*
- *"You shouldn't have…"*
- *"I can get it."*
- *"I'll get you next time."*
- *"That is too much…"*
- *"You are too kind."*
- *"I've got it."*
- *"Please don't…"*

Each of the preceding statements is poo-pooing on someone who wants to do something nice for you and treat you. It makes others feel good to give, just like you feel good treating others and giving to them! I mean, who are we kidding here, you are the queen of giving, right? Giving feeds your soul, right? So stop sucking *their* joy and taking all the fun out of it when they want to give to you! Just "Thank you." Period. End of story!

GIVING GAME #5: The Say Yes to Help Game. Give others the gift of feeling helpful. For one whole week, say "Yes" to anyone and everyone who offers to help you. Even if it is something you are perfectly capable of doing yourself. You are a strong, fierce, independent woman, and you can do it your damn self, right? Well, do you want to be alone forever? Do you want to condition people to never try and help you, ever? Do you want everyone to come to you for help but never reciprocate? Do you want one-way relationships? Do you want to build resentment because you are always the one giving and never feeling appreciated in return?

All of that is what *you* are creating by turning down others when they attempt to offer help. This game is about showing the universe that you are open to receiving help and support from others. Just try it. See what happens. For some of you, this one is going to feel sooo awkward. That means that this will be an opportunity to really stretch and grow. Yay!

You don't *have* to do *everything* by yourself. If you do, chances are you are going to experience more loneliness and isolation than someone who allows others into their life. Play with this concept as you play this game! Say YES to every offer of help. Give others permission to like you. I read a statistic once that said that people actually like people more when the person lets them do them a favor. This makes sense if you think about it. You are giving people the gift of feeling helpful. So stop being selfish and depriving people of this gift! Do yourself and others a favor; take a little help and love from them.

These Giving Games help you to become intentional about the energetic vibe you create and experience for yourself and for those around you. Be love! Be generous! Be an awesome receiver! Share your love and light with the world, let others share their light with you, and watch your own world ignite.

Oh, and one final thing… *Be generous with your smile!* It is incredibly beautiful. Your smile activates your light and the light of others around you. So *pleeeze* do us all a favor, yourself included. Share your smile!

GET YOUR SHARE ON *#epicsexyyou*

Work the Room. Don't Let It Work You!

Things have feelings too, you know! It's rude to ignore feelings, those poor things. OK, but seriously: things have energy. That painting you hung: feelings. The pictures in frames: feelings. The statues and artwork sprinkled around your home: feelings. The books on your shelves: feelings. Even empty spaces have feelings! That empty space on your wall where you've been meaning to hang something but haven't gotten around to it yet: feelings!

The good news is this: unlike *people*, who have feelings and will tell you about them if they don't like something you are or aren't doing, *things* don't give you any pushback if you decide to move them around. Things are here to *serve* you. Things act as energetic props for you as you create your Epic Sexy Environment.

Practice using the energy of things to create an environment that ignites your Limitless Self!

You can move things around, play with how they feel in different places, and even throw them out, all without an ounce of worrying about potentially hurting their feelings. These things are here solely to serve you. If they aren't serving you, then they've got to go! Sure, maybe a loved one gave you something that you don't like and you are experiencing guilt at the mere thought of wanting to throw it away. Time to celebrate, gurrlll!

Guilt and feelings of obligation are a signal to activate your Goddess Alert System. Let this experience remind you that you have been operating from Headspace Overload. Use this as an opportunity to ask, "What do *I* want?" Then, align your actions with your desires! That is where the magic happens!! A brilliant interior designer is a masterful creator of energy. She will evoke and elicit desired feelings by working the room in a way that leverages every nook and cranny to feed your soul. You can be a masterful creator of energy too!!!

Epic Sexy Q&A

Play with these questions to explore your awareness of the energy at play in your environment. Intentionally create something that ignites your soul and is aligned with your true desires.

✦ Where are the **top places** you spend most of your time? Do you spend most of your time at work, home, or another location?

✦ What do you **feel like** when you are in each place?

✦ Go **room by room**. How do you feel in each room? What do you *want* to feel in each of these spaces?

✦ What can you *do* to make each place feel more like how you would like to feel when you are there?

SPOTLIGHT EXAMPLE. Inspiring Quotes. I like to feel *inspired* when I am working. I also like to feel love as that is a core foundation of my business and my life. To nourish my soul and bring more of this feeling forward, I have inspirational quotes all over the whiteboards I face when I am sitting at my desk. I also have pictures of me and my man, my soul craving vision board, and spiritual energy stones that elicit more of what I desire to feel while I work.

In addition, I am surrounded by things that remind me to be grateful. For example, I kept a card that a woman gave me at a retreat. The card is bright yellow with a heart on it. Underneath the heart is the word, *Grateful*. I have intentionally created this energy of gratitude by strategically deciding what I wanted to feel when I sit down to have a coaching call with a client, to write newsletters and blogs to connect with and inspire my tribe, to write this book, or to have soulstorming sessions with fellow powerhouse soulpreneurs. As I connect with others to innovate, collaborate, and co-create love, ignition, beauty, bliss, and fulfillment I am surrounded by the energy I most want to bring forward in my life.

✦ *Create Your Hell Yes Environment* ✦

Intentionally *create* the energy of your environment rather than finding yourself at the mercy of it. Give yourself permission to get rid of anything and everything that is not an absolute Hell Yes for you! You can even use your Hell Yes scale to determine what stays and what goes. On a scale of 1 to 10, with 1 being Hell No, and 10 being Hell Yes, ask, "Do I really want this in my environment?" and "Will this help me create my Epic Sexy Environment?" Go on to play with more questions to help you decide what to keep.

"How much do I love this thing?" "How much value does this add in my life?" "What is the feeling that I have about this thing? And is that a feeling my soul craves to experience?" You can even use the Hell Yes scale as you play with the placement of said things. Maybe it is a Hell Yes to keep it, but you want to play with deciding where to put it. Use your scale. Yaaayyy! Look at all of these tools that you have to play with as you create your Epic Sexy and Limitless Life! You rock!! Get it girl!!!

· · • · •
THRIVAL PERSPECTIVE
· · • · •

Go room by room. Ask yourself, "How do I want to feel when I am in this room? How can I intentionally create that feeling in this space?"

The more you immerse yourself in your Heartspace, the more you will *feel* the energy in everything around you – people, places, and things! We are all energy readers; some of us just have the volume turned down. This journey is going to turn it up! Woo!!

234

Clear the Clutter, Make Room for Heartspace Relationships

We want to create a space for Epic Sexy You to grow and thrive. It's time to take a long, hard look at who you have around you. Sometimes the energetic currents that bond friendships and unite families are of a lower vibration but we are not consciously aware of it. The purpose for making room for more Heartspace relationships is to experience connections that are high-vibe, fun, loving, and generous. Let's look at the clear differences between a low-vibration relationship and a high-vibration relationship. This will empower you and give you the option to consciously create and cultivate relationships with high vibes.

Let's go back to section one of this book. There, we explored two opposite ends of the spectrum from which you can operate as you navigate life, forming connections with others. Each of these yields wildly different results. Think about how these descriptions apply to you as you experience relationships with other people. For each example, think of someone specific who comes to mind. This will give you a template of understanding for what each of these types of relationships looks and *feels* like for you!

Headspace Overload Existence: In this state of existence, you are *over*thinking and *over*analyzing. Typically, you are in analysis paralysis, overcomplicating things, and trying to force a solution. You may feel pressure to get something done. It's not an enjoyable state. Nor is it productive. In Headspace Overload, you do not have access to your heart and intuition. Your feelings get shut down, because you are operating from such a heavy thinking component.

You do not have full access to all of yourself, heart and intuition included. You know on a deeper level that you can't actually trust yourself *fully* to make decisions that will be guided, supported, and yield the results and outcomes you most desire for yourself and others. You keep thinking that if you keep thinking more and examine the problem from every possible angle that you will eventually get it right. Yet, without full access to your heart and intuition, you will only have a narrow field of possibilities, solutions, and options available to you. Inevitably, you will be left feeling depleted, exhausted, drained, frustrated, hopeless, and without the capability to be divinely guided in any way.

Common Headspace Overload Characteristics: Complexity. Complication. Restriction and Constriction. Hammer and Force. Struggle and Depletion. In Headspace Overload, it is impossible to yield the results that you desire for yourself and for others.

Possible Headspace-based Relationship Outcomes: Fear of intimacy. Coercion and control. Manipulation. Lack of trust in self *and* others, along with lack of trust in the journey and the universe's capability to deliver to you and for you everything that you desire. Walls are used for protection. Feels like you are out of control and that everything is happening *to* you!

In Headspace Overload, you may experience significant feelings of obligation. You may do things you don't actual want to do: *have tos*, *shoulds*, *ought tos*, and threats in the form of "You better do that or else..." You will encounter *lots of rules*! You will find yourself or the other person saying statements such as, "If you cared about me you would have…." or "If you were a good friend you wouldn't have…"

Your relationships will be chock full of arguing, bickering, nit-picking, and fights. You may compare yourself to others and feel as if you are competing with them or that they are trying to compete with you. You will feel *not enough*… not smart enough, not pretty enough, not thin enough, not lovable enough, and not successful enough. Or you will notice these patterns in the other person's behavior. There may be a feeling of keeping a tally: "I did *(fill in the blank)* for you, and you owe me *(fill in the blank)*."

Complaining, gossiping, judging yourself or others, and talking about others behind their backs become commonplace, as does a pattern of self-sacrifice. Verbally, you put yourself and others down. You may even talk about each other behind your backs. You may feel resentful and angry. You may often say, "I just need to get through today…"

You may do things that appear generous and kind outwardly but, if you are being super honest with yourself, it may be because you have an agenda. You may be doing these things because you actually want to get something in return for what you are giving, either in the moment or you have plans to ask for something or hopes to receive something in the future. It's the whole "What's in it for me?" energy vibe, which is a low vibration.

Your focus is on *me* but not from a "Me First" place that supports you in having me time that benefits *all* parties and where you are an active participant in creating a win-win relationship. Rather, you experience the energy of "I win, and if you win too, that's cool. But *I* win is my main priority."

Heartspace Immersion Existence: In this state, you have full-blown access to your divine guidance, your intuition, and your soul's wisdom in effortless flow and partnership with the sheer brilliance and pure geniustry of your mind. In this state of existence, you have an abundance of free-flowing limitless options, possibilities, and solutions available to you. This access allows for an effortless flow and ease instead of the feeling of having to *force* a solution such as what you experience in Headspace Overload.

You still get to use your mind when you are in Heartspace Immersion, but you do so with full expansiveness, full clarity, and the optimal ability to create and put into action the most epic of strategies. Those strategies will allow you to have *everything* that you desire and have a ton of fun doing it all. When you are in Heartspace Immersion, you have full access to every fiber of your being, and you are able to make informed decisions from the divine guidance and the full integration of mind, body, and soul.

Common Heartspace Immersion Characteristics: An open mind *and* an open heart. Connection. Activation. Clarity. Momentum. Effortless flow. Action with ease. You trust yourself fully, eliminate self doubt, and get results for yourself and others as you desire. Plus, you have a ton of fun along the way!

Possible Heartspace-based Relationship Outcomes: Thrival! Unconditional love. Trust in self, the journey, the universe, and others. A warm and loving embrace. Surrender to the magical and brilliant journey of the how. Everything feels like it is happening *for* you. Heartspace is desire-based with no limits and no rules. You find yourself feeling as if you are enough of everything. You are perfectly imperfect just the way you are and so is everyone else around you. Lots of laughter! Lots of fun! Lots of adventure! Lots of growth and expansion. Lots of feelings of desires and want tos!

You generously give without a single ounce of energetic vibration of desiring anything in return. You give because you love giving and because it feels sooo good to give! Celebrating!!! Joyful. Blissful. Complementing one another, and complimenting one another. Raving about the person *to* the person *and* to others.

From your Heartspace, you are generous with your emotions, your words, and your actions and easily express to others how much they mean to you, purely in the name of love. From your Heartspace, there is no hidden agenda. You feel grateful, carefree, and liberated. Actively and consistently, purposefully and intentionally, you create a win-win. We *all* win!! Always. Woo!

✦ *Identify Where You Are* ✦

As you learn to identify what Headspace Overload and Heartspace Immersion relationships look like for you and discover how each shows up in your life and how it feels when you are experiencing each state, you will have more opportunities to choose which kinds of relationships you would like to consciously and actively participate in and intentionally invite into your life.

The more clues you can gather for yourself, the more easily you'll be able to create intentional activation signals for your Goddess Alarm System. You can then use these to alert you when you experience a low-vibe connection or a high-vibe connection, paving the way for you to intentionally and consciously make room for higher-vibration bonds and connections with friends and family.

Epic Sexy Q&A

Explore the energetic vibration of your peeps. Who are the top three peeps you spend most of your time with? Yes, this can include family members.

✦ What are they **like**?

✦ What is their **typical energy** like?

✦ How do you **feel** when you are around them?

✦ What do you guys spend your **time** doing?

✦ What do you spend your time **talking** about?

✦ What are the **energetic patterns** you experience and create when you spend time together?

✦ How do you **help each other** move forward in life toward the things that your soul craves?

✦ How do you help make each other a **better person**?

✦ How do you **empower** each other to grow?

✦ Without asking each of them, do you know what their **top soul cravings** are? (If not, ask!)

✦ Do they know *your* **top soul cravings**?
(If not, tell them!)

✦ How do you help hold each other **accountable**
to being who you each crave to be? How do you
support one another in creating an Epic Sexy
Life?

✦ How much of the following do you do when
the two of you are together? **Complain. Gossip.
Judge.** Talk about others behind their backs.
Insert each of the Headspace thaangs from the list
we just covered. See "Possible Headspace
Relationship Outcomes."

✦ How much of the following do you do when
you two are together? **Talk about your dreams.**
Innovate. Create. Problem solve. Soulstorm. Play.
Laugh. Insert all Heartspace thaangs.

Step into your Heartspace. Get playful and curious. Explore the
energetic vibration of the people you spend the most time with. If
you see things from the Headspace list that are holding you both
back, play with how can you shift the time and energy you spend
together to include more things from the Heartspace list.

Yaaayy to creating Heartspace relationships and a thriving life!
Woo!!

Epic Sexy Q&A

Think of the various kinds of relationships you have and the roles you fill, such as Friend, Sister, Daughter, Aunt, Mother, Grandmother, Sister-in-law, Mother-in-law, Daughter-in-law, Wife, Girlfriend, and Lover. Use the following questions to further explore the values, gifts, and strengths you bring to your relationships.

✦ What do you *love* **bringing** to a relationship?

✦ What is it about you that makes you a person that others **want to be around**?

✦ Why are others **lucky** to be in relationship with you?

✦ What **values and gifts** do you bring to the table?

✦ What are some **strengths** that you feel that you bring to a relationship?

✦ What do you **help others to be**, feel, or experience more of when you are in relationship with them?

✦ What are some ways you **contribute** to making others' lives better?

Epic Sexy Thrival Actions

✓ **Explore and discover your strengths.** Begin to
honor them. Be aware of them. They help you
identify what gifts you bring to a relationship.
Share your gifts generously to others, and give
them to yourself! Me Too. Remember?

✓ **When you have assessed each of your current
relationships**, go back through the lists you have
made and discover what kind of relationship you
currently have with *yourself*! If you want to step
into Epic Sexy You, play intentionally with
creating a Heartspace Immersion relationship with
yourself.

✓ **Become the best bestie a girl has ever had.**
Become your own BFF! You do that by giving
generously to yourself the very gifts and strengths
that you are giving to and sharing with others.
Remember, Me Too is a win-win. *You* win too!
We *all* win! Woo!! High vibes feel soooo good.
Yaaayyy to consciously creating.

Be Prepared for When Your Growth Leaves Your Peeps Feeling Lost in the Dust

OK, so now that you've grown, you are having a hard time connecting to others who were once among your most effortless connections, right? WTF is that all about? Let's play with this. Together, we will explore some options and look at what you can do when this happens to you.

The truth is, when you grow and expand, you may notice that your loved ones don't know how to handle the new you. Truth be told, you may not even know what to do with this new you. In fact, you may not even realize just how much you've grown until you encounter the resistance of others!

Yaaayyyy resistance from others! Celebrate it, gurrrlll!! It's a signal to activate your Goddess Alarm System. This is validation that you have raised your vibration to the extent that you are now having a hard time connecting with lower-vibe relationships. Yaaayyy to resistance from others being an epic signal that you have expanded, evolved, and grown! Woo!!

I will share a story with you in an effort to help you see what might happen when you expand, morph, and grow in a direction that is no longer compatible with someone you love. I share this story simply to help you normalize what you may have already experienced, what you yet may experience in the future, or even what you may be experiencing right now. Whatever stage you are in, it is my hope that by sharing this story with you I can help save you from endless hours of searching for blame or fault, being confused, and or feeling totally pained by the disconnect from someone you love.

✦ *It's Story Time, Peeps* ✦

I once told a soul sister I needed a break from our relationship. I didn't know what else to say or do. It had been an epic year of growth for both of us. She got married, started trying for baby #2, got pregnant, and had the most beautiful little nugget. She was spending time creating her family unit, exploring and discovering how to be a wife, and learning how to be a mother to two now that she and her hubby had their second child.

My friend was busy creating her own version of a life she loved living, and I was busy creating mine, which happened to look wildly different than hers. Life began to take us in two entirely different directions. She was once the absolute center of my universe, but, slowly, without me even consciously realizing what was happening, I started to allow myself to be a priority.

This shift meant I was spending more time focused on me and less time focused on pleasing everyone around me. My life was no longer just about everyone else. I gave myself permission to make my life about Me Too! We all win! Woo!! Wins all around. I gave up being a hot mess and a sucker who settled for a life of mediocrity. I started my life coaching practice and began exploring the possibilities of leaving the corporate world. I wanted to devote my every moment to my life's mission to help others feel the level of bliss I had learned to access.

For the first time in my life, I was exploring what it was like to not date toxic assclowns. I quit drinking. I quit smoking. I got my yoga teacher certification. I studied holistic nutrition, and I uncovered a ton of food sensitivities that had led to me being sick for my whole life. I lost 35+ pounds and basically became a totally different person. I changed more in that one year, mentally, physically, emotionally, and spiritually, than I had in the sum of the first thirty years of my life.

I wasn't consciously aware of all of the changes that I made. I was most definitely not consciously aware of the true energetic impact of what had shifted. I genuinely thought my friend and I were spending less time together because she was busy with her new roles and responsibilities. I thought I was giving her space, yet missed her dearly and was excited for when the time would come so that we could spend more time together when she was ready.

Her experience and perspective of the shifts in our connection were wildly different. She sent me a message one day sharing that she was feeling hurt by our disconnect, and I started to notice that she was taking it incredibly personal. I was confused. I had no words. Through the course of our interactions navigating the complexities of our feelings, I began to feel attacked. I shut down.

I wasn't sure how to deal with what seemed to be her defensive reactions to what I felt were epic and mind-blowing shifts in the right direction in terms of my growth and expansion. I was lost. She felt hurt and betrayed. She felt like I was being a bad friend because I was no longer playing by the same rules of friendship we had once engaged in. I didn't realize it at the time; but, looking back, I had no idea how to engage in those rules anymore. In fact, I felt that to do so, I would have to squeeze my expansive, limitless, soul-awakened self into a tiny, limiting box that I no longer fit into.

I wasn't sure what to do. I felt it would have been more hurtful to just ignore the issues we were having. I did not want to pretend things were fine, or drop off the face of the earth with the "I'm busy" excuse I see other people utilize in similar circumstances. I decided instead to be honest with how I was truly feeling. I used the only words that I had access to at that time. I asked for a break.

I wish I had known the actual words to use. I have words now that I did not know then. When I finally found the words, after three months of my friend and I not speaking to one another, I reached out and shared them with her. I sent her a message that said something to the effect of the following, sprinkled in with some new awareness points I've gained since then as well:

"I can understand that the changes in my life may be difficult for you. For the longest time I made you feel significant by making you the center of my world. In fact, you *were* my entire world. I was nowhere to be found on my own priority list. I wasn't thriving emotionally. I was incredibly unhealthy, actually, and didn't even realize that until now. Now that I am consciously aware of what I want, who I want to be, and what I need I've chosen to take a little time to put myself at the top of my own priority list and sort my life out so that I can create and sustain my optimal thrival zones for living fully and experiencing this life as the new limitless and expansive version of me. I have chosen to make myself the center of my own world until I truly fall madly, deeply in love with myself so that when I emerge from my Me First cocoon I can truly soar! I can then give to you and others from a true place of generosity, desire, fullness, love, bliss, and joy!

However, I realize that this shift may feel like I care for you less now that I am spending more time focusing on me. I can assure you that I still love you with every piece of my being. Actually, I now have even more to offer you in regards to authentic, connected, raw and real, deep love. I can now actually give myself to you from a place of complete fullness in my own oneness of self. You are my soul sister. I miss you so much. I love you, please forgive me."

Unfortunately the words had come too late, and the desire to reconnect was not mutual. I am not going to lie. I still mourn the loss of that friendship in the depths of my soul. The unintentional pain that my loss of words and self-awareness caused her obviously left a wound beyond repair and for that I am apologetic. I still send her loads of light and love, and I am so incredibly grateful for the years that I spent connecting with her and growing together side by side. I cherish the epic adventures and the abundance of laughter we shared. I celebrate all the magic and beauty we co-created in our time together as friends.

I learned so much from that experience about how to handle resistance from a loved one.

✦ *Learn From My Mistakes* ✦

Do Not Take Others' Resistance as a Personal Attack. Part of why things fell apart in my friendship was because we were both taking the other's feelings, emotions, words, actions, behavior, and perspectives personally. I've learned to step outside of the situation, get curious, and explore on a deeper level to discover what's really going on!

I wonder what I might have discovered had I allowed myself to ask, "What if this has nothing to do with me? What if there is something going on with her, and she is just projecting it my way unconsciously. What might that be?"

I might have seen that she had just had a baby and that maybe her hormones were off a bit, causing her to be a bit more sensitive than usual. Or maybe she was having a hard time adjusting to her new roles. Maybe she missed me. Maybe she was feeling insecure in our relationship. Maybe she thought that if I loved her I could have focused my energy and efforts on showing her compassion instead of defending and protecting myself! Did you see that? Curiosity bred compassion. BAM! Get curious!!

Get Some Face Time! In my situation, there was an obvious disconnect, because we were both avoiding getting on the phone or taking the time to get together in person. Yes, I realize this is one big, huge duh factor, and I am not proud of myself for not having the courage to be bold enough to make a face-to-face happen before the tiny little baby monster of an issue became the incredible hulk issue and destroyed the whole entire city! Lesson learned. It is a lesson that will be with me forever, and for that I love you soul sister, and I thank you.

Get Vulnerable. Ask yourself, "What am I *really* upset about?" Truth was, I was hurt. I felt like she wasn't being supportive or understanding of my growth and that she never would. I felt she had said some incredibly hurtful things to me, and I should have just said I was hurt instead of reverting back into the Spicy McChicken routine of shutting down and being cold. I got upset and shut down because she canceled a dinner we had finally scheduled to reconnect and resolve our differences. I felt I wasn't important enough to her and I became equally insecure about our friendship. Instead of sharing my feelings and finding the strength in my vulnerability, I shut down and said I wasn't interested in resolving the friendship at that time.

Looking back now, I also realize I could have phrased that desire for Me First time in a much more loving and compassionate way that would have still allowed her to feel loved and appreciated, to know that she mattered to me, and that I just needed time to sort my feelings out and find my words. Doing so would have allowed the friendship to still feel like a sacred and safe space for connection. Instead she was left feeling as if I had dumped her coldly, and who the hell wants to make someone you love feel that way? Not me. I am eternally grateful for all of these blessons.

Explore Your Assumptions. What are some of the potential assumptions I am making here? Where do I need greater clarity? I assumed that my friend was not open to hearing me out. I assumed that she was avoiding jumping on the phone with me because every time I did ask her to jump on a call it wasn't a good time for her. I could have had more compassion and understanding that she had a newborn and maybe there really wasn't a good time. I assumed that it was too messy to be resolved, and I stepped into the land of "Why bother?!" Remember, assumptions are limiting. Celebrate assumptions when you catch yourself making them. They are signals to activate your Goddess Alert System to explore what limits you are putting on yourself. This is a way that you can break free from them!

Ask Yourself, "What Do I Want?" I was so busy playing defense that I never took the time to stop and ask myself what I really wanted. I missed my friend. I loved her. I wanted to spend time with her. I wanted to stop fighting and make up. I never said those things to her. Lesson learned.

Ask Yourself: "What are some things that I can do to help create what I desire to feel and experience in this moment?" I could have picked up the phone. I could have said "I love you. I'm sorry. Please forgive me. Thank you." I could have told her I missed her and that there was nothing that she could ever do that could make me love her any less, even a fight.

Friendships Evolve. When you or the other person changes, it doesn't always mean that the friendship needs to end or even that you need to take a break. Sometimes it means the friendship may not look *exactly* how it was before. That's OK. Maybe it just means you accept them for who they are, a fellow soul on their own journey. Maybe you find ways to create a new normal that is a win for all parties.

Your Boundaries and Happiness Are Your Responsibility. I realized long after the breakup of our friendship that I resented my friend for giving me so much pushback when I started saying no to her so I could say "Hell Yes" to me. I took it personal. I felt that she wasn't honoring my boundaries. I felt crappy, and I wanted it to be someone else's fault instead of my own.

What I know now is that my boundaries and my happiness are *my* responsibility. If I am not happy it's often because I am not honoring myself, I am giving too much of myself to others, I am not asking for what I want, I am saying yes when it's not a Hell Yes, I am saying no to myself so that I can say yes to others

251

(people-pleasing), or I am avoiding exploring and / or expressing how I truly feel. I now have the tools to honor myself, to create my own happiness, and to sustain loving, Heartspace Immersion, thriving relationships.

Now, when I find myself unhappy, I know the path back to the limitless Epic Sexy Me. I have new choices and options available to me now. I use my own unhappiness as a signal to activate my Goddess Alarm System and explore what *I* can start doing or stop doing so that I can get back to me.

Sometimes It Is OK to Be Busy. Time heals and reveals all. Had I just allowed myself to be "busy" for a week or two instead of saying that I was not interested in resolving the relationship at that moment, maybe I would have cooled off and had a fresh, new perspective that opened up a space for a rescheduled dinner. Maybe "honesty" doesn't mean sharing every single emotion, thought, and feeling with the other person. I am still working on this one for my own journey of expansion! Yaaayy growth!!

Stop Looking for Fault and Blame. Aside from this example, along my journey I have also learned that with some people the vibrations of energies are aligned in a way that you are not able to create and sustain a Heartspace relationship where true thriving is possible for all parties. This does not mean that it is anyone's fault; it is merely an energetic magnetism that is either there or it isn't. I have learned from mistakes I have made. In the past, there have been times when I tried to find fault in the other person and shared said fault with them so that *I* could feel better about my decision to disconnect from them. For me, that always makes things worse in the long run because later I feel bad that I parted in a way that may have left a crappy residual energetic vibration on their end. I do not ever want to hurt anyone else, and I'm constantly exploring new ways to navigate the complexities of life. This goes back to the fact that maybe you do not have to announce your disconnect. Instead, you can allow the energetic vibe to run its course and naturally go your separate ways.

Energy *Never* Lies. If it's not you, and it's not me, then maybe it's just the energy! Sometimes, if the energies are not aligned between two people you may even feel magnetically repelled when in the presence of that person, even if you are not sure why. Let me save you a shit ton of time... Trust that feeling. Energy *never* lies!

Redefine Honesty. I've realized that there is an opportunity for me to redefine "honesty" for myself. Historically I felt that I wouldn't be being "honest" if I did not share how I was feeling in every moment. The truth is that sometimes you can feel one way in the heat of the moment; yet, if you allow yourself to take time to let things settle, you may cool off. You may naturally make your way to a totally new perspective. You can then take action from a calm and loving place. Yaaayy for redefining things that are not getting you the results and outcomes you desire! This is *your* life. *No Limits. No Rules.* You define things in whatever ways you find to be "true" for you!!

Ask Yourself: "What are my new values and priorities?" Often we make points of connection and bonding with others based on our shared values and experiences at that given time. As we evolve and shift, so do our values and priorities. It can be helpful to explore what specifically has emerged during your period of metamorphosis so you can identify what may be causing these new disconnects in your relationships.

This process of exploration helps you do four things: 1) realize points of disconnection, 2) get to know your own self better, 3) explore and discover new opportunities for intentional connection with that person, and 4) find new peers who have similar values as those from which you are currently operating. The acts of awareness, discovery, and exploration are sooo high vibe! Woo!! Get your high-vibe self on! Woo!!

Extrapolating the lessons, blessings, and gifts that come from a situation allows you to change the energetic pattern that is present in the memory of an event. We grow from such experiences.

Right this moment, I am all, "Wow! I learned so much from that experience and all the friendships lost along the way!" I am also reliving all of the beautiful magic of the friendships, instead of allowing myself to be stuck in a singular, limited point of reference when I think of them. This is what I mean by raising the vibration.

You literally expand yourself. You open yourself up to new memories and experiences that you don't have access to when you are experiencing life in a lower vibration! I am infinitely blessed to have known every soul I have ever had a point of connection with regardless of the outcome in the end. I love them all in the depths of my soul, and I learned so much as a result of these experiences. I am eternally grateful for each soul and for all the memories we shared. To anyone I have hurt I'll keep sending vibrations of "I'm sorry. Please forgive me. I love you. Thank you."

What I know now is that it is OK for friendships to morph, shape-shift, and change. It is OK to spend less time with a person than you once did and still love the shit out of them. It's OK to get together less frequently than before while still fully immersing yourself in the love that the two of you share for each other when you have the occasional chance to catch up.

You are the only one who can decide what you truly want out of each relationship. You get to decide what's right for *you*. Explore, discover, and play with what works for you. Know that you'll grow as a soul through your own trial and error. Everything is happening *for* you. Even amidst perceived pain there is an abundance of blessons, and surprise gifts waiting for you!

GET YOUR SHARE ON *#epicsexyyou*

Leave the Self-Sacrifice in the Giveaway Pile

There are some people whose energetic vibrations are on such a different level than yours that it is truly painful to be in their proximity. These people, sometimes unknowingly, act as energy vampires. You will know who they are based on how you *feel* after spending time with them. See the next section, "Drain/Gain Game" to help you identify who they are.

Let me be clear. This does *not* mean these people are "bad" or that there is anything "wrong" with them. Or you for that matter! We all have different energetic vibrations. Some people aren't your energetic match. If they were your soul tribe, they would ignite you! People who are truly your energetic tribe members are those who you spend time with and, as a result of doing so, you feel even more ignited than you felt before being in their presence!

You're going to have to navigate this journey based on what *feels* good to you, but I'll share my own philosophy and you can take what you want from it. Personally, I refuse to subject myself to relationships where the energetic vibration is one where self-sacrifice is involved or where the rules of engagement are set up where someone has to lose.

I am of the belief that if we can't *all* win, then I don't even want to play! This one is especially hard when it comes to family, so let's lovingly approach this in a way that maybe you haven't thought of this before. If you *really* love someone, why would you want to reinforce a belief that they have that is limiting them and you from having an Epic and Limitless Life? Self-sacrifice is a low vibe. It is a restricting, limiting energetic pattern that will confine them to a life of mediocrity at best. It will prevent them from living a life they absolutely *love* living. It will prevent them from experiencing their life fully and having abundant access to *everything* their soul craves. Why are you participating in stunting their growth and your own growth by actively participating in the low-vibe energetic exchange of "I win, you lose?"

Some people get addicted to bouncing back and forth between "You sacrifice a lot for me" and "I sacrifice a lot for you." As you expand beyond the vibration of self-sacrifice, it will be difficult to connect with others who still operate at that vibration. Sacrifice is a very low vibration. It's *old* news! It's a stale and outdated energetic pattern that has been passed down and unconsciously recycled from generation to generation. Many who take on these energetic patterns simply do not know there is a better way. Until now. Yaayy for a new way!

There is another option that is available to us all should we consciously chose to embrace it. It offers a high vibration of win win win win. We *all* win! As a collective, we are getting creative to make sure that we don't play unless we all win. There is no need for self-sacrifice when we can *all* win. Isn't that awesome! When you are having a hard time connecting with a loved one who is operating in the energetic pattern of self-sacrifice, *celebrate*! This is validation that you've raised your vibration to one that extends beyond the restrictions and confinements of self-sacrifice. Celebrate that growth girl, get it.

Here is what goes through my head when I love someone and they are stuck in the old energetic exchange of self-sacrifice: I think to myself, "I am actually enabling you if I stick around and participate in this energy drain exchange game. That game is completely disempowering you, preventing you from doing your own work, and keeping you from upleveling your own life like you deserve to experience. I may be the *only* person in your life that has enough love and respect for you to *not* engage in energetic patterns that are keeping you from putting in your work and claiming a life of euphoric bliss that is yours for the taking."

People can't always see it at the time, but one day they'll get it. Or maybe they will never see it, and that's OK too. If they do see it, maybe they'll never even let you know that they get it. Just know that, when you participate in rules of engagement that require someone to sacrifice, be unhappy, or lose in any way, you are preventing the other people involved from taking their own inner journeys.

When you consciously decide to disengage from this energetic pattern with your loved ones, just express a silent "Thank you" and "You're welcome." Thank you for the opportunity to have engaged in this pattern with you, to experience, witness, feel, and now consciously choose a higher vibration! THANK YOU!! Woo!

You are more than likely never going to hear a "Thank You" from this person. Sometimes you are the *only* one who can see the true vision, and sometimes that just has to be enough. What if this is about loving yourself *and* someone else enough to offer a new standard of relationship to them than they've ever been offered before. What if you are offering love to them in a new way?

You are extending a high-vibe, empowering, expansive kind of love. If at any point they decide to choose to actively participate in a consistent we-all-win, Me Too, high-vibe relationship, then by all means open your arms and your loving heart to them. Let's do this!!!

Epic Sexy Thrival Actions

✓ **Do a deep dive analysis** of your peer group and make sure that you are intentionally, purposefully, and consciously spending your time and energy with people who ignite your soul.

✓ Ask yourself **whether those you engage with empower you** to live a full-blown, epic Heartspace existence? Do they actively engage in and co-create a "We *All* Win" expansively energetic vibration?

Play the Drain / Gain Game

This is a fun, playful way to identify what is igniting you, and spot what is draining you. This game will open you up to the opportunity to choose to do, be, feel, and experience more of what energizes you and to do, be, feel, and experience less of what depletes you.

✓ **Pay attention** to when you feel ignited, invigorated, energized, and on fire!

- *Who are you around?*
- *Where are you?*
- *What are you doing?*
- *What is going on?*
- *How do you feel physically?*
- *What are you thinking?*
- *What are you feeling emotionally?*

✓ **Pay attention** to those times when you feel exhausted, burned out, and depleted.

- *Who are you around?*
- *Where are you?*
- *What are you doing?*
- *What is going on?*
- *How do you feel physically?*
- *What are you thinking?*
- *What are you feeling emotionally?*

✓ **Look for recurring patterns.**

- *What are common triggers for your drain?*

- *What are the most common recurrences —
  people, places, things, activities, or thoughts
  — that activate the ignition of the gain?*

✓ **How can you create more gain and less drain?**
Brainstorm from the masterful brilliance of your
Headspace in tandem with the expansiveness of
your Heartspace.

Hit Pause on the Over-Connected World

Let me ask you something. When was the last time you turned your cell phone off? Not put it on silent or vibrate. But turned it off. Completely. Off, as in not even using it as your clock or camera when you are out of the country. Off, shut down, and put away. That kind of off. The time it fell in water and stopped working? Doesn't count!

When was the last time you intentionally turned your phone off? How long was it off for and why was it off? When was the last time you took an intentional break from this over-connected, over-stimulated world? When was the last time that you went rogue, off the grid, completely MIA with the full purpose of disconnecting from the world and reconnecting with all things you. When was the last time you were fully present and immersed in every second of living?

✦ *Do a Tech Cleanse* ✦

Five years ago I hit a wall. I was burned out, unhappy with my body, feeling awkward in my own skin, single and dating one toxic assclown after the next, lost, frustrated, confused, sad, fatigued, depressed, and feeling sooo stuck! I realized it had been *four years* since I had taken a vacation without bringing my laptop with me. Four *years*, people! Ahhh WTF, right?!

What I didn't know then but found out later was that I was a massive workaholic. The "workahol" me was constantly trying to prove my significance, and the alcohol and cigarettes (my social drugs of choice) were numbing the shit out of the pain I had from feeling un-lovable. All the while, I wasn't consciously aware of a damn thing that was going on! This was the era of Spicy McChicken, who I was telling you about earlier.

After four years without a break, I had had enough. Being connected 24/7 for *four* years was one of the biggest energy drains I had ever experienced. I was there, always at the beck and call of others: coworkers, clients, the employees that reported to me, my boss, my boss's boss, my boss's boss's boss, the endless lists of peeps I mentored at work, friends and family members. Whoever needed me, I was there. No matter the day or the time.

I worked 18+ hour days. I *never* said no. I handed away my energy all day every day and never had a single ounce left for myself. If any of this sounds even remotely familiar, then boy oh boy are you in the right place! At some point I finally hit rock bottom. I booked a trip to Sedona, Arizona and left the laptop at home. When I got there, I turned my phone off for the entire week so that I could focus on all things present and all things me. This was my first experience with full-blown Me First time.

Even my camera stopped working while I was there. The beautiful irony of that is not lost on me. The universe and my spirit team that watches over me have the best sense of humor ever. They were saying loud and clear, "Be fully present in this moment. Connect with yourself. See things through your own eyes and not through the lens of a camera."

It was liberating. No one died. No catastrophes happened. That experience taught me to take intentional tech breaks from my 24/7 connection to the world. I needed a break from over-stimulation, from responsibility, and from the chatter of the outside world. I needed to just focus on me! Me First. I needed to just be present in the moment. I needed to focus on adventure and connection with real people, connection with myself, and connection with nature.

• • • • •
THRIVAL PERSPECTIVE
• • • • •

Sometimes you've got to disconnect in order to find WHAT TRULY MATTERS. Sometimes you've got to disconnect from it all in order to find YOURSELF.

Plan your own tech breaks on purpose! Whether it's an hour a week, a weekend each quarter, or twice a year, plan them. Don't rely on awesomely epic accidents. Be intentional. A Tech Break will help you experience the feeling of liberation from the energetic vibrations of technology. Get unplugged and get intentional: be fully present as you play with the expansiveness in true Heartspace connections with loved ones, and sprinkle in some magically delish Me First.

✦ *Don't Pick Up Shitty Vibes* ✦

News, TV, Magazines, Books, Games. You pick up the energetic vibration of whatever you expose yourself to. You can intentionally choose the vibes you pick up or you can operate unconsciously. I challenge you to start *consciously* choosing the media you consume. Let's start, for example, with the news. When was the last time you watched the news and heard about the hot fireman (or firewoman) who saved that cute little kitten that climbed up the tree? Hey, whatever tickles your fantasy fancy! No limits. No Rules. Just do you.

Or when was the last time you tuned in to hear about all of the good souls in your neighborhood who are changing the world by spreading love and light to everyone they encounter? Yeah. Never. It isn't because this *isn't* happening. OK, so maybe the hot fireman (or firewoman) and the kitten doesn't happen *every* day… But the thing is that these things aren't highlighted on the news, because the news has a *very* negative energetic pattern that perpetuates fear as its underlying current.

And let's look at those gossip magazines that tell you all about all of the awesome celebrity couples who are going strong, the longest-running celebrity couples who are so cute together, the ones who have made it through and are in it for the long haul, the celebrities who give back and volunteer their time to epic causes that feed their soul... *Oh, wait!* In fact, the stories in the gossip magazines are the complete opposite of that, right?

I just heard this statement the other day on a local radio show: "Go to our website to see this year's list of celebrity couples who have broken up." Seriously? No wonder so many people have fears about marriage. We are inundated with news of divorce constantly, and rarely ever hear of all the inspiring Epic Love Stories. Unless of course there is a dramatic twist, such as cancer or an untimely death that plays a starring role in the story.

I am not saying *never* to watch television again. I'm not even suggesting you *never* pick up a gossip magazine. To each their own, sister friend. No Limits. No Rules. If you are going to expose yourself to these laser-focused downsides and negativity, gossip, and hearsay, I simply challenge you to do it consciously and to observe the impact these choices have on your mood, your emotions, and your thoughts.

For me, the news hurts my soul. It acts as a toxin, eating away at the very core of my being. I personally have *way* more important things to do than sit in front of a TV and listen to a skewed, one-sided, negative, shadow-infiltrated, dark version of a story, one that will tear holes in my heart and rip away at the fiber of my being. I gave up on news almost ten years ago and I never looked back.

This is about how you *choose* to spend your energy and your time. I hope you become *consciously aware* of the impact of every one of your choices. Again, I am not suggesting that you never watch the news ever again. I am merely challenging you to become more aware of how what you choose to watch and / or read impacts you.

Epic Sexy Q&A Part I

As you engage in said activities, get curious and ask yourself:

✦ How does this make me **feel**?

✦ **Why** am I watching or reading this?
What is my purpose? What is my intention?

✦ Is this how I **intentionally** want to choose
to spend my time and energy?

✦ Is this a **good investment** of my time and energy?

✦ **What** am I getting out of this?

One Week News Cleanse. Play with a one-week cleanse. Can you go seven days without any news, gossip magazines, or newspapers? See if you notice any differences in how you think, feel, and act. Don't forget to capture your insights, writing them down so that you will consciously have access to them moving forward as you place them at the forefront of your awareness radar and ingrain those blessons into the fiber of your being.

Epic Sexy Q&A Part II

For those of you who will not even entertain the idea of a One Week News Cleanse because you enjoy seeing what is going on in the world, I would challenge you to focus on asking yourself the following questions as you watch or read the news:

✦ What can I **do** about this topic I'm reading about?

✦ How can I **help**?

✦ What is within my control that I can actually **do**?

✦ How can I **take action** and impact this issue?

If you are going to be a participant, than be an active one. Be a do-er. Make a difference.

Be Fearless, Fierce, and Free!

Let's play with transforming your energetic patterns around resistance. Let's shift those patterns from activating historically low-vibe, conditioned feelings of *Lag* (Meh) and instead allow your choices to be powerful, high-vibe activations that signal a new and expansive option to *Launch* (Woo). Let's turn resistance into a launchpad! Let's program your Goddess Alert System to activate celebration when you are experiencing overwhelm and resistance. Let these be a signal for you to choose another option, one that you may not have access to yet. Let resistance be a signal to launch you into a more expansive, epic, and limitless you!

SPOTLIGHT EXAMPLE. When I first rolled out my newsletter, I promised it would be "Epic" and "Sexy." I told my peeps they were going to learn how to create their very own Epic Sexy Life as a result of being on board the ESY Newsletter Rocket to the Moon. Then, nada. Zip. Zero. Zelch. Crickets. I never seemed to find time to even write anything and send it out. I dug deep inside and asked myself, "WTF is going on?!"

Sure, I had a long list of excuses that came to mind that could explain why I was not making the newsletters a top priority. I'd been prepping for retreats and events in Costa Rica, in Mexico, in South Africa, in Toronto, and in Chicago (the list is endless really). I'd been writing a book. I'd been connecting with and enjoying my sister friends and enjoying spending time with the love of my life. I'd been spending solo time with yours truly and experiencing some good ol' self lovin' like doing my nails, getting massages, doing yoga and meditation.

If I am being *really* honest with myself, there were many procrastination activities I'd been participating in as well. A love affair with Netflix. Staring at the ceiling. Then there was napping, a strange new procrastination activity that I uncovered along the way. Sure, I enjoy a good nap every now and then, but come on, what the hell?!

Be honest with yourself when it is *just* a resistance nap. Oh you'll *know*. It is so incredibly bizarre. Those moments come where you know that you are doing something that is a completely self-sabotaging behavior and you can't even stop yourself. It happens to us all, and it is infuriating! Am I right? As I was asking myself what the hell was wrong with me, the first thing that came to mind was this: "Writing is vulnerable as hell! You're pouring your soul onto the paper and or screen in front of you."

An intuitive download brought a reminder of a quote I truly believe in in every single fiber of my being to be true. The quote is from Steven Pressfield's *Do the Work*:

The more important a call or action is to our soul's evolution, the more resistance we will feel.

That was the moment the epiphany sunk in; writing must be tied to something *super* important to my soul's destiny, because I am not often met with this much resistance about *anything*! Which immediately lead me to my Game On attitude. OK, well, if I am being honest, first it was a nap of the epic procrastination kind, and *then* it was game on. Don't judge me! Haha!

Here is a reframe I would like to offer you for those times when you are experiencing the energy of resistance:

What if your overwhelm and resistance are the exact clues that you are on the edge of something Amazing and EPIC. Life-altering! Mind-blowing!!

Sure, your current pattern may be to shy away from whatever has you feeling this way and just let the overwhelm and resistance stop you dead in your tracks. But what if there was a way to break free from these patterns and step into the beautiful rewards that await? I am a pattern-breaker, and the whole intention behind this book is to help you break the underlying energy currents that are creating patterns above and below the surface and keeping you from what you want.

So let's do this!

✦ *Break Free From Overwhelm and Resistance* ✦

✓ **Identify and Acknowledge the Resistance**. Ask yourself: Where am I experiencing resistance in my life? How is it showing up? What is this resistance holding me back from?

✓ **Reframe the Resistance.** Explore these options.

Reframe Option #1: What if this resistance meant that, once you do the exact thing around which you are experiencing resistance, your life will change forever and you will unlock an epic code that will send you skyrocketing on a trajectory of success? What if you programed your Goddess Alert System to have resistance and overwhelm be signals that you are on the *precise* path that will give you the most yummy, delicious, and limitless expansion your soul craves? Woo!!!

Reframe Option #2: What if resistance and overwhelm hold a powerful message for you? What might that be?

Reframe Option #3: What is the even-better-than-best-case scenario of what can happen if you do that very thing? Really get crazy here, and allow your imagination to go buck wild. Give yourself permission to dream big and have fun. Be playful.

Get grand with your vision. Hell yes, you can meet Oprah. OK. OK. That last part is *my* dream, but it can be yours too! There is enough Oprah love to go around people!! She is Oprah, for God's sake! I love her beautiful bright light of a soul. Call me Oprah! Woo! Get it girl. Dream big, damn it!

✓ **Lean Into It. Do It. Do That Very Thing.** Honestly, this is where I lose a lot of people. They are all, "Yeah, if it was that easy I would already be doing it!" I swear, when some people come at me with this statement, it is as if they are about to turn into a huge green hulk of a monster with massive amounts of rage. That rage and frustration makes perfect sense because, somewhere along the way, they have developed a pattern that has prevented them from the habit of doing it.

"Doing it" is easier said than done, right? Right! Learn to lean into overwhelm and resistance with the following "Get Busy Doing It" techniques and finally buy a one-way ticket out of Stuckville.

✦ *Outsmart Overwhelm and Resistance* ✦

✓ **Think Smaller**. You may be at the bottom of the massive mountain, staring at the top of it. Try this: look down at your feet and determine you will take one step at a time. Whatever your mountain is, it is quite possibly too large of a thing to be done in one sitting. So you are experiencing the "why bother" or the related "I'll do it tomorrow" syndrome. If "it" can't possibly be done in one day, then break "it" down into something more digestible, something smaller, something that does not max out your attention span. Ask yourself, for example, "What is something that I can do in thirty minutes or less that would make me feel like I am moving one step closer?" Do *that* thing.

✓ **One Thing at a Time.** Just focus on putting one foot in front of the other. One step at a time. Each morning when you wake up, ask yourself, "What is *one* thing I can do today that will move me one step closer to the completion of my goal? Then, do that thing.

Remember, thirty minutes or less. Actually, even ten or twelve minutes a day will make a huge impact, especially if that is the limit of your current maxed-out attention span. You can develop and strengthen your attention span in the same way you build muscle in the body. If your span is short now, over time you can increase it to twenty minutes, then increase that another five minutes.

Don't limit yourself to a locked-in identity of "I have a short attention span" and then just accept that *as is*. That will just keep you in the exact same place you are now, with the exact same patterns, and the exact same undesired results. Push yourself a little past your comfort zone every single time, and break free once and for all of a limiting belief that you have about yourself!

✓ **Try a New Approach.** One of the most common approaches I see people try, myself included, is committing to a chunk of time on their calendar to do "it" but then sabotaging themselves by using that time to do something else. I notice that many people don't allocate a particular time of day at all. They just say, "I'll do it on Sunday," or, "I'll do it on Sunday night." Sunday comes and goes, and "it" was never done. Some people pick a time and day, but something always comes up at that time. Look at *your* most common patterns. Ask yourself:

✦ What **approaches** do I keep trying that are not working well?

✦ What are the most common **reasons** I keep telling myself I can't? Note: If you are stuck here, go back to the section of the book where you dispel your "cant's" and play with those goodies some more!

✦ What are the **patterns** that I see myself repeating that are yielding undesirable outcomes?

✦ What are all the possible **new approaches** that I can try? If you are completely stuck, think of three crazy ideas that you don't even think are possible, and pick the best one and just *try* it!

✦ What are the **best times of day** for me to do "it"? What are the **worst times of day** for me?

✦ What can I change in my **environment** to set me up for success and increase the likelihood that I will actually get "it" done?

Get try happy! When you experiment you learn. When you try new things, you see what works for you and what doesn't. You grow. You get new information that can help you crack your own codes, find your missing pieces, get answers to questions that have been plaguing you for years, break your old patterns, and create a life you love! So, try new ways of doing it, whatever "it" is. If you don't, I can promise you that years will go by and you will find yourself in the exact same situation, with the exact same patterns and habits, and the exact same undesired results.

✓ **Remove Obstacles.** Ask yourself, "What are the most common procrastination activities I am participating in? How can I eliminate those activities?" When I first went full-time with my business, I noticed that I would sit in front of the TV and just get sucked in, watching God knows what for *hours*. It became clear I was using the television to masterfully avoid being productive, which was wildly opposed to my desire to get shit done and create a thriving empire. I made the decision to break up with my cable provider. They didn't understand. "It's not you. It's me," I assured them again and again. I stood strong through their stalkerish behavior (calls, letters, non-stop tantalizing offers to get me back) and have been TV-free ever since. Until my love affair with Netflix, that is. Damn you, Netflix. I actually had to end that relationship to devote myself to a committed relationship with this book. As you see, this step requires being incredibly honest, constantly checking in, calling bullshit on yourself, and having the courage to *do* something about whatever is getting in your way! The key to pattern-breaking is in the action of doing it.

✓ **Create a Habit Out of It.** On a daily basis, integrate your particular "it" into your life. Maybe even just start with fifteen minutes a day. The cool thing is, even if "it" is a project that will come to completion at some point, with a finished masterpiece to show for all of your hard work, you will have created a habit of *action*. If you do have an "it" that comes to an end, cue up your next hottest "it" and so on and so on. Repeat, repeat, repeat.

• • • • •
THRIVAL PERSPECTIVE
• • • • •

A habit of ACTION is hands down one of the most powerful game changers.

✓ **Finish One Step Before Starting the Next.** Make it a habit to stick with one thing at a time and finish it. Meaning *full* completion. If you constantly change your "one thing" and never finish what you start, you will never move forward. Without forward momentum, you will always feel stuck! Always.

It's important to ensure that you are always completing pieces so you can build upon them with the next piece, instead of just having a ton of half-done pieces around you and BAM you're back in Stuckville! Being surrounded by a bunch of unfinished projects immerses you in a heavy, chaotic energetic pattern. All of these random projects, each with their own energy, are just hanging out there, looming, waiting for you to finish them.

There are two ways you can begin to clear the energy: The first is to finish each one. The second way to clear the energy is to put them away, out of sight, and cross them off your "to do list" for now. Give yourself permission to say, "I will get back to you, but for now this is my one thing." Insert your hottest burning desire of the thing you choose to focus on in that moment.

✓ **Sometimes Good Enough Is Better Than Perfect.** "Don't let perfect be the enemy of good," Voltaire said. If it looks like "perfect" is turning into "never," then ask yourself, "What, if anything, do I want even more than 'perfect' right now?" It's better to deliver something good than to never deliver anything at all because you are waiting for a perfect that never comes. Eventually, as you create a habit of breaking free from perfection, your versions of "good" get better and better and better!

To illustrate this point, I am currently aware that the layout of my blog sucks. Perhaps by the time you read this some pieces may have been given a makeover, but if you have been following the ESY goodies for a while now you will have seen the hot mess. The newsletter sign up on the right hand side all squished and jumbled. No matter what device you are reading the blog posts on, there is an obnoxiously large text after every post that invites you to subscribe so you always get posts directly to your inbox!

Here's the thing: I hate the look and feel, and I know some thaaangs need to be changed. But I am not even actually sure how to change them just yet, because someone else set them up. So I can either not post and wait until the page is perfect or I can share my magical yummy goodies and figure the design part out later. Since waiting for perfection that never comes is something I am most definitely working on breaking free from in my own resistance pattern blocks, I just hit post, thank my tribe for their patience and their forgiveness of my imperfections, and call it a day.

I have to do the same while writing this book. There might be typos. After the book is published, there may be things I wish I had included. I might even change my mind on a point I made, and then I have a forever reminder of the old viewpoint I once had, one that I don't even want to be associated with any longer! If I took even more time, I could have included more pictures to illustrate the story or created designs and layouts I loved even more.

So I'll just write another book. I'll share the new insights in my next book. I'll add things there I forgot to include here. I'll incorporate the things that worked and exclude what didn't, and I'll continue to share my soul with the world. I can't allow my fear of imperfection to stop me from sharing my divine messages with the world! Don't deprive the world of your talents and soul gifts because you are waiting for a "perfection" that will never come. That is selfish. Remember, our convo earlier about re-defining selfish? Apply that. The world needs your gifts. Don't be selfish. Share them. You are perfectly imperfect exactly as you are.

I am a work in progress. We all are. My blog posts, website, and newsletters, even this book, could be better and better and better and better. I will continue to make small, incremental shifts of one "good enough" after another until it's all pretty damn great! Then, I will find something else to improve on, to grow, stretch, and uplevel, and so on and so forth until I take my last breath. I love growing!

How would you ever get opportunities to grow and expand if you were perfect?! BOOM! Activate your

Goddess Alert System. Mistakes are merely opportunities for growth! Yaaaayyy for making mistakes! Make as many mistakes as you can!! They are like little golden nuggets encoded with growth activations.

Let's play with how to actually use the "Get Busy Doing It" techniques we just covered so you can avoid your head spinning, activating even more intense overwhelm, and turning into the Hulk. Because, let's face it, that look is not sexy on anyone. OK, maybe Spicy McChicken thinks that's hot, especially if you are an incredibly toxic man, but she is a sucker, remember?!

Settling is for suckers! Don't be a sucker! Haha! Woo!! Let's leave mediocrity in the dust, shall we?!

Epic Sexy Q&A

Here is how you can actually use the seven techniques we just covered to "Get Busy Doing It."

✦ Ask yourself the following essential question:

   Which of these is the piece of the puzzle that is going to be the most impactful for where I am at right now on my own journey of resistance?

✦ Then, **play with that *one* piece!** Have fun with it!
   Keep it at the very forefront of your mind all day every
   day. Own it. Play with *just one* piece at a time! Get
   good at that one piece and *then*, and *only then*, try
   adding another piece to your puzzle.

278

For example, right now I've noticed that I need to finish one "it" before going to the next. Do you know how many half-written, code-breaking downloads I have for all of you? But then I break another pattern, crack another code, and get busy writing about that one instead of completing the first!

Also, I need to face the vulnerability and fears of something just being "good enough" as opposed to waiting for perfection. I need to let it rip, imperfections and all. I need to post it, share it, publish it, and give all of you Epic Sexy Souls access to the growth and expansion that my clients and I have been able to experience as a result of these code-breaking, pattern-shattering insights that have been revealed to me through my own first hand personal experience. Try different things, play with this, and have fun pattern-breaking the energetic reins behind your resistance!

Now that you have ditched the baggage, let's take step four of four simple steps to Epic Sexy You.

*Create the Ultimate
Love Affair with Yourself*

Step 4: Get Naked and Slip into Your Epic Sexy Body

Get Naked and Slip into Your Epic Sexy Body

Let's talk about that human body suit you are in. Let's play with loving it, listening to it, feeding it, and honoring it.

Imperfection is beauty, madness is genius and it's better to be absolutely ridiculous than absolutely boring.

Marilyn Monroe

Do you see that brilliant, magical temple that you are in? Let's explore *your* Epic Sexy body. I know a lot about this topic, and it is impossible for me to include *everything* for you here. What is included here will most definitely give you an epic kick-start to loving your body, connecting with your inner goddess, honoring your temple, and feeling comfortable in your own skin. We've got lots to cover, so let's jump right on in, shall we?

EPIC SEXY THRIVAL TIPS

We have so many goddess goodies for this section that we are just jumping right into all the *Epic Sexy Thrival Tips* you can play with to slip into your Epic Sexy Body in a new way than you ever have before. No diets, no counting calories, no more deprivation, and no more looking out into the world for answers that are already pre-programmed into that magical body suit you are in! We will cover what you are doing that is getting in your way of loving the skin you are in and what you aren't doing that, when you start doing it, will actually help you thrive mind, *body*, and soul.

Remember, pick one thing at a time and play with it for a week. Pay attention to how it makes you feel. If you experience an uplevel or insights, keep doing it. Play, experiment, and have fun with it. Once you've got the hang of that thing, add another approach while sustaining the first thing. And repeat.

This is about laying one solid brick at a time to your foundation and building upon each one, all the while having a ton of fun. These are not isolated, individual pieces, but rather many pieces to a whole. Let's go find your custom roadmap to a thriving existence and your Epic Sexy Limitless Body!

Ditch the Societal Labels

In our society, it is commonplace to put labels on everything. This pattern is a part of the old energy system we are accustomed to operating within. There is a new option available to you. This option is high-vibe, sexy, limitless, liberating, and free. Labels are low vibe energetically. They diminish our ability to own our power and take responsibility for the less-than-desirable things we are experiencing. Without accepting responsibility for what we may or may not be doing that has had a hand in creating these labels, we are unable to take our health and sexiness into our own hands. This can and often does feel like a life sentence. Trust me, I get it. I've been there. There's another way!

By the time I was thirty years old, I had been diagnosed with the following at one point or another in my life: sinusitis (inflammation of the sinuses), fibromyalgia (which basically just means, "you have chronic pain and we don't know what it is"), rheumatoid arthritis (inflammation of the joints), chronic fatigue (exhausted, depleted, burnt out, never any energy for anything other than the obligatory responsibilities of the day to day), and asthma (inflammation of the lungs and upper respiratory system). Not to mention the fact that I was a walking pharmacy.

You see, prior to studying nutrition and specializing in holistic healing, I thought it was normal for your stomach to hurt after eating. I assumed everyone was like me and needed Pepto Bismol and antacids as an after-meal treat for pretty much every single meal. I took Claritin daily and had Benadryl with me everywhere I went, just in case I had an out-of-control allergy attack that needed the big guns! I always had an inhaler on me, along with a nasal spray, just in case my nostrils decided it was going to be a mouth-breathing kind of day.

Shout out to my girl Kris Carr who wrote the book *Crazy Sexy Diet*. Serendipitously, my path crossed with Kris and her book when I was thirty years old. The collision of our worlds inspired me to do a cleanse. It was a complete and total, accidental elimination diet and allergy testing adventure. I did not even know consciously what I was doing at that time.

I basically went raw vegan for 28 days to detox my system and to help me quit drinking and quit smoking. For the first time in thirty years I felt what it was like to be "healthy." I could breathe.

My stomach didn't hurt after I ate. I had more energy than I even knew what to do with. I lost ten pounds within the first week. My skin was glowing. My cellulite diminished. Bloating and indigestion took a hike, and I didn't need a single thing that I had once relied on daily in my very own walking pharmacy.

At the end of the cleanse, I reintroduced all sorts of foods back into my system and, boy, did I get a rude wake-up call! What I accidentally uncovered through this experience was that my body was allergic to (or as some say "sensitive" to) dairy, gluten, and meat. The reason for thirty years of feeling like absolute crap was the fact that I had been unknowingly poisoning myself!

Once I got a taste of healthy, lean, and svelte, and experienced a nibble of that energized, sexy, alive-as-all-can-be feeling, I did not want to go back. When I went back to the doctor, a "miracle" and a "puzzling anomaly" happened. Inexplicably, I had none of the things I was once diagnosed with or labeled to be, which had been considered at one point, with one hundred percent certainty, beyond a shadow of a doubt, legit diagnoses.

Yet, here I was: Nada. Zip, Zero Zelch. I had none of those things. Just another "medical mystery." Or, as I like to believe, just another example of proof that every single body is different. There is no one-size-fits-all solution to "health." When you tune into what your body is telling you, you can defy limitations and "labels" that exist in the medical world.

Oh, and then there are the societal "norms" and "labels" we like to put on our youth. We continue the trend into adulthood. Labels that I was assigned at one point or another in my life include "bipolar" and "depressed." As I explored further, I realized these "diagnoses" were actually just me not having a single healthy coping mechanism to support me in actually processing and dealing with my emotions of anger and the underlying currents of sadness and deep insecurity that had been lingering in my energy field since childhood.

I didn't have any healthy coping mechanisms because no one ever taught me any. No one ever stopped to even ask me why I was so angry. Or, if they did and they heard my answers, they didn't really hear me. I was just dismissed as being an "angry teenager." As far as doctors were concerned, the answer was meds. Always.

The impact of these labels carried into my adulthood, where I continued to accept the limiting and constricting imprisoned life-sentence of mental illness which I had been given. As a result (you know, being that I was helpless and there was nothing I could do other than just accept that that was who I was), I mastered the art of chronic numbing through alcohol abuse. Paired with after-drinking depression and all the unhealthy food I was eating, which all had significant impacts on my energy and mood, no wonder I was "depressed" and moody!

The truth is I was unhappy because I didn't like my life or myself. I wasn't consciously and intentionally creating my WHO. I was just showing up, getting triggered, and reacting to life as it came my way. This is how a lot of people are living. It is impossible to be happy in this state of being.

Once I realized what was really going on, in both my mental and physical states, I decided that I was no longer going to accept limiting labels. I was no longer willing to accept something as true, even if it was a doctor who said it. So, sure, label me whatever you want. As far as I'm concerned I look at your "labels" as a "Game On" challenge for me to prove you wrong.

You have the power to create your own labels, and you get to decide for yourself if a diagnoses is a permanent life sentence or if it is merely a temporary state of being and a signal to activate your Goddess Alert System and get curious about what your body is really trying to tell you. When you decide to change the game to be one of seeking the root cause of a labels-driven existence, everything changes. You become the master of your own life and the creator of your health and sexiness – mind, body, and soul.

● ● ● ● ●

THRIVAL PERSPECTIVE

● ● ● ● ●

Labels are not prison sentences... at least not if YOU don't allow them to be.

We have learned to feed our bodies with our eyes and our mind instead of letting our bodies do the talking. We also inherited a pattern of accepting the prison sentences unwittingly forced upon us by societal "norms" which violate the essence of our ninja warrior goddess power and our soul's ferocious being.

Epic Sexy Q&A

Get out that pen and paper and let's explore this together.

✦ What **labels** have you been given with regard to health? Examples: asthma, rheumatoid arthritis, sinusitis, or fibromyalgia.

✦ What are the **limiting beliefs** associated with those labels? Take, for example, asthma. I believed I needed an inhaler to breathe, that there was something genetically, permanently wrong with me, and that there was nothing I could do to alter it.

✦ What are you doing that may be **feeding into** these labels? What can you stop and or start doing to challenge perceived limits? When I was in my mid twenties I went to an ENT (Ear Nose Throat physician) who told me that he wouldn't work with me unless I quit smoking, moved out of my parents moldy basement, took an allergy test to see what might be in my environment, and explored what I could potentially be ingesting that could be contributing factors to my shortness of breath and the constant inflammation of the sinus cavities and lungs. He was proposing that I had the power to actually alter what I was experiencing. Instead of stepping into my power and making the lifestyle changes, the very ones that did eventually heal me, I decided at that time it was easier to just find another doctor. I found a doctor who confirmed that asthma and sinusitis were genetic and permanent. He validated all of that with drugs that made me feel better and even recommended a surgery that could help. I didn't have to make any changes in my lifestyle or feel responsible for any of it. What are you doing that may be keeping the limiting beliefs alive? What might be some things you could explore looking into that would create new options and choices for yourself – mind, body, and soul – so you can be the best you in optimal health and vitality?

✦ What if the labels and beliefs **weren't even true**? How would that change the way you live your life? When I quit smoking and drinking, moved out of my parents moldy basement, and cut out all of the foods I discovered had in fact been flaring up my sinus cavities and contributing to the lack of Oxygen flow, I never needed an inhaler again. I never needed Benadryl or Claritin. The experience taught me to explore, discover, and create my own truths in every area of my life. It opened the door to possibilities that I had not had access to before. I mean, if this isn't true and I have believed it for 15+ years, what else am I believing that may also not be true? This experience also keeps me in a beautiful state of accountability to ensure that what I put into my body and allow in my environment is clean. Now, when my sinuses get clogged, instead of thinking "Asthma," I ask myself, "What might be the root cause of this? What did I just eat that could have contributed to this? What is in the environment that could be a contributing factor? What changed externally that could have triggered this?" I become a detective instead of a pharmacist.

✦ What do you **want to be true** instead? I now know that I am a limitless being who is in full control of my beliefs, thoughts, actions, and optimal energetic health and vitality, mind, body, and soul! There are always things you are doing or not doing that remain fully within your control. Those things can change the intensity or frequency of less-than-desirable symptoms you are experiencing. Instead of masking the symptoms, ask yourself, "What might be the root cause of this?" Get curious. Become a detective.

Listen to Your Body!

When it comes to "nutrition," question everything! Have you ever read one article about a topic in nutrition that proves something to be true and then came across another article on the very same topic that proves the complete opposing fact to be true? How infuriating, right? The reason this happens is due to bio-individuality. One person's medicinal miracle is another person's poison. No two bodies are the exact same.

That being said, just try things. Experiment and play. Test things to feel what works for you. Become the scientist in a laboratory that is to your own liking. Your body is your guide to your optimal peak performance, so stop navigating your health with the "shoulds" of the nutritional world. Learn what you can and then test your newfound knowledge to see what works for you.

Remember that whole "should" and "can't" thaang? That applies here. You should or shouldn't do something? Says who? You can't? Says who? Is it really true? Do you want it to be true? Take your power back. Create your own truth. No Limits. No Rules.

✦ *Question Everything* ✦

As I said, I have been misdiagnosed more times than I can even count. I have witnessed endless accounts of others getting advice from medical practitioners that make no sense to me. Let me be very clear: I am not a doctor. If that was something running through your mind: "What does this girl know, she isn't a doctor?" then you are on the right path.

Seriously, question everything! The whole point is for you to learn to let your body do the talking. I am not saying that advice from a doctor cannot be amazing, transformative, and life-saving. What I am saying is just because someone says something is "true" does not mean that it is so. Even if that person is a physician.

When I decided I wanted to learn more about nutrition, take my health into my own hands, and get certified to help others do the same, I enrolled in a program that had a predominant emphasis on holistic healing. Around the same time I got to the section where we were studying diabetics, I started to notice the fact that a friend of mine constantly had a sports drink with her. Because she is a diabetic, I was perplexed by this. I asked her why she was drinking a sports drink. She told me her doctor told her it would help with muscle cramps.

I looked at the label: 21g of sugar. Other bottles she had were at 35g of sugar. In a single bottle there is more sugar than what most sources would recommend for your entire daily consumption! Why would a doctor recommend that a non-active, non-athletic woman with Type 2 Diabetes consume a sports drink to help with her leg cramps? I stared at her like she had three heads.

"What?!" she asked. Me: "I don't understand why you would be drinking all this sugar, especially being that you are a diabetic!"

"The doctor said it has electrolytes in it, which are good for me," she said. I stared at her like she was crazy, trying to process the powerful marketing clearly in full effect here. She continued, "OK, well then, how would you recommend I get rid of these muscle cramps? You don't understand how painful they are! What else am I supposed to drink?"

"Ummm, I will give you one guess" I said. She paused, and then came the lightbulb moment.

"Oh. Water?" she said. Yes, water! As humans, we are more water than anything else in our physical composition. Water is the natural cure for many ailments, from muscle cramps to hunger pangs, from dry skin, dry lips, dry scalp, and dry mouth to headaches, constipation, and fatigue.

Another example: a few years back, about three months into my new vegan lifestyle which came as a result of uncovering my allergies when I did the cleanse, I started to get really sick. I had the most epic head congestion. I had dealt with "sinus infections" my whole life, now known to me as my body's natural response to the allergens I was unknowingly putting into it, but this one felt wildly different.

My entire head was pounding. For the first time ever, my thyroid was swollen. I knew something was wrong, so I went to the doctor. I chose to go to the same doctor who told my friend about the sports drink. Let's call this Clue #1.

While I was explaining to this doctor what I was experiencing, he quickly wrote me off. He told me it was a sinus infection. He would often get irritated with my use of Google and remind me that he was a doctor. I told him repeatedly that this was different; I had never felt this way before, my thyroid had never been swollen, and it was most definitely not a sinus infection. He assured me that I was wrong. He suggested he knew my body better than I did.

After all, what do I know? I am not a doctor.

He gave me a script for a Z pack and said, "Give it three days and you will be feeling back to brand new." My Heartspace was speaking to me, and I could feel in the depths of my being that he was wrong, that he was missing something. But it was my Headspace that led to me dismissing this thought. Who am I to think that I know my body better than a doctor, right?

Let's call this Headspace Overload self-doubt and dismissal of my own Heartspace intuitive knowing Clue #2. Before I left his office that day, he looked at me with concern. "I can't let you leave the office without sending you for some blood work to get tested for diabetes," he said.

I was dumbfounded. Where was this coming from? "I'm confused. Why do you want to test me for diabetes? I am in the best shape I have ever been in in my life. I've lost 35 pounds since you saw me last. I quit drinking, quit smoking, and stopped eating processed foods. I hired a personal trainer, I work out now, and I have never felt healthier and more alive in my life. What am I missing here?"

"Exactly," he responded. "You have lost a lot of weight since I saw you last. It is quite drastic, actually, and I am concerned by that. Being that diabetes runs in your family and that this extreme weight loss might be a sign that you could be diabetic too, I am going to send you to the lab to get tested. Just to be sure. So I can have a clear conscious." I was confused. I thought to myself, say what?! Am I hearing you right? Are you hearing me at all???!

I didn't lose weight because I am sick. I lost weight because I quit drinking, quit smoking, quit eating pizza, mozzarella sticks, and hamburgers, hired a personal trainer, and changed my entire lifestyle. I work out now instead of couch surfing. None of this is cause for the weight loss? Let's call this Clue #3.

I went home and, against my own bodily intuition, I dutifully filled the script and started taking the Z pack. Three days in and I was not feeling as he had promised. Nothing had changed. It was still just as bad as it was on the day when I walked into his office. This was Clue #4.

How many more clues did I need? Yes, sometimes we need a brick upside our head! OK, doctor, I thought, you had your chance. Now it's my turn. So I began my own research. I started by Googling the following: "What foods cause a swollen thyroid?" I was playing with different variations of this and then BAM!

There it was. Soy. Soy was the only thing I had changed in my diet since I started this new vegan lifestyle. I had added in tofu as my primary source of protein. Tofu is soy. Soy is one of the most common causes for thyroid inflammation and mucus buildup. I took soy out that very day, and I have never felt that kind of congestion again. My thyroid is completely back to normal and I have not had a single problem with it ever again.

Got it! Boom. I added Soy to the ongoing list of my allergies. Often times, people question the validity of my use of the word "allergies." Here's the thing... If I eat fish, I throw up. If I eat gluten, meat, or dairy I end up with symptoms so severe that in the past I was actually misdiagnosed with auto-immune disorders such as asthma, fibromyalgia, sinusitis, and rheumatoid arthritis. Hello, inflammation city here I come.

If I eat soy, my whole head blows up along with my thyroid. So much so that a doctor prescribes me a Z pack. Yeah, so I am going to go ahead and listen to my body and, while you are more than welcome to call it what you will, I am going to go with calling it "allergies." This word helps people, including myself, not accidentally poison me when I am out and about daily trying to get my eat on. Word.

I still have that diabetes test order he gave me that I never used. I keep it as a reminder of this experience. I know my body better than anyone else. Even better than a doctor.

Again, that does not mean that a doctor is worthless. Doctors most certainly have value to offer. All that I am saying is that a doctor should be more of a partner with you and your body and not the end-all, be-all holy grail. Like the magnet on my fridge says, "Trust yourself. You know more than you think you do." That's from Doctor Spock.

Booyah! Get it, girl!!

Knowledge is power, and what you learn from firsthand experience is the most powerful knowledge of all. You are the BOSS of your own knowledge. Experiment and play with what works.

✦ *Get Your Body Logging On* ✦

Body logging allows you to play with learning the language your body speaks so you never have to be on another fad diet, count calories, or read diet books or nutrition guides ever again, because you will let your body do the talking. Play with this. Experiment, test it out, and have fun with it. Pretend you are a scientist in a lab and mastering your own body talk is the mission.

This is something you can do on your own for a period of two weeks, then look back and see what patterns you observe. This is the best way I know to begin to explore what your body is trying to tell you. Maybe you will notice that you are only drinking one glass of water a day. You may see that this might be correlated to dry skin, chapped lips, headaches, muscle aches, fatigue, and a long laundry list of other symptoms getting in your way of connecting with your inner goddess.

You may realize that every time you eat milk or cheese you get gassy. Umm, hello, *not* epic or sexy! Or maybe every time you eat gluten, you realize you experience bloating, indigestion, skin blemishes, gas, sneezing, feeling depressed, and / or brain fog. There is a long list of things related to gluten sensitivity that many people don't know about. Again, you can't be powerfully connected with your inner goddess while experiencing the aforementioned things.

Epic Sexy Thrival Actions

✓ **Keep a body log.** We're going to play a version
of twenty questions, but with the top twelve power-
hitters instead of an overwhelming twenty. The
insights you gain from these twelve mini-actions
will prove invaluable.

Mini-Action #1. Log the *what* and *when* of food, sleep, and
liquids!

Mini-Action #2. Log all emotional, physical, and mental
symptoms. Think brain fog, fatigue, and exhaustion. Think
feelings of sadness and annoyance along with light-
headedness, dizziness, skin blemishes, sneezing, and itchy
eyes. Take notice of skin issues, gas, bloating, having a
hard time breathing, asthmatic symptoms, and swelling of
any kind. Look for swelling and puffiness under your eyes
and beneath your eyelids as well as on your hands, feet, and
/ or tummy. Pay close attention to achy joints and aches in
general. Be specific about where they are. Examples: lower
back, knees, or hands. Record indigestion, acid reflux,
tummy aches, tummy gargles, diarrhea, muscle cramps,
backaches, headaches, and dry skin, lips, or mouth.

Mini-Action #3. Look for the patterns.

Mini-Action #4. Notice what is happening every time you
are experiencing an undesired symptom.

Mini-Action #5. *Exploration Question:* Notice whether there is a certain food you eat a half-hour before a recurring symptom occurs.

Mini-Action #6. *Exploration Question:* Are you getting ample sleep?

Mini-Action #7. *Exploration Question:* Are you drinking enough water?

Mini-Action #8. *Exploration Question:* How do you feel after you consume each of the following: Milk and Cheese, Gluten, Sugar, Caffeine, Pesticides, Chemicals, GMOs, Alcohol, Eggs, and Meat (especially red meat)?

Mini-Action #9. *Exploration Question:* What happens thirty minutes after you consume each of these?

Mini-Action #10. *Exploration Question:* When looking for patterns, take into consideration common culprits for the symptoms you are experiencing. Get curious and Google, "What foods cause (insert symptoms)."

Mini-Action #11. See the Dirty Dozen / Clean Fifteen Lists in "The Truth About Pesticides" section. These lists reveal which foods have a ton of chemicals in them and are totally getting in the way of you getting your sexy on!

Mini-Action #12. Experiment and test your hypothesis. When you find something you think might correlate to a physical symptom, play with it! Take it out of your diet for seven days and log how you feel, then put it back in on the eighth day and log like the boss babe that you are! Get curious, and put your curiosity into action, because action is where new outcomes await you, girl.

Be a detective. See what correlations you can come up with and what hypothesis you can form. This is about you finding your body's truths.

✦ *Sample Body Log* ✦

Here's an example of a Body Log. See what you notice.

Friday

7:10	Wake up (late)
8	Water x 2. Oatmeal and raisins (no milk). Have a headache.
9	Water x1. Feeling positive about getting back on track with diet.
10:20	Water x1
10:40	Water x 1 and watermelon
11:30	Cranky. Don't like the new coworker at work. Looking forward to weekend, really excited.
12	Water x 1 Stressed about thinking about how I don't like new coworker. Does this make me a bad person?
1	Light-headed, dizzy. Lunch. two flatbreads with hummus, salad (yellow pepper, cherry tomatoes, sugar snap peas, carrot, water x 1)
2:30	Water x 1 Feeling gassy and uncomfortable (no flatulence)
3:30	Water x 1
4:30	Water x 1
5	Water x 2
6	2 x pieces of toast, water x 1. Tired

7	Flatulence
7:30	Potato, sautéed leeks and mushrooms and roast butternut squash and zucchini with a teaspoon of sour cream
8	Apple and blackberry crumble and custard (made with milk)
8:30	Water x1
10	Water x2
10:30	Sleep; Have been feeling dizzy and light-headed all day

Saturday (out of town)

7:30	Wake. Really dry mouth and feeling light-headed.
8:30	Water x 2
8:45	Oatmeal and raisins
9	Water x1
10:30	Water x 1
12	Light-headed and hungry
1	Water x1
2	Lunch. Salad roll (lettuce, tomato, egg mayonnaise), carrot cake, cup of black tea
3	Feel a bit sick (carrot cake too sweet)
4	Feeling quite queezy and light-headed
7	Steak and caramelized red onion baguette with spinach, orange juice and tonic water, glass of champagne, mocha. Feeling a bit ill straight after mocha (milk or sugar?). Tired, but have energy. Little bit of flatulence, but ok.
8:30	Water x 1.5
9	Tired, bloated, sore feet, back and shoulders
10	Water x3
11	Sleep

Sunday

7:30	Wake
8	Get up, water x3 Feeling excited and motivated
9	Oatmeal and raisins
10	Water x 2
11	Water x 1
2	(Out for lunch) roast pork with cauliflower cheese, carrots,

spring greens, potatoes, Yorkshire pudding (oven fried batter) and gravy.

3	Orange and tonic, chocolate brownie and ice-cream (really didn't need brownie, I just wanted it)
4	Water x 1
5	Light-headed and sleepy
7:30	Water x 1 Ankles really achy
8	Water x 1 Flatulence
9	Bit of a wobbly tummy. Oatmeal and raisins
9:30	Water x 2 Hips, ankles ache, exhausted, light-headed, wobbly tummy and feeling cranky
10:30	Water x2 Sleep

✦ *Evaluate Your Body Log* ✦

Here is what I noticed about the above client:

✓ She was going **too many hours** between meals, causing her to become "hungry" and tired.

✓ **Sugar and bread** appear to be culprits for feeling sick, nauseous, light-headed, and dizzy.

✓ Tired, bloated, gassy, and epic inflammation of the body after eating **inflammatory foods** such as meat, bread, and milk.

✓ Common culprits of **meat, gluten, and dairy** appear to have a possible link to her achiness, gas, and crankiness.

What we were able to do with this log was to play with these possible correlations and then narrow down to uncover what her own unique poisons were. In her case, the two biggest poisons were dairy and gluten. Then, we were able to come up with a game plan for substituting alternative options into her lifestyle so she could move forward with her life with ease and eliminate the undesirable symptoms. Winning!

Remember, one person's medicinal food savior is another person's poison. This is about finding out more about your body, so you can make more informed decisions about what you eat and know how you will feel after doing so. The body log will support you in being the expert of your own body language. You will no longer look for an external, one-size-fits-all solution or for someone else to tell you what is best for your body. Your body already knows what is best. You just need to learn to listen to it! In order to help alleviate a bit of resistance that you may experience around this, you can play with looking at your own log as if it was someone else's (as we just did here).

It's often easier for us to see what is impacting someone else's ability to achieve the desired outcomes and results they are craving, right? So pretend it's someone else's log that you are reviewing! Review your log with a fresh mind. Be open and unattached, and resist the urge to be premeditative, such as thinking, "Oh, please don't be cheese! I looove cheese! Not cheese! Ahhh!!"

✦ *Eliminate Culprits* ✦

Once you start Body Logging, I encourage you to play with elimination testing. See how your body responds as you take things out and put them back in. For example, if you notice that you are having a less-than-desirable reaction every time you eat dairy (let's say you get bloated, have gas, and your sinuses become congested), remove dairy for a week and keep logging. See and feel the differences that show up. Then, add dairy back into your daily consumption after the seven-day elimination period and keep logging. See if the symptoms disappeared and came back. If you notice that there isn't a big difference, then repeat the process with another common culprit, such as gluten.

Do your own research. If you are experiencing undesired symptoms, explore resolving them in a new way than what you have tried before. The definition of insanity is doing the same thing over and over and expecting new results, right? So, let's try something new.

Open yourself to the possibilities of *new* outcomes and results! The next time that you are experiencing bloating, Google, "What foods cause (insert your undesired symptoms)" and see what foods if any you have ingested that may be contributing to undesired symptoms! When all else fails, drink more water!

✦ *Know the Truth About Pesticides* ✦

People don't always realize the impact that pesticides have on their health. These chemicals impact your ability to get your sexy on and connect with your inner goddess. They can have a detrimental impact on your energy throughout the day. The truth is that pesticides can wreak havoc on your health, body *and* mind.

Let's make this simple, shall we? When it comes to food, "conventional" means chemicals may have been used in an effort to kill bugs and small rodents that may otherwise eat the crops. I can only speak for myself here but, if I am doing the math on that equation, it might mean that, although it won't kill me *immediately* (because I'm a lot bigger than a rodent or insect), there is a possibility that pesticdes can in fact poison and kill me rather slowly.

These chemicals can have potential impacts on the brain, memory retention, vision, your digestive system, and your reproductive organs, including your ability to make healthy little "nuggets" (what others often refer to as "babies"). The list goes on! It's not *just* the body and brain that are impacted by chemicals and pesticides. Your emotions and energy levels can go haywire as well. Moodiness, feelings of depression, and fatigue are common.

Oy Vey! Experiencing these types of symptoms will hold you back from being able to look and feel the way that you want to feel as you create a life that you love living, and a *you* you love being.

✦ *The Dirty Dozen* ✦

Google "Dirty Dozen" and you will find many examples of lists of produce that have a higher concentration of chemicals than others. For each fruit or vegetable that you find on a Dirty Dozen list, it is highly recommended that you buy organic. To launch your research, here are some common produce that you'll typically see on these lists:

- Apples
- Bell Peppers
- Cucumber
- Grapes
- Tomatoes
- White potatoes

- Raspberries
- Spinach
- Strawberries

✦ *The Clean 15* ✦

Google "Clean Fifteen" and you will find a list of produce that are safe to buy conventional as they have been tested as having lower levels of chemicals and toxicity. This means you can save some bucks and stay healthy! The list below includes fruits and vegetables that commonly show up on "clean" lists. Here are just a few examples to kick-start your own research!

- Sweet potatoes
- Pineapples
- Onions
- Avocados
- Sweet corn
- Cabbage

Remember, this is *your* body. Own your power, make sure to do your own research, and use your research in a way that works for you. For example, you can take a picture of each list you find on Google and keep it on your phone for easy reference when you shop. When I first started playing with this, I took screen shots of each list and stored them in my "favorites" album folder for quick and easy reference.

Now, I just buy everything organic and only reference the list when the organic is out-of-stock in the store, so I can check to see if that fruit or vegetable is on a Dirty Dozen list. If it is, I opt to skip it and wait for the organic to be back in stock. As always, play with what works best for you.

✦ *Know Your Meat* ✦

When buying meat, think about the following. If you purchase meat that is not organic, then there is a possibility that the livestock that was the source of the meat you are now eating consumed food containing antibiotics, genetically-engineered grains, pesticides, or chemicals. If that is the case, then you are eating all of said things! Take the time to make a conscious decision about what you consume. Do your research on how your meat is prepared, and listen to your body for the feedback on what feels best for you.

Keep these new insights on your awareness radar. Start to experiment with organic and alternative food choices. Listen to how your body responds to each. Let your body be your guide to optimal health. This includes looking and feeling amazingly sexy in your own skin!

The key in all this is to let your body do the talking and to chase the feeling. If it feels good, do more of it, eat more of it, and drink more of it. If it makes you feel bad, do less of it, eat less of it, and drink less of it! Decide how you want to feel. Then, go find all the possible ways that you can help support your brilliant body to experience more of that. You and your body are partners in shine. Do your part, sister!

GET YOUR SHARE ON *#epicsexyyou*

The remainder of this section is chock full of *Epic Sexy Thrival Tips* that cover everything from nutrition to skin and body care. I'll share ways to improve your posture, keep your legs sexy, and get your body lovin' on. I've got you, girl. Let's work your way back to Epic Sexy You one thrival practice at a time.

Epic Sexy Nutrition, Simplified!

Here are some Epic Sexy thaaangs you can experiment with and implement. They help you move step by step in the direction of creating the body that you *love* being in and to look and *feel* sexy in your own skin. Remember, pick just one thing at a time.

Dirty Dozen / Clean Fifteen. Find a list for each of these and take them with you when you shop. Buy your produce accordingly. Avoid the toxicity of pesticides as much as you can, and pay attention to how you feel when you eat conventional versus organic. Do more of what feels good and less of what doesn't.

Eat More Whole Foods. Whole foods include those without a label, such as fruits and veggies. That whole foods section in the grocery store is full of fresh produce. That whole section is yours for the picking! Try one new dish a week that includes whole foods.

Eat Fewer Processed Food. Look at labels. Decrease the consumption of processed foods that have more than five ingredients. Also eliminate foods that include ingredients that you can't pronounce or you have no idea what they are. Start with just a little bit less of it than you are currently consuming. Baby steps will work wonders!

Think of it as a spectrum of choices. On one end of the spectrum you have pizza, mozzarella sticks, ice cream, and potato chips. On the other end of the spectrum you have broccoli, kale, organic produce, and whole foods. Look at where you currently fall on that spectrum. Then, move incrementally towards the end that is going to help you get your lean on, minimize cellulite, make your skin glow, and most importantly *feel* sexy, energized, vivacious, and alive!

Chew Your Food! Help your digestive system out and consciously *chew* your food into pieces as small as possible before swallowing. Consuming large chunks of food at once can lead to bloating, gas, and discomfort. Play with conscious awareness around chewing. As an example of a challenge to help you focus on chewing, count a minimum of thirty chews before you swallow. Yes, that is a bit extreme, but play with this to build awareness around it. Over time, you will create a new habit of intentional chewing. Obviously, you will not do that forevaaaaaa, but just doing it for a couple of days with intention, full awareness, and curiosity will allow you to slow down, breathe, chew, and enjoy your meal instead of wolfing it down and ending up with symptoms of bloat, gas, and discomfort.

Drink More Water. Seriously, you have no idea how much this can rock your world until you try it. Go on with your bad self and give it a go. Here are some thaangs to consider:

✓ **Symptoms** related to lack of water include dry skin, dry lips, dry mouth, dandruff, fatigue, backaches, headaches, digestive problems, and cramps.

✓ We often mistake hunger for what is really **thirst**. The next time you think you are hungry, drink a glass of water, wait five to ten minutes, and then eat if you are still hungry. Yes, water can help you lose weight. Get it girl!

✓ Water is the most **natural elixir** of life, one we often take for granted. We easily forget its natural and epic medicinal healing properties.

Get More Sleep. This will only apply to some of you, and you know who you are. I get it, you are *busy*. Just start with getting fifteen minutes more per night than what you are getting right now. Baby steps can be life changing. Sleep is not just about quantity but quality too. How comfy is your bed? What is the ambience and energy of your bedroom? What are you doing right before you go to bed? Is this aiding your sleep or hindering it?

Listen to Your Body. Don't drive yourself mad listening to all of the contradicting information that can be found on "nutrition" today. We are all different. Listen to *your* body. Once you learn to listen to your body, you will never have to be on another fad diet, count calories, or seek answers from external sources.

No more reading conflicting truths in diet books or nutrition guides ever again, because you will let your body do the talking! Play with this area of your life. Experiment, test it out, and have fun with it. You are a scientist in a lab of exploration, and mastering your own body talk is the mission. If it feels good do more of it, if it feels bad do less of it.

✦ *Labels Made Simple* ✦

✓ First of all, try to **eat more things** *without* **labels**. Yeah, visit that epic sexy produce section in your grocery store! Woo!!

✓ If a label has **ingredients you can't pronounce** or if your mind is confused by what's on the label, your body will be confused by the ingestion of it. If the label has chemicals listed and you put those chemicals in your body, you'll be poisoning yourself slowly but surely and that leads to all that not-so-epic-or-sexy stuff, to include bloating, skin blemishes, weight gain, puffiness, inflammation, moodiness, gas, irritability, and achy muscles and joints.

✓ **More than five ingredients** and you are starting to get into a potential highly processed somethin' somethin' and your body will retaliate accordingly.

✓ **"Natural"** is merely a marketing buzz word. It is not regulated (at least not in the United States). When you see that word, know that unless it has the

USDA-certified "Organic" label, there is a strong possibility that it is not truly organic. Some food companies even have the word "Organic" in their company name, an ingenious marketing ploy to make you think it's organic when it isn't. Explore further and find out for yourself what the "truth" is for *you*. And, remember, let your body do the talking.

✓ The **order of the ingredients** matters. The first ingredients listed on the label are the most prominent ingredients in that thaang! For example, if "high-fructose corn syrup" is the first ingredient, that is basically what you are eating. Oh, and high-fructose corn syrup basically means *sugar*. Hello sugar-crash moodiness and not so Epic Sexy You!

✓ If you **aren't sure what an ingredient is,** get curious. Google it! Know what you are putting into your body and serving to your loved ones.

✓ The longer the food's **shelf life**, the shorter your life. Think about it this way, the longer something is able to sit on a shelf, the longer it is able to sit in your body taking up space and wreaking havoc instead of being absorbed to nourish the beautifully magnificent and brilliant machine that you live and play in daily! Think about eating things that your body can take in, absorb the nutrients, and digest efficiently. The longer it's in your body, the more it's going to weigh you down.

Sure, there are a *ton* of other things you can look at when you read a label, these are just a few things to add to your awareness radar. Looking out for these things will move you incrementally toward becoming a more educated consumer as you create an Epic Sexy body you love being in! xoxo

Get Your Natural Skin Care On

We've been talking about cleansing your body and eliminating the ingestion of chemicals and toxins. Girl, the same damage from chemicals applies to topical treatments that you put *on* your skin! Think about it: makeup, shampoo, conditioner, lotion, makeup removers, deodorant, hand and body soap all go directly onto your skin and seep right into your pores. Whatever ingredients are inside all these goodies and potions goes directly into the stream that is within you.

Make educated decisions. Read Labels. *Know* what you are putting directly into your pores. This can feel overwhelming at first, so just pick *one thing* to play with at a time. As an example, you can start with your deodorant. Start experimenting with alternative options that have fewer chemicals but still keep you fresh and clean.

Don't let some of the inevitable "fails" of the not-so-fresh-and-clean experiments deter you from your journey in the search of a lower-chemical option that works for you. For example, it took me quite a while to find a deodorant that was lower in chemicals and could prevent me from smelling like a complete zoo by midday. Currently I am experimenting with a deodorant that falls in the middle of the spectrum.

On one end of the spectrum, you have choices that are *loaded* with chemicals and fragrances, so you smell yummy but you've got the whole chemical thing going on. On the other end of the spectrum are choices that are completely and utterly organic. These have no chemicals but do not necessarily get the job done in regards to a yummy fragrance department. So you will have to play around with different ones to see what works best for you.

This is *not* about removing all the chemicals immediately, or never again using anything that has chemicals in it. Rather, it is about you choosing to start your journey and then progressively moving toward the end of the spectrum that has less toxins going into your body. Just start with *one* thing and move incrementally, step by step, selecting options with fewer chemicals than what you are currently utilizing. It's a journey, not an overnight overhaul.

As an example, I want my face to glow and shine. I want the outside to match the inside, so I use natural eye makeup remover. I currently am using organic jojoba oil and love it. There are a ton of options you can play with: olive oil, almond oil, jojoba oil, Shea butter, coconut oil, and grapeseed oil to name a few.

Remember: Read the labels on everything. Read the labels on your shampoo and conditioner. See what you are putting on your hair. Especially for my souls sisters who have thinning hair, it's time to get conscious. Own your power. Do the research. If you don't know what an ingredient is, Google it.

Know what you are putting onto and into your body. Explore utilizing an alternative that would be less toxic. Remember, what works for one person may not work for another. Each one of us is a unique being. No two of us are the same, which is precisely why you are so incredibly *special* and deserve to feel Epic Sexy You.

Get Your Twist On!

I literally mean getting your twist on. Google "Yoga Twists" for a plethora of options. Twists help detox your organs of all the junk that gets all up in there. Toxins are neither epic nor sexy. Twists can also improve digestion and relieve backaches, headaches, and stiffness in the body. Help your body help you. Take breaks in the middle of your day and get your twist on!

Circulate Those Sexy Legs!

Google "legs up the wall" and you will get a picture of one of my fave restorative yoga poses. I always incorporate this pose when I teach yoga to my tribe. Spider veins and varicose veins are most definitely not epic or sexy, and this restorative pose will help recirculate your blood flow and prevent those bad boys. This pose is also soothing to individuals who experience lower back pain.

As a little bonus, here's a song I listen to while I do this pose, perhaps it will tickle your fancy too. Google, "Ut 396 Hz, Liberation from Guilt & Fear, Solfeggio Meditation, Tom Soltron" and give it a go. I'd recommend using your headphones to get the most out of this therapeutic sound melody. I find this song to be beautiful, moving, and aligned with the pose. It allows me to just sit still and zone out for twelve minutes, which is what I have found is *my* sweet spot attention span for this pose.

Remember, we are all different. Find your fave mood-setting song and your own sweet spot for length of time in the pose.

Breathe!!!

Breathwork is linked to relaxation, rejuvenation, weight loss, clearer skin, more energy, mental clarity, and all things that will allow you to look and *feel* sexy! Yeah, that's right. I said weight loss. *Breathe*, sister, breathe! Here is a quickie, go-to breathing exercise to do as needed and or desired:

✦ **Breath in** to the count of 1, hold for the count of 1, breath out for the count of 1, hold for the count of 1, ... Repeat to the count of 2... 3... 4... 5...

✦ If you have more time, feel free to count up to 7, and then **count backwards** all the way back down to 1. If you have less time, just go up to 5, and reap the benefits and the rewards.

✦ If you are **nervous**... *breathe!*

✦ If you are **angry**... *breathe!*

✦ If you are **tired**, fatigued, exhausted, and have brain fog.... *breathe!*

✦ Just *breathe!* ☺

Stand Tall

It is not epic or sexy when you are hunched over. Straighten up, sister friend, and own your bad-assery like the boss babe you are. If you need a reminder, you can go back to that section in this book on Epic Sexy Posture. Find it quickly by looking at the full table of contents up front, your easy-navigation tool to find whatever you are craving to reconnect with along your journey to Epic Sexy You.

Epic Sexy Workout Tips

Here are some tips to keep your Epic Sexy workouts a priority.

✓ **Trick Yourself into a Workout**. Sweaty, stinky gym time with muscle heads? Hey, if that is your thing, go on with your bad self, but personally, no thank you. That is totally not for me! Find something that *you* think is fun to do, and have the workout be the added bonus. Some ideas for you: skiing, ice skating, hiking, exploring the town, indoor wall climbing, snow tubing, yoga, or running around after kids. Go to museums, playgrounds, and fun runs such as the mud run or the runs that mirror the show "Wipeout." Sign yourself up for a flying trapeze class, take a Silk Ariel yoga class, go pole dancing, or try a hip-hop dance class. Dance around in your living room or check YouTube for a dance you want to learn, such as the Dougie, the Wobble, or anything Beyonce. Make it happen!

✓ **Think Outside the Box**. Get creative and have fun with it, girl! Make sure that you have ample things on the list that are *free* to do, so you don't even allow yourself for a single second to use the excuse that you, "Don't have the money." Also, make sure you have a list abundantly filled with endless fun, quick, and easy things that you can do so that you don't have the time excuse either! For example, take a three-minute dance break to get your body moving. Don't sell me the BS that you don't have three minutes. Set yourself up for success you Epic Sexy Goddess you! When you find things that work for you, share with the rest of us. Don't be shy. Help a sista out! Share by using #epicsexyyou on your fave social media platforms or e-mail me directly at morgan@epicsexyyou.com so I can share your brilliance with the rest of the tribe! WOO! Get it girl!

✓ **Look and Feel Good Doing It**! Wear whatever makes you feel how you *want* to feel. I like to feel vibrant, playful, and alive when I am out there getting my play on and tricking myself into a workout, so I wear bold, bright, vibrant colors and fun patterns. When I have a fun outfit that is going to make me feel the way I want to feel, I am automatically more motivated right out of the gates to go get 'er done! BOOM.

✓ **Chase the Feeling.** What do you want to feel more of? Find things to do and wear that make you feel more of that! Chase that feeling, girl! In some good ol' Me First fashion!

Get MEDucated

When it comes to medications, make an informed decision. I was having a conversation with a friend one day. This was a continuation of an ongoing convo about the fact that he has acid reflux and takes medication for it. I try really hard not to push my health knowledge onto others like it's a religion. It's hard though when you love someone and all you want is for them to be happy and healthy. It is hard not to share the alternative choices and possibilities that you know about with others when you know that those options can uplevel their thrival factor!

Sure, there are many ways to achieve an end result and to each his or her own. I like to look for the root cause of something so I can stop the symptom from occurring, and I personally feel that medicating something like acid reflux is just masking a symptom. Before you get defensive and start thinking, "You don't understand. It's the only thing that stops it. I've tried everything!" just hear me out.

Epic Sexy Q&A

Let's take out that pen and paper and get our exploration on, shall we? Write down undesired symptoms, diagnoses, and societal labels. This list might include things such as acid reflux, acne, skin blemishes, rosacea, psoriasis, diabetes, depression, bipolar, bloating, indigestion, gas, IBS, Rheumatoid Arthritis, or Asthma. For each and every one of these labels, take your time and answer the following questions:

+ Have you *really* **tried** *everything*? What are all of the things that you have tried already to help decrease the negative impacts of this symptom?

+ If you had to guess, what might be the **root cause** of this symptom? How much have you done to explore what the root cause of it may be? What are you doing and / or not doing that might be causing this?

+ What are the **holistic avenues** you have explored to treat the symptoms that you are experiencing?

+ What **research** have you done yourself with regard to your symptoms, diagnoses, labels, and ailments?

What I have seen with people who go the medication route is that they start taking one medication for one thing, and then, before they know it, they need another medication for something that the first medication caused. Pretty soon, you own a pill box to manage all of your meds. You become lost, imprisoned in a life sentence that you have *chosen* to accept, not knowing that you can actually choose an alternative route.

I was left with but one question for my friend. "Have you read the side effects of the meds that you are currently taking?" His answer?

"No. That isn't a bad idea. I think I'll do that." Here is my direct challenge to you: make an informed decision about the medications you choose to take. *Read about the side effects.*

Research them yourself if they are not on the bottle. Hit up my friend Google and see what other people are saying about the side effects and potential negative impacts they experience as a result of utilizing the meds to "treat" their symptoms. Do not be ignorant to the further damage and deterioration you may unknowingly be causing your body when you choose to take a particular medication.

- ✓ **Read the ingredients**. Know what you are putting into your body.

- ✓ Have you really tried **everything**?

- ✓ Is there **another way**?

✦ *Too Cool for School?* ✦

Have you seen the TED Talk by Sir Ken Robinson called, "Do Schools Kill Creativity?" If not, I highly recommend it! One of the biggest takeaways from the talk is the idea that we all have innate gifts and, once we tap into them, these gifts not only allow us to thrive, they also empower us to make the world a more enjoyable place to be for everyone who is touched by our gifts.

In this Ted Talk, Sir Ken Robinson tells a story about a little girl in the 1930s who was "fidgety." Her parents were told that there was something wrong with her and that she shouldn't be in school. This was according to the labels, standards, and definitions of the education system in that day. She couldn't sit still and pay attention. Her mother took her to a psychiatrist to find out what was wrong with her.

The psychiatrist noticed that this girl had the gift of movement, and he recommended that she be enrolled into dance immediately. Thank God there was no medication for "fidgeting" back then, thank God this psychiatrist was gifted and talented in his own right, and thank God there were no labels to put on this little girl such as the labels we have today, such as A.D.D. or A.D.H.D, which would likely have led to medicating the dance out of her mind, body, and soul and medicating the world out of being able to experience her gifts.

That woman is Gillian Lynne, famed choreographer for Broadway shows "Cats" and "Phantom of the Opera," the longest-running show in the history of Broadway. How robbed would we have been if there had been a way back then to literally medicate her talents out of her? Sir Ken Robinson goes on to talk about how, when Gillian finally was enrolled into dance school, she said, "The room was filled with people like me: people who couldn't sit still and had to move to think."

It's clear in her language that movement is her flow. Movement is her gift. Movement is her means and vehicle for processing. If you take movement away, merely to calm her down so that she is more "manageable" in a classroom, you deprive the world of an epic and unique talent that goes on to touch the souls of so many beings who otherwise would not have been touched unless you unleashed those talents within.

Embrace what makes you "you." Don't medicate the gifts, talents, and spiritual essence out of you!

We all came here with gifts. The sooner we can learn to embrace what makes us the unique, one-of-a-kind beings we are, the sooner we can light up the world and make it an even brighter existence to share with each other.

Epic Sexy Q&A

Get that pen and paper out. It's time to explore and play some. Consider these questions.

✦ What have **others said about you?** How have you been judged as "weird" or "crazy" or made to feel different, less-than, not normal, or an outsider?

✦ What are some of the **things that make you *you*?**

✦ What are the **labels** that others have tried to put on you as a result of your uniqueness? What are the labels that you have put on yourself?

✦ If you were to **release judgment** from yourself and embrace these things about you, what might that look like? How might that feel? How would you behave different? What would you gain as a result?

✦ What is the **best-case scenario?** What might happen if you unapologetically embraced Limitless You?

✦ What is it **costing** you to not embrace these things?

Love Your Body

Pretty much everything we've previously covered in this section is a piece of the puzzle when it comes to loving your body. There is an additional piece. If we did not address this additional piece, it would leave this section incomplete. Let's focus there:

How do you currently love your body in a Self Love and TLC kind of way?

I mean, think about it. Your body is a dumbfounding miracle. It's this super-complex system that somehow finds a way to adapt to whatever you put it through. It is constantly talking to you, telling you when you are leaving your optimal Thrival Zone. Miracles beget miracles. What you focus on grows, remember?

What you invest your time and energy in noticing, appreciating, and honoring will inevitably birth more of those very things. When you take time to intentionally create and engage in ongoing consistent practices of loving and honoring your body, you will gradually experience more and more love for yourself. You will experience that love for *all* of you – mind, body, and soul.

Let's leave mediocrity in the dust once and for all. Let's claim all of the yummy, delicious, sparkly, magical goodies and surprises that await you in your limitless Epic Sexy Life. Let's get our Body Love on, shall we? Woo!! ;) xoxo

✦ *Give Your Body Some Good Ol' Lovin'* ✦

How you treat your body says a lot about how you feel about yourself and what you will tolerate in life. If you are lazy with body maintenance, that low standard will spill into other areas of your life. Treat your body with kindness, love, and respect.

Epic Sexy Q&A

Get out that pen and paper. Some questions to consider:

✦ What are the current ways in which you **maintain, care for, love, and fuel your body**? What is the frequency of each?

✦ What are some **opportunities to explore** for how you might better love, honor, and care for your body in a more conscious and consistent manner?

✦ If you genuinely viewed your body as a **temple**, how would you treat it differently than you do now?

✦ If you genuinely viewed yourself as a **true goddess**, how would you treat yourself differently?

✦ What are some things in your life you can identify that indicate you are **settling for less** than Goddess Thriving Levels? Where are you currently accepting mediocrity? Get as specific as possible.

✦ What does your inner Goddess actually **crave**?

✦ What are some ways you can honor, love, respect, admire, and **appreciate your body**?

✦ *Gift Yourself: Treat the Root Cause and Forget the Magic Bullet, Band-Aid Approach* ✦

Again, the amount of time and energy you put into honoring, listening to, loving, sculpting and strengthening your body has a direct correlation to the results you get in every other area in your life. If you don't feel that you're worth investing your own time and energy and therefore ignore sculpting, loving, and honoring your body, then how the hell are you ever going to be able to get raw, real, and naked with anyone else? If you cut corners, have low standards for what you are willing to invest in yourself, and you half-ass this area of your life, then you're most definitely going to end up with a life that is mediocre at best.

For example, diet pills may help you lose weight, but your body is going to start breaking down as a result of the nutrients you are depriving it by taking those pills in the first place. When you do not invest the time and energy to change your lifestyle and make healthier choices for yourself over the long-term, you signal to your inner Heartspace GPS, your Goddess Power Source, that you don't believe you are worth it. Before you know it, that GPS is back on the shelf, and your Goddess Self is back sitting on the sidelines waiting for you to get your act together once again!

You see, your Goddess is the one who has full control of turning that Heartspace GPS on or off. She has impeccable boundaries and standards, and she is not going to tolerate your laziness or unhealthy and toxic shortcuts. She will just go sit down on the sidelines until you show her that you are ready. Until you show her that you deserve to have her epic force in full effect on your team, she won't be front and center. If you aren't going to put in the work, if you aren't going to invest in you, and if you aren't willing to play full-out, well then, sister friend, neither is she.

When you create lifestyle changes that support a happier and more fulfilling life over the long term, then and only then will your Goddess be by your side. Invest your time and energy in becoming a better version of yourself. Make healthy decisions. Move incrementally closer to the healthier end of the spectrum in the mind, body, and soul choices you make on a daily basis. With your Goddess by your side, your inner GPS will be fired up and lead you straight into peak performance. Be aware of this as you move forward on your journey. Intentionally make space for and invite the Goddess to be by your side.

Epic Sexy Q&A

When you feel disconnected from your divine guidance and intuition, ask yourself the following questions:

✦ Where am I **choosing the shortcut** that is the "easy" path instead of investing in the long-term solution? Where am I settling for the energetic vibrations of "this will do for now," "I'm fine," "I'll do it tomorrow," or "I'll do that when...."?

✦ What are the **unhealthy choices** I have been making recently? Mind? Body? Soul?

✦ What is it that I want? What are **healthier options** I have available to me to get where I want to go?

✦ How might I **have it all?** How can I be happy and thrive now *and* later. How can I achieve the results I want now and later? Explore possible ways. Having to choose between happy now or happy later is an old energetic vibration that is low vibe. There is another choice that is available to you, one that is limitlessly expansive in the options, opportunities, and possibilities that are available to you. It's what I call "The And Factor." What if you didn't have to choose? What if you could get creative and find a way to have everything that you want? All at once. Starting right now. How might you do that?

When you hear yourself saying, "Yeah, but…" followed by the insertion of reasons that that you think it's not actually even possible to experience what you want, replace that with this: "Yes, but what if I could? How might I be able to get uber creative and make that happen?" Let your imagination run wild and free!

If it helps, take yourself out of the equation. Pretend you are helping a friend come up with all the limitless possible solutions to their perceived dilemma. You are a pretty stellar problem-solver for others. Do yourself a favor, and be generous with that gift. Use it for yourself! Remember, Me Too! We all win when you choose Me Too and that means me too! Me too! Woo!!

✦ *Make Time for Body-Love Mirror Moments* ✦

Stand in front of the mirror and tell yourself what you love about your body. Take time to really explore. Look deep into your own eyes and see what they really look like. Eyes are so beautiful! Take time to discover and explore yours. See what they look like up close and personal. Look at your smile, your hair, your lips, your ears, your nose, your legs, even your butt. Find at least *one* thing that you really like about yourself and make sure to take time every single day to admire that thing.

Resist the urge to go down the path of seeing all of the things you don't like. What you focus on grows, so focus on what you do like. Every time you hear yourself focusing on what you don't like, stop and ask yourself "Yes, but what *do* you like?" Remind yourself to intentionally focus on the beauty, appreciation, and admiration for all things you.

As you progress in your journey, add more things onto your admiration list! Do *not* allow this to become an opportunity to beat yourself up. Just start with one single thing and do your best to ignore the mental chatter that says, "Yeah, but look at all these things you don't like." Do not "Yeah, but," yourself! Unless it's a yeah, but power reframe: "Yeah, but what do you like? Yeah, but what if you could find something that you like? What might that something be?" If this game seems too hard to play and the chatter is too loud, then play with another *Epic Sexy Thrival Tip* and come back to this one when it feels right for you.

✦ *Intentionally Gift Your Body Relaxation* ✦

What are you currently doing to intentionally gift yourself relaxation as your body reveals that it is craving some good ol' TLC? Take a minute and write out a list of ideas of thaangs you can do to honor your body when it is craving relaxation. Here are some ideas to get your creative juices flowing:

- Restorative Yoga
- Meditation, massages, and bubble baths
- Lying on the couch and watching a movie
- Sauna, steam room, or spa
- Mani / pedi

What else? What would your body like to experience in order to get its relaxation on? Take time and write it down.

Create Daily Rituals That ROCK

Now, let's take a look at what's going on on the daily, so that we can explore ways to get your Epic Sexy Swag on from sun up to sun down every single day.

Epic Sexy Q&A

Get out that pen and paper. Let's explore and play!

✦ What are your **morning Self Love** and body care rituals today? Be super-honest with yourself. You are the only person who is going to see this. Example of one of my old patterns from back in the day: Snooze one million and forty-five times because I went to bed super late, after working into the wee hours, and only had four hours of sleep. Grab the phone and check e-mails while lying in bed, still groggy. Spicy McChicken's heart gets racing as she deals with the fire-drill e-mails in bed. Now, I'm late and I'm overwhelmed. I rush out of bed, already angry, annoyed, and agitated. I brush my teeth, fix my hair in a random updo, quickly and haphazardly put on makeup, then grab whatever is clean and throw it on. I take my dog on the shortest, fastest walk possible, then run out the door late, hungry, and pissed, headed for work. Seriously, these used to be my morning Self Love and body-care rituals. Now, write out your morning routine. Be honest, girl. You're the only one who is going to see it.

✦ What would be **more empowering morning Self Love, body-care rituals**, ones that if you did them every morning would signal to you that you *love* yourself and that you are worth investing your time and energy in? To give you an example, here's my dream vision: Roll out of bed after eight blissful hours of beauty rest. Give man hugs and kisses. Find the dog and give her hugs and kisses. Make my way to the kitchen. Make myself a morning green smoothie with vitamins and nutritional goodies and yumminess. Grab my phone, headphones, walking shoes, and doggie. Dance and sing to my fave playlist as we take a long walk around the neighborhood. Come home, turn on the music, and dance myself to the bathroom. Dance and sing in the shower. Dance in front of the mirror while I floss and brush my teeth. Admire my beauty. Play makeup artist with my beautiful face. Pick out a poppin' bright, bold, and *fun* lipstick color. Style my hair in a way that matches the vibe I am going for that day. Dance to the room where my clothes, shoes, and accessories are. Pick out an avatar. Find outfit that matches my desired avatar's vibe. Creatively and playfully accessorize like the fashionista I am. *Then* start my workday. That's me. Now, it's your turn. Write out your dream morning routine.

✦ How would your days really be different if you implemented more **empowering morning Self Love, body-care rituals**? What comes to mind?

✦ Now let's look at your evening. What are your current **evening Self Love, body-care rituals**? Be super-honest with yourself. You are the only person who is going to see this. Example of one of my old patterns from back in the day: Distracting and numbing myself from my own loneliness and lack of Self Love by watching TV on the couch until all hours of the night while simultaneously working away. Putting in yet another 16+ hour workday.

Go to bed without brushing my teeth, because that is too much of a bother at this point. At most I might have gone into the bathroom to use a chemical-filled makeup remover wipe to take off my makeup. Fall into bed physically exhausted. Try to fall asleep. Cannot sleep because my mind is still racing from either whatever junk I was just watching on TV or whatever project I have been up late working on. Stare impatiently at the ceiling, pissed about the rapidly approaching hour that I need to wake. Toss and turn. Sleep restlessly, annoyed that yet another day has gone by. Ponder, "Where does all the time go." Back in the day, those were my evening rituals. Now, write out your evening routine. Be honest, girl.

✦ What would be **more empowering nightly Self Love, body-care rituals**, ones that, if you did them every evening, it would signal to you that you *love* yourself and are worth investing your time and energy in? For example, here's my dream routine: Tech cleanse starting thirty minutes before bedtime to prevent over-stimulation before I go to bed. Use organic jojoba oil to remove my makeup. Treat myself to a relaxing hot bath in a tub cleaned with organic cleaning products. Utilize organic bath salts. Light soy candles. Play relaxing music. Decompress from the day. Shave. Lotion my body from head to toe. Floss and brush my teeth as I admire my beauty in the mirror. Do some positive Self Love talk. Put on some comfy jammies. Listen to sound-therapy music. Meditate with yoga pose that opens up my heart and throat chakras. Go to bed reviewing the endless list of reasons that I am the luckiest and most blessed being on the face of the planet: thank you, thank you, thank you. *Zzzzzzz.* That's me. Now, write your evening dream routine!

✦ **How would your days really be different** if you implemented more empowering nightly Self Love, body-care rituals? Write down what comes to mind.

✦ What are your **ongoing Self Love, body-care rituals**? With what frequency do you do each? Some areas to consider: haircuts, dental appointments, massages, facials, body scrubs, manicures, pedicures, working out, and meditating.

✦ If you were playing **full-out** and loving your body at the highest level possible, what would your ongoing Self Love, body-care rituals be? With what frequency would you do each?

Honestly, the number one impact on loving your body is keeping up with daily rituals that show your body you care, that it matters, it is loved, and it is a priority. A ritual can even be just one isolated thing, such as paying yourself a compliment. It doesn't need to be a whole series of things!

Meet yourself where *you* are. If you have zero rituals right now, then start with picking *just one thing* you can do every day that will make you feel like you are loving, honoring, appreciating, and respecting your body. Then, do that thing every day.

When you skip a day, you send a message to yourself that you don't matter, and that couldn't be further from the truth, could it? The truth is you are a priority to you. You *do* matter!!

Think of it this way. Basically, you are managing multiple relationships with yourself. With your mind, you are breaking patterns that are limiting you. With your heart, you are allowing it to do the dreaming and have more of a leading role in your life. With your soul, you are connecting to your inner GPS. With your body, you are treating it like the temple that it is. In every area, you are choosing to treat yourself like the goddess that you are.

As you explore your own rituals, don't forget to research the products you are using directly on your skin, such as shampoo, conditioner, makeup, deodorant, lotion, soap, and makeup remover. If there are a lot of toxins and chemicals in these products, those are going directly into your pores and can impact skin clarity, texture, and tone. Toxins can also impact hair loss and your overall health.

Just start loving and honoring your body more by reading those labels! Build an awareness of what you are actually putting onto your body, as what goes on is absorbed and affects how epic and sexy you feel every day.

✦ *Have a Pamper Party or Go Solo* ✦

Invite some soul sisters over to your house or head to a spa and have a pamper party! You can even go solo and have a pamper day all to yourself. Think facials and manis / pedis. Pack some healthy and delicious, yummy, energizing, and luxurious snacks. Treat yourself to body scrubs, massages, meditation, relaxing music, and or restorative yoga. You could even make it a monthly thaang!

Take turns hosting it with your girlfriends, which means most of the time you literally just have to show up and be pampered. Bliss! Get creative, and think outside the box. And send me pics of your Epic Sexy Pamper Party! Share them on social media using #epicsexyyou or email them to me at morgan@epicsexyyou.com.

I'd love to see how you badass ninja warrior goddesses get your pamper on. Show me how you roll. Word.

✦ *Allow Yourself to Be Seen* ✦

Stop hiding in baggy clothes and dark colors. Stop letting the extra weight pile on. Stop avoiding taking pictures. Stop getting mad when someone posts unflattering pictures of you. Instead, start telling those people, "Thank you! I needed to see that so I can face the changes I want to make! Woo!!"

Turn triggers into the activation of your Goddess Alert System. Ask, "What specifically don't I like?" Great! Now that you know what you don't like, you can flip it. What you don't like becomes a clue to what you do actually want! Then ask yourself, "What are all of the possible ways that I might be able to go and make my desires a reality?" Yaaaay, triggers! Celebrate when you are triggered. Look at where they can lead you if you let them. WOO!

Be seen. Spend time with yourself naked. Wear lingerie around your house. Wear sexy undergarments everywhere you go. Do it all for *you*. Even if you are in a relationship with someone who thinks you are the most sexy woman alive, you will never truly believe them unless you yourself are comfortable in your own body. Self Love and body care are vehicles to get you there. This is about you seeing you. This is about *you* exploring and discovering new things about yourself that you absolutely, positively *love*.

Admire yourself. Notice all of your intricate details the way you would with a lover or best friend. Look closer! Shed the layers, both the literal, tangible ones *and* the metaphorical layers. The more you love you and the more open you are to others, the more of an energetic space you will open up to receive love from others! People follow your lead. Give them permission to fall madly, deeply in love with you by first falling madly, deeply in love with yourself.

✦ *Get Your Mirror Talk On* ✦

Practice positive self-talk in front of the mirror. Yes, I am super serious about this. Stand in front of the mirror and give yourself some compliments. Start with something like: "Guuurrl, you rock!" "You are so pretty!" "Look at those eyes..." "Your smile is really beautiful." "Look at those curves!" "You are such an epic badass." "You are sexxxyyy!" Insert whatever feels good to you.

If this is *reeeeaaaally* uncomfortable for you at the beginning, just start with one compliment every time you are in front of the mirror. It can even be the same one every day for a week. Then, add a new compliment to your daily rituals the following week. Then add another the week after that. Build up to it. Step by step. Eventually, you'll be telling yourself freely just how awesome you are and you'll be immersed in an abundance of some self lovin'!

GET YOUR SHARE ON *#epicsexyyou*

OK, now that you have enough Epic Sexy Thrival Tips to last a lifetime, it's time to get our simplicity on and revisit the key principles to Epic Sexy You...

Let's Recap, Shall We?

So that you have a quick and easy way to keep yourself on your path, let's recap the key foundations that have been sprinkled in throughout the entire book that will unleash your *LIMITLESS* and Epic Sexy Self. These foundations are critical if you want to create and sustain your very own Epic Sexy Life! Woo!!

*L*et Go of the How. Focus on the What.

What do you want? Utilizing the brilliance of your cerebral Headspace in tandem with the magical, euphoric flow of your Heartspace, allow yourself to create intense desires. Then program that burning desire into your Heartspace GPS, activating your Goddess Power Source, and embrace the magical and beautiful, serendipitous, divine surprises that await you in the alignment and flow of the how.

*I*ntentional Awareness.

Utilize intentional awareness to activate your Goddess Alert System. Get creative and playful! Celebrate mistakes, resistance, overwhelm, frustration, and confusion. Yaaayy! These signal growth and opportunities for even more limitless expansion! Woo!! Don't forget to preprogram all of your signals for activating the Goddess Alert system! Woo!!

*M*aster Creator.

You are the Master Creator of your Epic Sexy and Limitless Life! Own your power and make sure to consciously and intentionally live life on purpose!

*I*mmerse Yourself in a Heartspace Existence.

Live a "Hell Yes" life! Use your Hell Yes scale to make decisions and *only* say yes if it is a big fat huge "Hell Yes!"

*T*ry on Different Avatars!

Get playful. Get creative. Be conscious, intentional, and purposeful about who's on your roster and which position you've got each player in. Leverage players intentionally. Put them in positions that allow you a limitless experience. This will pave the way for the results and outcomes your soul craves!

*L*ove Yourself.

Love yourself in a Me Too, Me First, we ALL win, Self Love kind of way! Yaaayy!! Leave the self-sacrifice in the giveaway pile, and pack in all the brilliance, expansive beauty, and limitless possibilities that the high vibrations of Me Too can offer! Sprinkle in Me First time to rejuvenate, restore, and reignite whenever you want and or need it.

*E*pic Limitless You.

Be Epic Limitless You. You are an epic, limitless being and *You Can Have it All*! Remind yourself of this constantly. Intentionally keep this at the forefront of your awareness radar. You can even create an avatar that is "Epic Limitless Me" and, when you need to call upon her, you can ask yourself, "What would Epic Limitless Me do in this situation? How would she behave? What would she say here?"

You *can* have it all. Sometimes, you just have to stop and ask yourself, "Where are the limits I may be putting on myself unconsciously?" Another one of my fave questions, "But what if I could? How might I be able to make that happen?" Let your imagination run wild and free! Don't be afraid to dream. Dream so big that others, and perhaps even you, might think you are a permanent resident in Crazytown!

*S*ettling Is for Suckers.

Thriving is where it's at. Don't be a sucker! When you catch yourself settling, tolerating something less than what you know you deserve, ignoring your desires, or avoiding getting going, celebrate your awareness! This book is filled with infinite possibilities for you to come back to over and over and over again, so you don't have to stumble through the dark or haphazardly create your dream life. Use them.

*S*exy Time. Bring Sexy Back!

Redefine "sexy" and step into it on your own terms, in whatever way sexy looks and feels like to you! Embrace it! Love, honor, appreciate, admire, and pamper your body like the magically divine machine it is!

Now, for some final, inspiring words. Pay attention.
This is some serious business, ladies . . .

Burn Those Granny Panties!

Haha! As you may have experienced in our journey together here, one of my core philosophies in my life coaching practice, and pretty much in life in general, is that growth, discovery, self-exploration, and expansion can be tons of fun! So, let's ditch the serious pants and let's talk about granny panties, shall we?

This journey of aliveness in creating a limitless and Epic Sexy You is about having the ultimate love affair, a love affair with yourself. In most love affairs, all parties show up at their best in the beginning, right? I mean, you are on your best behavior, working out and eating well so that you can rock their world in the bedroom, putting your best foot forward, getting dolled up, and investing in the other person like it's your job.

In the beginning, you are thoughtful. You go above and beyond. You are kind and loving, and you constantly tell your partner how wonderful he or she is. You let them know they are your Numero Uno. You clean your house when they're coming over. You shave your legs. You wear sexy underwear. You lovingly and patiently tell them what you want and need. You greet them at the door with excitement, butterflies, and complete adoration.

Somewhere along the line, things shift. You get comfortable. As in the "Comfy Slob" kind of comfortable, not the "Comfort Goddess" kind of comfort. You stop putting in as much effort. You stop trying as hard. You lose your patience. You stop doing the very things that created the love affair in the first place.

You begin co-existing instead of co-creating. Then, the magic disappears, and you tell yourself that it is "normal" and that, at some point, "all things fade." You say, "That's just the reality of relationships." I call bullshit on that! I call that settling!

On the journey to aliveness, as you are stepping into the epic and limitless version of yourself, it is possible to keep the magic alive! It is possible to have the ultimate love affair that is endless. As in from now until forever more. The way to make that happen is to never stop the things you did at the very beginning that made you fall madly, deeply in love with Epic Sexy You.

You've got to live life on purpose, intentionally and consciously, thoughtfully and lovingly creating the magic, love, excitement, bliss, euphoria, laughter, joy, and adventure your soul craves and desires. Essentially, I'm asking you to consider burning the metaphorical Granny Panties and never ever allow yourself to get so comfortable (Comfy Slob) that you give up on intentionally and purposefully being your Epic Sexy Limitless Self! This book is filled with an abundance of things that you can revisit whenever you need a little Me First time. Connect, discover, and explore all that is YOU and keep the love alive, girl!

Create a Habit of Action, Become a Doer

Wow! A lot just came at you! Am I right? Wowzers! Holy cow of a-lot-ness! Yeah, all that just happened. So, here is the thing… Do not let your mind trick you into thinking that by reading this that you actually did something to change your life. Stay with me.

I'm sure after reading all of this, you are like, "What do you mean I didn't do anything??!! I did just do something, Morgan. I read hundreds of pages of goodness, and that was quite an epic feat and journey!" OK, so lets take a second and acknowledge that *yes* you did just accomplish absorbing a ton of content that will change your life forever! True that, sister friend. Take a second to give yourself a hug, a pat on the back, or a high five. Or all three.

Seriously, come on now, you should know by now that we are a tribe of DOERS. Amuse me. I'll wait. Pick one. Make it happen....

Awesome! OK, now that you have congratulated yourself and celebrated step one of your journey, the Learning Step, now it is time to go to step two, which is where the real magic of transformation awaits. Step two is The Doing Step, and it is all about the habit of action. Often times in life we trick ourselves into thinking we have "done everything" there is to do. We say, "Nothing has worked, so why bother?"

"Why bother?" is for those suckers who are looking for a life of mediocrity and settling! To prevent a trip to Whybotherville, take a look at doing instead of just learning. Put your learning into action. If you say, "I already knew this stuff, Morgan. I already know about Self Love, and I still feel like I am not living my Epic Sexy Limitless Life! This stuff doesn't work!"

My response to that would be that for you it isn't about learning it then. It is about doing it whatever "it" may be for you. If this describes you, I am challenging you right now to take a moment to think about one thing that stood out in this book that you can do this week, starting right here, right now, today, not tomorrow, but right NOW. What is one thing you commit to play with, experiment with, and put into action this week?

Write it down in your journal. Tell three friends! Find an accountability buddy who is willing to pick his or her one thing too. Choose someone who is just as excited about doing his or her one thing as you are. Make sure to choose a thing you want to do, not just another thing you feel like you have to do.

If you can't find anyone reliable or if you feel like you need help, hire a coach. If you are ready to leave mediocrity in the dust, come play with me! I would be beyond honored to work with you.

✦ *Welcome to the Epic Sexy You Tribe!* ✦

Want to know more about how we can work and play together? Visit www.EpicSexyYou.com for all the deets.

✦ *Connect and Share Your Journey with the Epic Sexy Tribe* ✦

Instagram: @epicsexyyou
Facebook: facebook.com/epicsexyyou
Twitter: @EpicSexyYou
Pinterest: pinterest.com/epicsexyyou
YouTube: EpicSexyYou

✓ **Email me** at morgan@epicsexyyou.com

✓ **Share your stories**, Aha moments, insights, epiphanies, lessons learned, and what's working so that we can all grow, learn, and celebrate together!!

✓ Let me know **what you are struggling with**, what you are craving more of, and what you could benefit from as your next steps. These insights help me create custom content,

events, retreats, and programs to support you in your
journey to a sustainable, Epic Sexy, and Limitless You.

✓ What do you think the tribe would benefit from next?
Share your ideas!

✓ Join the **Epic Sexy You movement**, and get social with
your sharing!! Use #epicsexyyou to connect, explore, and
celebrate with fellow Epic Sexy Souls along your journey.
Sharing ingrains every lesson you learn deeper into the
fiber of your being, which yields optimal sustainability.
This is about finding Epic Sexy You, and *never* going back.
Let's do this! WOO!

✓ **Create your own** Epic Sexy You Movement! Share your
journey with others: Start your own book club. Learn,
grow, expand, evolve, and celebrate together. Hit me up,
and if divine timing serendipitously aligns for our
calendars, I'll pop in for a Skype Q&A Book Club Quickie
in my glamorous gold sparkly gown.

✓ **Share your pics** on social media using #epicsexyyou or
email them to me at morgan@epicsexyyou.com.

• • • • •
THRIVAL PERSPECTIVE
• • • • •

ONE thaaang at a time will create the MOST EPIC, sustainable change and allow you to experience a LIMITLESS LIFE beyond your wildest dreams! WOO!! Go get it, Gurrrll!!!

✦ *I'm On Your Team, Girl* ✦

Let's *do* this! There are Epic Adventure Retreats, one-on-one coaching, online coaching programs, and a plethora of options to support you wherever you find yourself along your journey. Let's get you the life that your soul craves. Let's lay the bricks for the most Epic Sexy Self Love foundation you've ever seen! Let's make magic happen, so you can create an Epic Sexy Life.

You *can* have it all, and you *will* have it all. Remember, you do not have to do it all at once! For now, let's prevent overwhelm and epic resistance. Just pick *one* thing. Get started creating a habit of action. Start doing things that will move you forward in your lifelong journey of progress and growth. Then, when you get good at that thaang you selected, choose again.

Ask: "What is the *one* thing I can do consistently to make the biggest impact on my life and move me toward my soul's pursuit of epic fulfillment?" When that intuitive download comes in, make that new one thing your primary focus of awareness until you get really, really good at that one thing and you are ready for another one thing. Repeat! You've got this! Now, go DO it. Get it girl!! Woo!!! Insert me on stage, dropping the mic. "I'm out! Peace!"

In Gratitude and Infinite Love,

XOXO
Morgan

Morgan Field
Your Epic Sexy Soul Sister from Another Mister

EPIC SEXY GRATITUDE

My acknowledgments to the most amazing team of co-creators of all time. Thank you to each of you for helping me make my visions come to life! I Love You. Thank You.

To an awesome photographer, Kirsten Miccoli for an epic book cover. Basically, she is hands down the most talented photographer of ALL time. She was the only one who I knew could make my vision come to life in the way that she did. I love you. Thank you!

To the best hair and makeup team ever: makeup artist Stephanie VanHazebroeck, and hair artist Big Nat Capone, who both create true art through their talents and gifts! Thank you so much for sharing your sheer geniustry with me and making me feel so damn glam! You two ROCK!

To every single soul sister who read this soul work and shared their experience, feedback, insights, creativity, light, and love with me, I love you! Thank you! Ana Dominguez, Courtney Butler, Avril Marchegiano, Julie Bauke, Elaine Soul Sister Grace, Elaine Batho, Leecis Perry, Denise Stillman, Shawna Burkhart, Kat O'Heir, and Niki Payne. To each and every one of you, I love you. Thank you!

To Kat O'Heir for sharing the geniustry of her Wordstress ways with me. You provided me with a framework for this soul project that will live in my Heartspace Immersion forever when you said: *"Any woman who wants to dream big and dance with her own demons with a sense of adventure and lots of laughter should read this book."* I Love you. Thank you.

To Julie Bauke, one of the most Badass Ninja Warrior Goddesses of all time, who constantly shares her never-ending flow of brilliantly on-point ideas with me and who helped me come up with the tagline for this soul work: *No Limits. No Rules.* I love you. Thank you!

To Joel Londen, the most talented graphic designer of all time, who can do in mere minutes what takes others days or weeks to do, you ROCK! Thank you so much for sharing your talents with me, I am so excited for the continued partnership ahead! Thank you for working your magic on the book cover design. Nailed it!

To Catrice Jackson, who was my partner in branding shine and helped me organize all the yummy, magical, brilliant goodies that were in the depths of my soul dying to come out and who playfully peppered in her fun and edgy brilliance along the way! I love you. Thank you.

To my parents for hosting Gammy Camp for my little fur baby while I was in the final stretch of this soul creation and went down a total bookworm hole. I love you. Thank you.

To the epic sexy male models on the cover: Sean Field, Chris Thomas, Matthew Caucci, and Derrick Babinsky (and to Dan Rodriguez who missed the cover shot by mere minutes). This wasn't the first crazy idea you have each said, "Yes" to, and I am sure this won't be the last. I'll be calling you to discuss launch party details to share your handsome selves with the ladies of the world! I love you, thank you.

To Dawn Richerson who more than amused my epic and super-human desired timelines for this soul creation. She came, she saw, she edited, she designed, she conquered! I am beyond blessed that our spirit teams united us for this soul work. You were most def THE woman for the job. I love you. Thank you.

To Heidi Weise who is the best soul sister a girl could ever ask for, who truly held my hand and danced with me on this project, celebrated me and the soul work every step of the way, played with me, shared her sheer brilliance and geniustry with me along with her expansive, neverending, limitless Heartspace Immersion. I love you so much. Thank you. xoxo

To Leecis Perry for being the true leader in this whole equation, the very first one to stand and dance with me so that I wasn't just a lone nut. A true co-creator of ESY, whose soul has been with me every single step of the way. Words could never even come close to doing my gratitude for you justice. I love so much you. Thank you for sharing your light, love, laughter, humor, and epic analogies with me. My life is better because you are in it. Soul sisters for life! I love you. Thank you!

To every client who has opened your heart, mind, and soul in a partnership of exploration and allowed me to share your journey: I am beyond blessed, honored, humbled, and overwhelmed with an abundance of limitless gratitude to be by your side for this adventure that is life. You are my tribe. Because of you, I jump out of bed every morning with my soul on fire. I love you. Thank you.

To Spicy McChicken. Without her, there really is no story. She just wanted to be loved, and I am most def not going to deprive her of that. Spicy, I love you girl. Thank you. (But seriously girl, you've got to stop sneaking in through the back door!)

To my spirit team, the MVP of all spirit teams, you guys are the best! I have SO much FUN sharing this adventure of life with you! Thank you for expressing your divine wisdom through me in this soul creation. I am beyond blessed, honored, and humbled to be a part of such a mind-blowingly, life transformative, powerhouse team. You blow my mind more and more every day. Thank you for always having my back, for always going along with my crazy ideas, and for always showing me the way. I love you so much! THANK YOU!

And last, but *most certainly* not least, to JoJoBa who is the consigliere to my spiritual gangster. You are the most amazing soul I have ever encountered. You are my favorite in the whole wide everything. In all the universes and all the dimensions. My life is better because you are in it. Thank you for your never-ending support and free-flowing creative geniustry that you have generously poured into my life and into ESY. You are the most creative and talented being I have ever encountered. Just like I told you at the very beginning of it all, that day in the Mac Store, "You have no idea just how much of **everything** you are." You truly are the kewlest. There is no one else in the entire universe who even comes close. I love you more than words will ever be able to express. I love you. Thank you!

Made in the USA
San Bernardino, CA
25 February 2016